D1576783

Wine, Women and Westminster

CHRIS MONCRIEFF

Wine, Women and Westminster

Behind-the-scenes true stories of
MPs at play over 50 years

JR
BOOKS

First published in Great Britain in 2008 by
JR Books, 10 Greenland Street, London NW1 0ND
www.jrbooks.com

ISBN 978-1-906217-80-8

1 3 5 7 9 10 8 6 4 2

Printed by The Cromwell Press, Trowbridge, Wiltshire

To Maggie with love

Contents

Acknowledgements   ix

Foreword   xi

Introduction: The Dank and Dark
Corridors of Power   1

Sleeping Dogs and Flying Saucers   10

Work is the Curse of the Drinking Classes   23

Westminster – The Good Life   35

POINTS OF ORDER   44

Caught with their Trousers Down   49

Armed Neutrality   58

POINTS OF ORDER   71

Name-Calling and Narcissism   77

TV: And Parliament Powders its Nose   96

POINTS OF ORDER   109

Liberal Helpings   114

Perilous Days on the Knocker   122

The End of the Peer Show? Not for a While   127

POINTS OF ORDER   131

Keeping the Show on the Road   136

Thatcher the Fashion Icon   142
Crimpers and Curling Tongs   147
POINTS OF ORDER   150

Travels of a Fitful Flea: The Hurricane in Skirts   154
The Man in the Raspberry Turban   172
The Whispering Valet Supreme   179
The Lady's not for Spurning   181
POINTS OF ORDER   185

Fresh Air and Fun   190
Telephones from Hell   197
Soaked in Guinness as the Troubles Raged   204
POINTS OF ORDER   212

Enoch the Unflinching   217
The Slow-Motion Downfall of the Iron Lady   224
Galloping Major to the Rescue   237
POINTS OF ORDER   244

The Raging Bull   249
Who Goes Home?   253

Acknowledgements

I would like to thank my wife Maggie and all our children (in chronological order) Joanna, Sarah, Kate and Angus, as well as my sister Ruth Whitfield for their invaluable help.

Special thanks also to Iain Dale, Maggie Scammell, Avril Ormsby, Jennifer Sym, Vivienne Morgan and Rachel Musson, without whose help I would never have got the show on the road. And, of course, I am eternally grateful to my employers, the Press Association.

Finally, a huge thank-you to our MPs whose buffoonery and antics made the whole thing possible.

Foreword

This is a book about politics and politicians. But it is utterly devoid of analysis, it has no depth and as for gravitas – forget it. *Wine, Women and Westminster* is largely a collection of anecdotes and trivia assembled in some sort of order from the past 46 years I have spent working at Westminster for the Press Association.

I am fortunate to have travelled around the world both with Margaret Thatcher and with John Major, in each case a source of much unwitting comedy. I shall never, for instance, forget the spectacle of the late Denis Thatcher trying to feed an elephant a bun through the wrong orifice in Kandy, Sri Lanka.

Nor the occasion when I was asked to ring up a hospital to enquire about the condition of a particular patient, namely Harold Macmillan, the then Prime Minister. By accident, or possibly because they thought I was somebody important, the hospital switchboard put me through to the bedside phone of Mr Macmillan himself rather than to a spokesman. I nevertheless enquired how he was and he replied gruffly: 'I was fine until you bloody well woke me up.'

Then there was the flamboyant, handlebar-moustached Tory, Sir Gerald Nabarro. I met him once in his Worcestershire constituency, and offered him a drink at the bar. 'A large scotch, please, Christopher,' he boomed. So I bought him one, and myself a pint of Guinness. When we had downed these, I asked if he would like another, assuming, wrongly, that he might say it was his shout.

'Another large scotch would do very nicely,' he said. So I bought that, too, although not with much relish that time.

A few days later Sir Gerald tabled a Commons question, asking whether we Britons would be forced to drink 'unpalatable' continental beer once we had joined the Common Market. I went down to the members' lobby to expand on this story. He said: 'Take this down, Christopher, quotes on, "Speaking as a total abstainer, I…"'

At which point, somewhat pained, I stopped him in his tracks, saying: 'What about those two large scotches at Evesham last week?'

'Scrub that,' he said. 'Take this down, Christopher. Quotes on, "Speaking as a connoisseur of British beer…"' He didn't bat an eyelid. You had to admire the cheek.

So you see, there are as many laughs as there is solemnity at Westminster, as much farce as there is heavy drama, and as much rollicking fun as there is tedium.

I hope you enjoy it.

Chris Moncrieff

Wine, Women
and
Westminster

Introduction:
The Dank and Dark Corridors of Power

The Hampton Court maze has nothing on the Palace of Westminster. I have been a Westminster journalist based there for almost 50 years and I still find myself lost on occasion. It may be the seat of Parliament, but it's also a sprawling complex of dank, dark corridors, subterranean passages, and forbidding staircases in the most unsuspected places. In one area there is actually a door high up on the wall. No one has ever been able to explain how this architectural blunder came about. I have never found the other side of that door, but I trust it is securely locked, with the warning: 'Mind the drop' – which is about 15 feet.

The most public part of the entire edifice is the central lobby, a large, busy circular area, the Piccadilly Circus of Westminster where constituents go to lobby their MPs. It is always busy and bustling. As you enter it, to your left is the Chamber of the House of Commons and to your right is the House of Lords, also known as the Upper House and, by those in the Commons – in a typically bizarre tradition – as 'another place'. The Commons Chamber was bombed during World War II, and afterwards rebuilt almost but not exactly the same as the original one. For instance, the present Chamber has no pillars holding up the galleries.

There is a strict colour coding distinguishing the two Houses: the benches and other items in the Commons are green and red in the House of Lords. The long committee corridor, which stretches virtually from one end of the palace to the other, starts with green furnishing and ends with red, signifying that you have entered the Lords' area of the building.

To get into the Commons Chamber from the central lobby, you pass through a short corridor with huge paintings of historical events on the walls and into the members' lobby to which, generally speaking, only MPs and political reporters have access when the House is sitting. In here are statues, larger than life, honouring, among others, Winston Churchill, Lloyd George and Margaret Thatcher – who became the first person to have her statue erected there while she was still alive. Most visitors have to climb stairs, elsewhere, to get into the public galleries. Only MPs are allowed to sit on the benches surrounding the members' lobby. Reporters have to stand.

And then into the Chamber itself. Smoking was banned in the Chamber from the 17th century (and is now banned everywhere else in the palace), but a snuffbox is attached to the portals entering the chamber for MPs. The Speaker's canopied chair faces you at the far end of the Chamber as you enter. Elected by MPs from among their own number, the Speaker controls the debates in the sense that they make sure that parliamentary rules are not breached. MPs who want to speak in debates stand up when the previous speaker has finished and the Speaker chooses which one to call.

To the left, as you enter the Chamber are the Government benches and to the right the Opposition. It is a confrontational cockpit of a place. The two sides are officially two sword-lengths apart to prevent skirmishes when swords were allowed in the Chamber. There still remain pegs on which members were once able to hang their swords. The Serjeant-at-Arms is the only one who still carries a sword into the chamber. He is often a retired military officer and is responsible for discipline throughout the palace. His office dates back to medieval days. If, for instance, the Speaker suspends an MP for breaking the rules and that MP refuses to leave the Chamber, then the Serjeant-at-Arms has to eject the miscreant, physically if necessary.

On important occasions, such as Budget day or the state opening of Parliament, MPs will queue up before the doors of the Chamber open at 8 am to bag their seats. They take a prayer card – which admits them to prayers which precede each day's sitting – and once they have placed that card in a slot in front of the seat of their choice, that remains their seat for the rest of the parliamentary day. Prayer cards superseded tall hats – once de rigueur in the Chamber – which, once they were placed on a seat, reserved that seat for the owner of the hat for the entire day.

All visitors or employees in the Commons who were not MPs were described as 'strangers', a term that has only just been abandoned after centuries of use. The public gallery was always known as the Strangers' Gallery – and actually, informally still is, because old habits die hard. The Strangers' Cafeteria and the Strangers' Bar (so called because MPs are allowed to bring visitors into them) were renamed the Terrace Cafeteria and the Terrace Bar (because, surprise, surprise, they run alongside the terrace). Even so, they are still referred to as The Strangers.

The Strangers' Bar is also jocularly known as The Kremlin because it is a favourite haunt of Labour MPs. Annie's Bar – named after the first barmaid to run it before World War II – now exists in a dank, windowless dungeon in the bowels of the building. Admission to this is supposed to be confined to MPs and political correspondents, and it has the reputation of being the place where political plots are hatched and exclusive stories are born.

Across the road from the main palace is recently-built Portcullis House which bears an uncanny likeness to the ill-fated

Titanic. In here, there are fig trees, water features, a coffee shop, a cafeteria and a waiter-service dining room called The Adjournment, as well as scores of offices for MPs.

The Commons part of the palace is normally rowdy, busy and bustling. But there is an air of calm and serenity as you approach the Lords. There is a much smaller lobby ahead of the Chamber and the rules here – as everywhere else in the Lords – are much more relaxed than they are in the Commons. The Chamber, which escaped the bombing, is far more ornate than the Commons. Straight ahead, as you enter, you will see the throne from which the monarch reads the Queen's Speech on the state opening of Parliament day. This speech is in fact written by Government ministers and sets out, in broad terms, their programme for the coming session of Parliament. The monarch actually has no input.

The famous Woolsack, which looks like an uncomfortable red bench, is where the Lord Chancellor (now known as the Lord Speaker) sits. The occupant of that office does not have the same powers as the Speaker in the Commons. Quite recently it was discovered that the Woolsack was not filled with wool but with horse-hair. It is not, therefore, a very comfortable place to sit, especially for hours on end. The Government side sits to the right of the Lord Speaker, facing the Opposition parties on the other side. There are also seats facing the Lord Speaker for cross-bench peers – those with no party political affiliations. Bishops entitled to seats in the House of Lords sit on the Government side, invariably wearing their robes. The Lords' debates are generally far less rowdy than those in the Commons, and are often regarded as superior. The Lords contains many people who are great experts in various fields – something which is woefully lacking in the Commons. This often means Lords' debates are far more instructive.

The favoured watering hole in the Lords is the Lords' Staff Bar, a breezy, bright place alongside the terrace. The nearby Lords' cafeteria, where the food is regarded as superior to that in the Commons, is also hugely popular. Both the Commons and the

Lords have their own shops where visitors can buy any manner of souvenirs, drinks and chocolate, all bearing the imprimatur of one or other of the Houses.

Back in the Commons, the press gallery seats are just above the Speaker's chair. But the press gallery 'estate' is far more than just a grandstand. Behind the chamber the press gallery members enjoy a bar and restaurant (named Moncrieff's Bar – probably because I have spent so much time there) as well as a cafeteria and library. There are also numerous offices scattered over the press gallery where several hundred reporters – on a busy day – will be thundering out their stories. These include reporters from national and provincial newspapers, as well as those from TV and radio organisations.

There are two kinds of journalists at Westminster: parliamentary reporters who report debates in the Chamber and political reporters (or lobby correspondents), who hobnob with ministers, attend Downing Street briefings and generally find stories beyond the Chamber itself. There is no doubt that the Palace of Westminster is the country's biggest single source of stories under one roof.

Relations between political reporters and politicians are often strained: MPs do not like their affairs being probed by journalists. On the other hand, most MPs are desperate to get their names in the papers, particularly the local papers in their constituency. MPs usually blame the press for their shortcomings. For instance, if Tony Blair didn't like a story he would publicly denounce it as 'media froth'. That was usually a sign that the story was actually correct but that it was embarrassing to the government.

I came into the House of Commons almost by accident in 1962. I had always wanted to be a newspaper reporter from an age when most small boys wanted to be engine drivers. My parents put up with this until I was about 15, when they started to get alarmed that I might join what they regarded (maybe correctly) as a disreputable occupation. So they thrust me into a solicitors' office in central London with the horrendous prospect of a legal career ahead of me. I spent most of the time I was there (about six months) writing round to local newspapers in London and elsewhere, asking for a job. It was when I struck lucky with the *Harrogate Herald* in 1949 that my parents realised that the game was up.

I spent four years at Harrogate and its sister papers in Thirsk, Ripon, Knaresborough and Northallerton, getting kicked around by a stern news editor who taught me most of what I know about the job today. I still think this is a far better way to learn the trade rather than, as is the custom now, to go to university and emerge with degrees but no practical knowledge of what the job is all about.

I had to break my career to do national service in the Intelligence Corps during the state of emergency in Malaya. I was in the unusual, if not unique, situation of being busted twice during that period. The first time I was stripped of my single stripe after losing a security pass in Taiping in the north of the country (it turned up, months later, in a schoolboy's exercise book and was posted to me in England by his teacher). Later, I was given the stripe back, but this was virtually ripped off my arm when the troopship taking us home docked at Liverpool. This was because it was what was known as a 'local, acting, unpaid' stripe and it ceased to have any validity once I left Malaya. Enoch Powell once said that the greatest promotion in his entire life was from private to lance corporal (he eventually became a brigadier). I can boast that I was promoted not once but twice to that Olympian level. However, unlike Mr Powell I went right back to where I started – being a private.

I returned to Harrogate briefly after demob before moving to the *Coventry Evening Telegraph* as a general reporter and then to the *Nottingham Evening Post* and *Nottingham Guardian-Journal* in the same capacity. In this last post I spent a considerable amount of time in the paper's Grantham office, the town where Margaret Thatcher was born and brought up. I never knowingly met her father, Councillor Roberts, who instilled in her the work ethic which she never lost.

At around this period I had two spells abroad, one working in a factory near Poitiers and the second in an office in Dusseldorf, the object being to learn French and German properly. It was not a huge success and as it turned out I didn't end up becoming a foreign correspondent. I decided to seek my fortune in London.

I stayed in a house in Barnes run by a friend of mine, Ray Anker (a former colleague on the *Coventry Evening Telegraph*), and occupied largely by journalists and out-of-work actors. It was here I first met my wife-to-be, Maggie, who was far more modest than her then impressive name (Margaret Fotheringham Ferguson) would imply. She was a repertory actress from Scotland, waiting for the phone to ring with job offers.

We were married in 1961 in the very upmarket St Columba's Church of Scotland, in Chelsea, where my sister made disparaging remarks about the state of my shoes. The reception was in a nearby pub with no carpets on the floor, much to the disgust of my new mother-in-law. We had nowhere to go, but my mother insisted we left the pub so that the guests could leave in time to get their trains back to Scotland. We meandered around the pubs for the afternoon in the pouring rain, went to watch comedians the Crazy Gang at the Victoria Palace in the evening and returned to our flat in Finsbury Park on a no. 29 bus. The following day I returned to work. As far as I am aware, there were no snaps at all taken of our nuptials. I have never seen any, anyway. We went on to have four children, but try as I might I was unable to seduce any of them into journalism.

Back then I tried my hand at freelancing in southwest London, but it was a failure. I applied to the Press Association for a job as a general reporter and was told there were no vacancies, but that I could have a job in Parliament if I wanted. This was the last thing I was after, but I could not turn down this opportunity to get into Fleet Street.

The Press Association is the principal and only comprehensive news agency in the country. It supplies stories of all kinds: general news, sport, fashion, the arts, you name it, to virtually every daily or evening newspaper and radio and television organisations in the UK and the Republic of Ireland. When there is a huge story breaking, the PA will put out a 'flash' with just the bare headline. The full story will follow minutes, if not seconds, behind that.

Set up in 1868, the Press Association was conceived primarily as a means of providing provincial papers with national news at as modest a cost as could be achieved. It is, in fact, a kind of co-operative, owned by the various branches of the media who pay a subscription for the service they receive. The PA has no political views, writes no editorials, and conducts no campaigns. In that way it is anonymous and yet an enormous amount of material in the national newspapers and elsewhere comes from the PA. And although the PA gives bylines to reporters, these are usually dropped by the newspapers who, understandably (since they pay a subscription for them) like to give the impression that the stories are their own. Those who work for the PA are expected, naturally, to be loyal to it. And that means that their reporters should not sell their stories directly to newspapers.

And although the PA is oriented to the UK, it has staff reporters in Brussels and New York and elsewhere abroad. It also sends journalists overseas with prominent politicians, royalty, or to cover, for instance, major trials, with a British interest, on foreign soil.

The watchwords of the PA are 'speed and accuracy'. That is why I grew to love working for the PA. The stories have to be done quickly and there is no bias whatsoever in any direction.

But to begin with I was not so much apprehensive as terrified as to what I might find at Westminster as a journalist. My fears were well grounded when I watched Hugh Gaitskell, Harold Wilson and the rest going head-to-head with Harold Macmillan. I thought I would never be able to cope.

Oddly, the place grows on you, and you suddenly realise you

are enjoying yourself. I spent some 12 years in the gallery reporting the debates and then I was given Lobby credentials which enabled me to seek out stories elsewhere. In 1982 I was made the Press Association's chief political correspondent, a title which soon changed to political editor. Much of the time, subsequently, was spent chasing prime ministers and other prominent politicians around the globe.

Both the Lobby journalists and the Gallery journalists have their own committees which, generally speaking, look after their affairs and also to keep at bay those minority of MPs who dislike us to the extent that they would like to curb our freedom. I was chairman of the Lobby and then the Gallery committees in 1985 and 1986. I was brought back as chairman of the Gallery just after the millennium, the year in which the Gallery's bicentenary was celebrated. This marked the occasion when the House authorities first allowed reporters into the Chamber, thus making legal what had been going on illegally for years: reporters had long illicitly sneaked into the galleries and, because they were forbidden to write, sometimes had to later make their reports from memory. I was formally retired in 1994 at the age of 63 with a massive party on the terrace, but was asked to stay on as a political reporter in retirement, a situation which prevails until the time of writing this, 2008, and, I hope, beyond. I may still not always know my way around the palace's remotest corridors, but I have never lost my attachment to the place.

Sleeping Dogs and Flying Saucers

The House of Commons, when at its most spectacular, can be better than the London Palladium on a Saturday night; when at its most sonorous and pompous, it can rival the grandest of grand opera at Covent Garden; and when at its most skittish it outdoes the fluffiest of light comedies. And all the seats are free. But behind all this lies the press gallery, its seedy music-hall offspring, once illegitimate – you would never have called it a love-child – now still treated with caution, fear and even contempt by some politicians. There remain, indeed, a few who would not touch it with a bargepole.

James Cran, an obscure and now ex-Conservative MP, is one such. When approached by a reporter in the autumn of 2001 he reportedly said: 'I am quite prepared to speak to every life form down to the level of vermin. Below that is where I put the press and I am not prepared to talk to them.' So we know where we stand with him. However, most MPs are amiable enough towards political reporters and some virtually fall over each other in their feverish desire to get into print or, preferably, on the TV screen.

The press gallery is the home of gallows humour, boisterous drinking and cynicism of a very high order. By the time the millennium arrived the place had become extremely high tech, with every word uttered in the Commons recorded for posterity (not that posterity would make sense of much of it) and thus accessible to a reporter whose shorthand or miniature tape machine or powers of hearing had let him down. But it was not always like that. There was a time, within living memory, when newfangled typewriters were barred because of the cacophony they generated. They were later allowed in certain areas to compete with the scratching of nibs.

When I arrived, frock coats were a distant memory, there were virtually no women and you were told off if you stood at the bar having a drink wearing a raincoat. One of the very few women there when I arrived was called Pat Newton. She had been engaged as a reporter on one of the agencies as the result of an exchange of letters rather than a face-to-face interview and her employers were surprised and, I suspect, dismayed, to discover that she was not a man. It never even crossed their minds that 'Pat' was in fact 'Patricia' and not 'Patrick'.

In those days, a reporter in the press gallery lived and died by shorthand. There were very few handouts of major ministerial statements made in the Commons and on Budget day in particular, the Treasury offered no help whatsoever. It was a wonder we got so few things wrong. I used to wake up on those mornings wondering whether I would still be in employment by nightfall. And there were moments during the actual Budget itself when I thought my number was up.

The Press Association had the use of a bank of half-a-dozen telephone kiosks just outside the Chamber with a direct line to our copy-takers in Fleet Street. They were used by breathless, perspiring PA reporters rushing in and out of the Chamber with news flashes and running stories to be dictated straight down the line from the notebook and the hieroglyphics which was an apology for shorthand. By the end of Question Time these phone booths were dense with smoke and fug, reminiscent of the old London pea-souper. Everyone smoked in those days and one entered these kiosks to be greeted by swirling clouds of tobacco smoke and the agreeable aroma of singeing wood (people left half-smoked and still-lit cigarettes in the booths for their successors to puff on). The kiosk windows were themselves caked with carcinogens and the telephones probably harboured enough germs to wipe out a decent-sized town. If the Health and Safety Executive people had been around at the time, they would have gone spare. They would probably have closed down the entire press gallery and fumigated it. Smoking was eventually banned in Parliament, along with the rest of the country's buildings, in the early 2000s.

Back when the press gallery still operated in a cloud of smoke, it was nonetheless hectic, particularly on Budget days. There was never any time to check anything and if your superior spotted you trying to check a dodgy word or an indecipherable shorthand outline (and there were plenty of those and so little time), he would virtually frogmarch you into the telephone box. You were flying by the seat of your pants.

What is more, no Chancellor I have ever come across was able to say simply 'six pence on a bottle of wine' or 'two pence on ten cigarettes'. That would have been too easy. They would, instead, clothe these workaday statements in florid Whitehall language and technical jargon that would, to the lay ear, make them sound like algebraic formulae of immense profundity and impenetrable complexity. The Budget, from a press point of view, became far smoother, far simpler and less traumatic. But it certainly lacks the danger, the heart-stopping thrills and spills and the obligatory dense and comforting tobacco fug of those splendid times.

If there was a particularly difficult speaker (which was most of the time), or a tricky exchange between the Prime Minister and his opposite number, we would huddle round the table outside the Chamber and check our notes at very great speed. Usually we could make some sort of sense of it, but there were occasions when even the serried ranks of Fleet Street's finest could not decipher a particular passage or indeed an individual crucial word.

In which case, since time was always desperately short, the answer was simple if not exactly one hundred per cent ethical. We hastily agreed on a suitable word or phrase to fill in the blanks and following the admirable principles of solidarity and safety in numbers, we all – Hansard included – inserted our unanimous choice and went merrily on our way. In those halcyon days there were, mercifully, no videos or tapes or other electronic paraphernalia on which an aggrieved MP could check his words against what appeared in the papers and we always got away with it.

Those were relatively minor transgressions. For the most part, the rules and regulations governing and restricting reporters in the House of Commons have always been clear cut, and transgressors were likely to get it in the neck, either from their own kind or from what are called 'the authorities'. So I knew I was chancing my arm when I entered a lift in which a stern notice proclaimed: 'Strictly for the use of MPs only.' To my dismay, the lift stopped at the next floor and in walked, of all people, Enoch Powell, strict guardian of all that was right and proper. He gave me – looking my most sheepish – a withering look, then ostentatiously studied the notice, before transferring his uncompromising gaze to me once again, uttering the words: 'Oh, I'm sorry. I hadn't noticed there had been a by-election.'

But I was not so lucky in 1965, when I climbed up the steps of a forbidden tower in order to gain an illicit glimpse of the body of Sir Winston Churchill being laid on the catafalque in Westminster Hall before the great man was to commence lying-in-state. As I mounted the spiral steps, I heard the dreaded footfall of police officers behind me. I swiftly concealed myself in a shadowy recess, hoping, in the tradition of the Keystone Cops, that the constables would carry on climbing past me and that I would be able to slip down and escape undiscovered. It was not to be. They caught me fair and square, and frogmarched me off the premises. But not content with that, they despatched a complaint couched in the most vitriolic language both to the Lord Great Chamberlain, Lord Cholmondeley, and to 'the authorities' of the press gallery. To have broken the rules was bad enough. But to have done that in relation to Sir Winston Churchill was unforgivable. I had to brace myself for the imminent storm. Nor did I have to wait long for the storm to break.

The Lord Great Chamberlain had himself written a letter, no less virulent than the one he had received, to the press gallery, about my 'reprehensible conduct'. I was duly summoned to appear before the then honorary secretary of the press gallery, Gordon Campbell, in the library, which was to become the Press Bar, to receive the mother-and-father of all dressings-down while Stella Thomas (since an MBE), the paid secretary of the gallery looked on. Ultimately, I had to write a letter of grovelling and abject apology to the Lord Great Chamberlain, which seemed to work, because I heard no more about it. But I was a marked man. It was not my finest hour. I did not even have a story to show for my ordeal.

There was a sequel to this story some 30 years later. In December 1993, ITN political correspondent Mark Webster was travelling in a cab in London when the driver recognised him. The cabbie ascertained that he knew me. 'When you next see him, please pass on my greetings,' he said, 'and then say to him, "Remember the lying-in-state of Sir Winston Churchill?"' It transpired that this cab-driver was one of the 'arresting' officers on that occasion, one of the men who took me in charge. I am not surprised that he did not forget the event either.

I got into further serious trouble many years later. One afternoon, the House was in a rowdy mood when discussing Northern Ireland. The great Dr Ian Paisley, firebrand leader of the Democratic Unionist Party in Northern Ireland, was sitting in one of the side galleries adjoining the press gallery.

I thought I would lean over the barrier to get a quick quote from Dr Paisley. As I did so, there were frantic cries of 'Order! Order!' from down below. What I had forgotten was that the gallery in which Dr Paisley was sitting, although on the same level as ours, was technically the floor of the House of Commons. So I had broken one of the strictest rules by trying to speak to a member who was actually in the Chamber. Needless to say, there was yet another a portentous complaint and I had to write yet another letter of abject apology, this time to Mr Speaker Weatherill. I was becoming quite an old hand as a groveller.

It's best to be humble about these things. One reporter, Nigel Nelson of the *Sunday People*, was rash enough once to pass some remarks in his paper about parliamentary security and was peremptorily banished from the Palace of Westminster for a number of weeks. His immediate response was to set up his 'office' in the bar of the Red Lion public house in nearby Whitehall, where he was regularly visited by his contacts. The galling thing from the viewpoint of the authorities of the House of Commons was that Nelson did not seem to miss any stories during his exile. Indeed, he profited from the sympathies of those who thought he had been hard done by.

Even in the sanctuary of the press gallery, life is not always calm and tranquil. Punches have been thrown in full view of MPs below. Blood has been spilt. Two *Daily Telegraph* reporters, each of them determined to occupy the same seat, suddenly exploded into fisticuffs in the full view of MPs down below. An unerring right hook was thrown with devastating effect. Then a desk top slammed. But by the time MPs looked up to see what was going on, peace had been restored. It was the fastest fight I ever saw, over in a flash, but not before drops of blood had cascaded on the writing desks.

On another occasion, I was sitting in the press gallery cafeteria minding my own business when a cup and saucer whizzed past my ear and smashed on the floor nearby. I cannot be sure who hurled the crockery but it certainly came from the direction of the volatile columnist Edward Pearce. I, of course, would be the last person to accuse him of that sort of conduct.

It's even worse for those who don't know the etiquette of the gallery. There was the case of the Estonian lady who must have wondered what hit her when she pulled her camera out in the press gallery in April 1994 and proceeded to take a snap of Prime Minister John Major answering questions. It must rank as one of the most heinous crimes in the book. I do not know how officialdom reacts in the legislatures of Estonia at the naked spectacle of a camera in the press box, but this budding David Bailey soon found out the hard way what happens at Westminster in such circumstances. It was as though she had been caught photographing a gunpowder factory in Albania. The Westminster stormtroopers, namely the doorkeepers, had her bundled out of the gallery and thrown on the mercy of Parliamentary security – the Serjeant-at-Arms' department.

I have often wondered what it is that gives cameras the status of something approaching an offensive weapon in Westminster. At one time, in the not too distant past, visitors were forbidden even to take snaps of the fountain in New Palace Yard, something which could anyway be done with impunity and ease from the pavement outside – but once you are within the precincts of the building, it suddenly becomes a very different matter indeed.

At least we are now allowed to take tape recorders into the gallery – and even the permission for that was only granted in the new millennium. It's of immense benefit to the likes of me because deafness is setting in and I could hear only those whose diction was clear and whose decibels were impressive. Even so, I tried to avoid using the tapes when I came out of the gallery because although they are an admirable back-up (and more than just a back-up in times of crisis) their use tends to slow things up. And that, for a news agency, is bad news.

Mobile phones are still looked on with horror in some parts of the Palace of Westminster. In the old library of the press gallery they were barred – a rule, I have to say, I simply ignored. Reporters have to be on call at all times, so it was a ban that pretty well everyone joined me in cheerfully flouting. Mobile phones were also barred in the Strangers' Cafeteria, a room which is so full of clatter and chatter that you would not think the occasional tinkling of a telephone would make the slightest difference to anybody or anything. I had no idea of the ban when I was joined by Conservative MP Dame Marion Roe and immediately answered a call. Dame Marion banged on the table in front of me a small wooden block depicting on one side a mobile phone with an angry red line drawn across it. I affected not to understand what she was getting excited about and completed the conversation.

The mobile rule doesn't generally apply to MPs, who can use them when and where they like, even in that holy of holies, the members' lobby. However, the Chamber itself remains an area where even MPs are expected to switch them off. The great Michael Heseltine forgot to do this and once, to his huge embarrassment, his mobile rang out loud and clear while he was delivering a speech of great passion and fury. Needless to say, this put him off his flow and he had immense difficulty in finding the right button to press to stop the infernal thing, while the Speaker and the formidable, bewigged clerks looked on with scorn and even contempt. Those of us who were fortunate enough to enjoy this scene of humiliation from above in the press gallery indulged in our usual bout of infantile giggling. In pre-mobile days, it was an old-fashioned alarm on a wristwatch that troubled the venerable Dick Mitchison, Labour MP for Kettering. He was plunged into confusion and embarrassment by this disturbance.

Now those old-fashioned watches are as rare a sight at Westminster as Pitmans shorthand. Only a few reporters now use it, the majority writing Teeline which is reportedly much easier to learn than Pitmans (it could scarcely be harder) but, again according to its exponents, is actually not so fast.

Even Charles Dickens, when he was a parliamentary reporter, wrote shorthand. It was Gurney's shorthand, which was itself disappearing by the start of the 20th century. Dickens entered the press gallery as a boy. But he was soon to make a name for himself there as 'the fastest and most accurate man in the gallery'. Indeed, he was so successful, with a number of journals printing his reports, that with his new-found prosperity he went out and purchased 'a new hat and a very handsome blue cloak with velvet facings.' However, he did not have a very high estimation of MPs, denouncing most of them as 'pompous' men who seemed to spend most of the time 'speaking sentences with no meaning in them'.

In those early days, when Dickens had to contend with MPs, he was said to have 'literary abilities of a high order with reporting capacity of a superior kind which are seldom found in conjunction. They were so in the case of Mr Dickens in a measure which never were before in any other man since parliamentary reporting was known.' It would no doubt be churlish to suggest that the same may be true even in the years since the great novelist left the press gallery for greater things. But he found working there in the 1830s 'exhilarating and exciting' although pretty arduous.

'I have worn my knees by writing on them on the old back row of the old press gallery of the old House of Commons,' he wrote afterwards. 'I have worn my feet standing to write in a preposterous pen in the old House of Lords where we used to huddle together like so many sheep, kept in waiting until the Woolsack might want restuffing.'

Charles Dickens is not the only parliamentary reporter to have had difficulty with his shorthand. Once an agency House of Lords reporter misread his outline for 'physical' as 'bicycle'. Somehow, he managed to make a sentence of it which, astonishingly, made sense, although, it has to be said, it bore little resemblance to what had been uttered in the Chamber of the Upper House. Even more bizarrely, the same reporter misread 'child' for 'trout', which did at least cause a hawk-eyed subeditor to inquire of the reporter about the prevalence of 'trout abuse'.

Soon after the millennium, the politicians cast covetous eyes over the press gallery premises. Even though they had built at great expense that great monstrosity Portcullis House, they were still after more space for their pampered MPs. The number of MPs in the Commons had not increased hugely since 1950, and at that time, before all sorts of annexes were put to use for MPs' accommodation, there was no great clamour from the authorities to hijack space used by the press. However, I suspect MPs were envious of our facilities. We have nothing, really, to grumble about. However, a lot of journalists would probably prefer to have their offices outside the Palace of Westminster, to avoid being controlled by the Serjeant-at-Arms' Department, which effectively rules the roost. Although we can argue our case whenever they wish to make changes to the press gallery we do not have the final say.

It did seem odd, however, this sudden official interest in our premises. Bureaucrats came round – I as chairman for part of the time had to help show them round – looking at every nook and cranny. They asked for instance: 'Why do you want a library?' 'Why do you need a bar?' 'Would you be prepared to give up your dining room?' We have retained all the facilities.

There was more official interest in the daily running of Parliament after spring 2004, when some of the Fathers 4 Justice campaign members threw contraceptives containing purple-dyed flour at Prime Minister Tony Blair. There were to be new security measures, introduced at the behest of the Speaker, Michael Martin. The main new restriction for reporters was that day passes were banned, making it difficult for one-off reports to be made. A lesser change was made to the dress code. Men have always had to wear a jacket and a tie. But it had been the custom for as long as I could remember for us to enter the gallery in shirt-sleeves in the summer months (although you still had to wear a tie) and this is no longer allowed.

That seemed unnecessary, given that people in the public gallery can come in in fancy dress if they wish. It was all part of the perpetual petty cold war between 'us' and 'them'. And perhaps it's not entirely a bad thing. It could be said that MPs have been subject over recent years to far more mockery than they have been used to for a while, particularly from the pens of the parliamentary sketch writers, and above all by the brilliant Quentin Letts of the *Daily Mail.*

* * * * *

When I was chairman of the press gallery for the second time, it was part of my job to find speakers each month for the press gallery lunches. In the late spring of 2005 I managed successfully to invite Lord Archer of Weston-Super-Mare at a time when the novelist was still serving his four-year sentence for perjury. He was to appear at our September lunch, although when I made the arrangements, the parole board still had to meet to decide whether to let him out in July of that year. I thought it wise not to mention this to anybody because if it appeared in the papers, the board might have regarded it as arrogant on the part of Lord Archer to be making lunch dates for September when, in theory at least, he still had some of his sentence to complete. The parole board reached the predicted decision that Archer should be freed in July and it was then that I thought it would be all right to tell my colleagues on the press gallery committee.

The initial response was that it was quite a coup. But a few days later I was approached and told that it was not such a good idea after all. Various people had been mulling over it and I was told that it would be bad for the press gallery's reputation to have a convicted criminal as our guest of honour. This hot news property would have made his first speech on his release from prison to the press, which would have been revealing, but I was told to cancel the invitation. The result of all this, when the story leaked out (it shouldn't be difficult to guess the source of the revelation), was the press gallery bigwigs were labelled as 'boobies' in one diary column.

By that time I was used to the ways of the press gallery. I have always been of the John Major school of thinking, namely, 'if it ain't broke, don't fix it'. For my second election, I wrote a light-hearted piece in the parliamentary *House Magazine* to this effect, describing myself as a 'do-nothing chairman'. My wife improved on this with the expression 'a sleeping dog chairman', a phrase which also went into this piece. It didn't go down as intended. That article was ripped out of the magazine and stuck on the gallery's notice board with the offending passage prominently highlighted. The gallery's secretary, Benedict Brogan of the *Daily Telegraph*, and incoming vice-chairman Chris Fisher of the *Eastern Daily Press*, both resigned when I won the election without having campaigned at all. Yet in the end, the absence of a vice-chairman seemed to make no difference whatsoever and Greg Hurst of *The Times* volunteered for the secretary-ship. I must say his mastery of detail, his diligence and thoroughness were an eye-opener for me: he was a superb performer and just the man to have when the press gallery is in the hands of a 'sleeping dog chairman'.

The high spot of that year was the bicentenary banquet which was brilliantly masterminded by Brian Shallcross, who went on to succeed me as chairman. I sat between Prime Minister Tony Blair and the Speaker, Michael Martin. The deal was that the Prime Minister should speak right at the outset, stay for at least the starter and hopefully the main course and then leave with his wife Cherie. Blair was a highly genial, amiable and entertaining character. Immediately he sat down after making his speech, he turned to me and inquired, 'Well, what do you think of the Government so far?'

I have to say it was not precisely the sort of inquiry I had expected. I suppose if I had been a political animal this would have been a magnificent opportunity to unburden myself. But not being a political animal, I feebly said: 'I require notice of that question…' and proceeded to attack the starter. It transpired that he regularly asked this question of his neighbours at dinner engagements. Blair himself pecked at his food like a bird and stayed only for the starter course. I expressed my worries that he would be leaving the event under-nourished. 'Don't worry,' he replied, 'I'll get something back at Number 10.' Was it, perhaps, that he had previously endured a meal at this particular London hotel?

Work is the Curse of the Drinking Classes

Clement Attlee, the first post-World War II Prime Minister, was a stickler for propriety and a man, it was said, who would never use one syllable where none would do. He always advised new Labour MPs: 'Keep out of the bars.' But judging by the crowds, not to say scrummages, sometimes seen in the parliamentary bars, one wonders how much Attlee's advice was followed, not only by his contemporaries but by later generations of parliamentarians as well.

I have been in trouble before for talking about MPs' drinking habits. Let us suffice it to say that quite a few of them have a jolly good time. To suggest, from the press gallery, that a member in the House was the worse for wear through drink used to be one of the worst 'offences' a parliamentary reporter could commit. So nervous, at one time, were newspapers and news agencies about even the most oblique suggestion that an MP might be asleep in the chamber or – horror upon horrors – the worse for wear, that sometimes strange behaviour was totally ignored. Fairly late one night, a Tory MP entered the Chamber, swaying from side to side, collapsed on one of the leather benches and fell into a noisy slumber. As usual, no one took the slightest notice.

But in the story I wrote from that, I said that this member entered the Chamber and then 'sat tight', hoping to give the impression that he was inebriated without actually saying so. But the sub-editor, so nervous was he, even removed that expression from my copy.

Labour MP Clare Short was not so nervous when she publicly declared that the late Alan Clark, then a Defence Minister, was inebriated as he made a statement from the Treasury Bench. It was something which Mr Clark, to his credit, did not, indeed could not, deny.

In the autumn of 1987, a distinguished psychiatrist almost found himself hauled before the Speaker for suggesting that Members of Parliament were not always as sober as they might appear to be to the unpractised eye. He said, in as patronising a manner as he could muster: 'I shall be delighted to help any honourable member and their noble colleagues who find themselves in thrall to the demon drink.' Well, as invariably happens to people who are 'only trying to help', he soon began to wish that he had kept his mouth shut. He had succeeded in bringing a ton of bricks down on his head. Sir Nicholas Winterton, the doughty Conservative MP for Macclesfield, led the protests. He described the remarks as 'thoroughly offensive and insulting' and reported them to the Speaker, who, fortunately for the psychiatrist, declined to pursue the matter.

Around about the same time, an eminent neurologist also publicly expressed doubts about the mental state of Members of Parliament. He outraged Westminster by suggesting that politicians and national leaders should be given regular tests for brain disorders which, he claimed, would open the way to 'preventive maladministration'. And he warned, too, that ageing politicians were 'potentially dangerous because they might be in a state of concealed brain failure while controlling the lives of thousands of people'. To drive home his point this expert, totally oblivious to the fury he was provoking, named Ramsay MacDonald, Stanley Baldwin and Neville Chamberlain as the three Prime Ministers who, in his view, became inept through mental disability yet remained in office.

Reading of these antics, you will not be surprised to hear that one day in November 1993 I stepped into a cab at Westminster, shortly before midnight, and the driver looked at me with some astonishment. He then said, to my great surprise: 'Good grief, sir, you're sober!' I had, by that year, already stopped drinking for a decade, so I wondered whether this particular cabbie still retained a vivid memory of some spectacular performance by me when I was still hitting the Guinness. I waited somewhat apprehensively for the driver to recount to me some embarrassing episode which I probably had not remembered the following morning, never mind 10 years on.

But, no, it was not that. What he then said was this: 'You are the first person I have picked up at the House of Commons for years who has not been verging on the paralytic.' Which tells you probably as much as you need to know about the place…

However, it is true to say that soon after the millennium, the drinking cult at Westminster subsided considerably. This must have had a lot to do with the drastic changes in the hours of sitting. MPs used to congregate in the bars waiting to take part in late-night divisions. In more recent times, most days of the week, the House sits through what the civilised world would call the lunch break and often rises in the evening at an hour when one would normally be between the soup and the fish at dinner-time. The result is that the bars and the dining rooms and cafeterias are by no means as busy as they used to be. Equally, the figures have shown that the consumption of alcohol has dropped as well.

The so-called Strangers' Bar, overlooking the terrace of the Palace of Westminster, has perhaps been the rowdiest bar in the building and that includes the Press Bar, which must run it a very close second. The Strangers' Bar, sometimes known as The Stranglers, was a traditional haunt of Labour MPs more than anyone else and often their trade union friends – it was also known as The Kremlin. I have even seen MPs rolling around the floor in mortal combat, with the police having to be called. Once, a 'way out' sign, complete with arrow, suddenly appeared outside the Strangers' Bar. It was affixed to the wall and was, wait for it, just four inches from the ground. When I inquired whether the place had been invaded by a colony of dwarfs, I was sternly rebuked and told by an official: 'The sign is where it is to accommodate those who leave the bar on their hands and knees.' Since he said this with a totally straight face, I am assuming that it was not meant to be a joke.

One former Serjeant-at-Arms, the late Sandy Lennox, whose ruddy complexion betrayed a liking for gin, used to get into trouble with his wife over what she regarded as his excessive intake. She banned him from visiting the St Stephen's Tavern opposite the palace, which had been his practice, to consume large quantities on a regular basis, still attired in his formal robes, silk stockings and all. But he had a cunning plan to circumvent this little problem. He used to leave his overcoat hanging on a particular peg, with enough cash in one of the pockets to cover a bottle of gin. One of his minions, a doorkeeper, used to fish the cash from the pocket, repair to the pub, buy the bottle and stick the bottle in the coat pocket. The perk for the doorkeeper was that he could keep the change.

Winston Churchill once said that when he was younger, he made it a rule never to take strong drink before lunch. Later he somewhat revised that: 'It is now my rule never to do so before breakfast.' As a result, and with a clear conscience, he would regularly tuck away a bottle of hock with his bacon and eggs. But even that degree of self-control was barely met by some of the Cabinet Ministers in the late 1960s. Fred Peart (Agriculture) and Ray Gunter (Labour) were regularly to be seen in the Lords Staff Bar at around 9am, sometimes waiting, with some degree of impatience, outside the door of this hidden-away drinking den before it was unlocked. The idea that any present-day Cabinet Ministers would indulge in early-morning drinking, presumably to top up their hangovers from excesses the previous evening, could not even be contemplated. The hard men have disappeared and ministerial hangovers are a thing of the past.

The hardest of hard men was probably George Brown, whose drinking feats were heroic. When President Kennedy was assassinated in 1963, Brown, as Foreign Secretary, was wheeled on to television to express the horror and sorrow of the British Government at this outrage. However, it being latish in the day, Brown was not at his most sober or articulate. In fact his on-screen performance was so spectacular that a po-faced BBC official 'explained' to the nation that the Foreign Secretary's demeanour could be attributed to the fact that he was 'tired and emotional'. Never before or since has an innocent expression found its way so quickly into books of quotations. The satirical magazine *Private Eye* instantly latched on to it – and the rest is history. Harold Wilson once described Brown as a brilliant Foreign Secretary – until four o'clock in the afternoon. Brown once said: 'Many politicians drink too much and womanise too much. I never fell into the second category.'

Once during a general election campaign when I was drinking copiously with him in a pub in Middlesbrough, Brown made me swear a solemn oath that I would not tell his wife Sophie that he was back on the bottle again. He was lucky, because I was feeling in a pretty malevolent mood at the time. Earlier in the day, I had inquired of his driver whether he would give me a lift the eight miles into Middlesbrough from where we then were. It was pouring with rain and I had no transport. A few minutes later the driver returned to tell me that Brown's message to me was: 'Let the bugger walk.'

* * * * *

The press bar has also had its moments. There have been occasions when the barman has come in in the mornings to clear up and start afresh to find some of the customers from the previous evening laid out in a state of inebriated stupefaction on the benches in the bar. One member of the press gallery was actually physically carried downstairs to the Westminster underground station platform. While he was waiting for the train he slumped on the platform. An ambulance was called and the medics initially thought they had a corpse on their hands.

The body was covered, the ambulance sent away and a more suitable vehicle was summoned to take the body to the mortuary. When it arrived the corpse suddenly perked up and the muffled words, 'A large scotch, please. And no ice,' emanated from under the blanket. That vehicle, too, was sent away, and the 'body' staggered on to the next train home and to a wife who would probably not be full of the joys of spring when she witnessed what was reeling up the garden path.

Police officers regularly used to come up to the Press Bar, probably to escape from MPs, who were rarely found there. One regular visitor, known as 'Wickets' (the number on his uniform was 111), used to run a clandestine convenience store on the premises whose principal – and probably only – stock-in-trade was contraceptives. From time to time superior officers banned the police from coming, afraid, no doubt and with some justification, they would fall into bad company and emerge in a state incompatible with doing their constabulary duties. One such policeman, Ken Thomas, a relative of the then Speaker, George Thomas (later Lord Tonypandy), consumed an entire bunch of daffodils which were on the bar, in an excess of Welsh patriotic fervour on St David's Day, washing them down with Carlsberg lager. They did not appear to have done him too much damage, because he was back at his post the following morning, looking no worse than usual.

In those days, the Press Bar was at the end of the cafeteria counter, where it is again today. At one end, there was raucous drinking and carousing and at the other end our more demure colleagues (we christened them Ovaltinies, I am ashamed to recall) sipped their tea, munched their toast and looked on disapprovingly.

It was not long before the state of antipathy – which did once or twice spill out into open warfare – between the boozers and the Ovaltinies was ended. The press gallery library, in which I had been well and truly carpeted some months earlier, was moved to the next room and what was the library became the Press Bar.

A new machine appeared in the cafeteria which, according to its manufacturers, would quickly cook you a snack. It was, I suspect, the crude forerunner of the microwave. However, the press gallery was an immovably conservative organisation and any new mechanical object was viewed not only with the deepest suspicion but also with something akin to resentment. The machine's days were clearly numbered even before it was installed.

Happily, the suspicion in which it was held soon proved to be justified. Freddie Barnett, a veteran Press Association parliamentary reporter and a wartime hero of the Palace of Westminster Home Guard, invited this contraption to grill a kipper for him. This it did, but in the process it managed to reduce a regular-sized kipper to the size of a healthy tadpole. It was with ill-concealed glee that Mr Barnett presented this offering for inspection by the catering management, demanding his money back. This was denied him. He was told, however, he could have another item instead of the same value. When he said he would like a boiled egg, the staff told him that was not on the menu. A hugely disgruntled Freddie Barnett stalked off, threatening to make an issue of it. He was as good as his word. This soon became a cause célèbre. The matter was put on the agenda of the press gallery committee, which gravely considered this injustice. The issue became so prolonged – like Jarndyce v. Jarndyce in *Bleak House* – that it was still unresolved when Mr Barnett expired, never having reclaimed his outlay.

The bar itself had once remained open until midnight or the rising of the House, whichever was the later, but eventually the rules were changed to read 'whichever was the earlier'. Usually, when the bar was supposed to close, there was a crowd of well-imbibed but still thirsty customers around and barmen could sometimes be bribed successfully to keep it open a little longer, even a lot longer. Dawn occasionally broke and the morning rush-hour was in full swing before the shutters went up in the Press Bar.

There was at least one member of the bar staff who could not be bribed or cajoled in any way to keep the bar open beyond its appointed hour. Her name: Jean Hanratty, a stern and uncompromising guardian of the rules and a devout Roman Catholic. She was not regarded as the world's speediest bartender. Indeed one of our colleagues, who must remain nameless as he is now in the Government's service, became so impatient as he waited to be served that he muttered to a friend sotto voce: 'If the service had been like this at the Last Supper, there never would have been a Crucifixion.' Unfortunately for him, it was not sotto enough. Jean Hanratty's sharp ears picked it up and he was not merely ordered out of the bar but banned from it for three months. And one Edgar Copestick, an experienced Press Association parliamentary reporter, did not exactly endear himself to the daunting Miss Hanratty when, in a cutting statement on the quality of the beer, used to ask for 'a pint of cloudy, please, Jean.' Needless to say, Jean did not find this reflection on her professional abilities at all amusing. However, Copestick was sentenced to no more than what in military terms would be called 'a severe reprimand'.

Sam Anderson, until his untimely and sudden death at the age of 50, was the most famous barman the press gallery has had – probably even the entire Palace of Westminster. Although there was regularly a notice on the bar, 'Do not ask for credit, because a punch in the teeth often offends,' Sam actually handed it out to all and sundry as if there were no tomorrow. He was equally malleable when it came to closing time. Determined imbibers used to queue up around the back of the bar, pleading for more. Sam would start off being adamant. 'No more!' the cry rang out. However, he could invariably be persuaded to change his mind, although his tormenters usually had to perform the complex rituals of something akin to the courtship dance of the praying mantis before he surrendered to their intense blandishments.

On one not-so-celebrated occasion, when he had quite definitely gone home, there was an incident which demonstrated that the grille he put up at closing, daunting though it was, was not sufficient deterrent for really resolved drinkers. Between us, we manufactured a Heath Robinson contraption resembling a gigantic drinking straw. This we poked through the grille and, despite our trembling hands, managed to insert it in the top of a bottle of Pernod which the ever-trusting Sam had carelessly left open. Through this bizarre means, and seemingly defying many of the laws of gravity, we were somehow able to consume a large quantity of the contents of this bottle. Neat Pernod is never a good idea. I can tell you that although there are many things that happened in the Press Bar over the years about which my memory is distinctly hazy, this was an event which has stuck in my mind all these years, not least the prolonged hangover which followed. I might add that the following day the grille was replaced by an impenetrable iron sheet which remained until the bar closed in 2007, which was shortly before it was replaced by a 'state of the art' (dreaded phrase) drinking den that bore my name.

In Sam's day I sometimes felt that more business was done and more money changed hands in the ludicrously-styled 'dry' hours, when the Press Bar was supposed to be shut, than when it was legally open for business. The challenge of wheedling Sam round to your own point of view seemed to be much more enjoyable than legitimate drinking during the official opening hours.

On another occasion, Sam was himself – to employ a Glaswegian expression – hopelessly refreshed, and the business of counting out change was far too tiresome and complex an operation for him to undertake. So he simply charged a straight £3 for each order, whether it was a single, small glass of lemonade, or half-a-dozen large scotches. The following morning Sam, with some trepidation, cashed up. To his, and everyone else's astonishment, the money taken tallied precisely with the amount of goods purveyed.

Sam once had to pop over to the House of Lords on an errand. On his way back, he was accosted by an American businessman in the corridor outside the House of Commons banqueting rooms. The American asked him where he was from. When Sam replied, innocently and accurately, that he had come from the House of Lords, his interrogator immediately handed Sam his business card and was given the telephone extension number of the Press Bar in return.

'You will be hearing from me,' the American said. Sure enough, a few days later, the telephone rang in the Press Bar and the American voice at the other end inquired: 'Is Lord Anderson there?'

Sam, unabashed, replied: 'That's me…' The outcome of that was that the American invited Sam out to lunch at the Savoy Grill, because he believed that this humble barman was actually an influential British nobleman with whom he might be able to transact some useful business.

Once a meddlesome Labour MP with overdeveloped nannyish instincts suggested to *Daily Express* reporter George Lochhead, who was slumped on the bar in a posture which told you all you needed to know about his condition, that it was time for him to go home in a taxi. George staggered out of the bar and tumbled into the taxi. Meanwhile, the MP was negotiating with the reluctant taxi-driver to take Lochhead back to Orpington, and finished up paying the fare out of his own pocket. Imagine, therefore, the MP's chagrin and dismay when he returned to the bar, having performed his good deed for the day, to find George ensconced again, the MP's own money being irretrievably driven away in a taxi without a passenger. While the MP had been negotiating with the taxi-driver, Lochhead surreptitiously slipped out of the other door and had stumbled back to the bar.

You always knew, incidentally, that when Lochhead began to sing (a charitable use of the word) 'Falling in Love with Love' he was well on the road to boozers' bliss. And whenever MPs appeared in the Press Bar, to our great glee he used to inform them in his unique high-pitched rasping voice: 'You are all pigmies…the lot of you' He once came into the Commons swathed in bandages.

'What happened, George?' we inquired.

'I slipped on the slopes of Glen Fiddich,' came the reply.

With all of these booze-fuelled adventures, it will come as little surprise to learn that the Press Bar has also been the scene of late-night sexual adventures. It was highly fortunate for those involved that the in-house constabulary and security guards who now infest the place, never once, to my knowledge, ever set foot in the bar at crucially embarrassing moments. My own manifold misdemeanours would have paled into insignificance if 'authority' had caught the Press Bar with, metaphorically, its pants down. There would have been a regular snowstorm of memos to higher authorities and the rules governing our conduct would have been tightened to such a degree as to confine us in a straitjacket.

* * * * *

Annie's Bar – named after its first barmaid – was created before World War II. It was bombed out during the war and reopened only in the 1960s. But in the 1990s, the powers-that-be at the House of Commons decided they wanted the room for something else. So Annie's was abruptly moved to the windowless, airless dungeon, which was the Commons Staff Bar, leaving the staff, so to speak, to hang out to dry. Annie's Bar always, misleadingly, had the reputation as the place where reporters would do business with MPs and where stories were born. But, in fact, although the clientele was limited to lobby correspondents, MPs and a few senior officials, it was far too public a place for such clandestine activities.

In my case, when I was illicitly filled in on the activities of the Labour National Executive meetings by the late Labour MP Tom Bradley, we used to resort to the dingy Staff Bar, from which we were technically barred, to conduct our business. Annie's Bar, like the Press Bar, closed in the afternoon. But you could make an agreeable arrangement with the very accommodating bar staff to leave you drinks behind the voluminous window curtains. So there was, mercifully, very little danger of dying of thirst during the dry periods of the day. If you think that all this implies that Parliament used to be awash with drink and its occupants – or at least some of them and mainly reporters – in a state of induced merriment, you might not be far wrong. However, the place has deteriorated to a condition where sensible drinking is now practised. Fings ain't what they used to be. So we must fight back to restore the culture of bad habits in tune with those wise words of Sammy Davis:

'What shall we drink to?'

'About four in the morning...'

Westminster –
The Good Life

The late Lord Fitt – better known as Gerry Fitt, the one-time leader of the Northern Ireland SDLP party – used to stand on the terrace of the House of Commons watching crowded pleasure boats cruising up and down the River Thames. You would rarely find Gerry without a large tumbler of gin in his hand. Whenever a boat, crammed with tourists, came within earshot, he would brandish his glass in the air, crying out: 'It's all free!' This splendidly mischievous fellow was helping to spread the story – fictitious, of course – that Members of Parliament, whether in the House of Commons or the Lords, live a hedonistic life, guzzling subsidised drinks in bars which never seem to close and eating sumptuous meals, part paid for by the taxpayer, in lush surroundings.

When not doing that, they can be sitting around watching television, playing chess, snoozing in the library (or sometimes in the Chamber itself), indulging themselves in their own private work and whizzing abroad to the most exotic places on trips which are officially called fact-finding missions, but which in reality are nothing more than freebies. Or so the stories go. As the Labour MP Dennis Skinner once said: 'You never find MPs going on fact-finding tours to Greenland in the middle of winter.'

What is more, the late and splendid Tory MP Alan Clark embarrassed his colleagues hugely when he publicly pointed out: 'Free telephones, subsidised food, air-conditioning, strawberries and cream on the riverside terrace, watching the peasants go by in their vulgar pleasure craft.' There was more: 'The Palace of Westminster is the most wonderful place. A "tawny male" paradise, 11 bars, seven ticker tapes giving you the news, devoted staff who work 22 hours a day, special rooms for interviews, watching television or parking members of one's family. Champagne and toasted teacake at any time of day. Leather armchairs bigger than those of any club in St James's. What more could they want?' I think they would probably have wanted Mr Clark not to have spilled the beans quite so comprehensively...

Well, the truth may not be quite like that, but it can be very near to it. An MP who has no particular political ambition can, if he chooses, enjoy the cushiest of lives at Westminster and yet can be seen by his constituency party – the real boss of a Member of Parliament – as a hard-working backbencher, always attending to his local problems. I remember one case, in the 1960s, where a Conservative backbencher spent nearly all his time making vast sums of money in the City of London. Each week, he would table two questions to ministers for written answer (which meant he did not even have to attend to get the replies) about local issues. When the answers appeared in Hansard, the *Official Report of Parlimentary Debates*, he tore out the relevant pages, scribbled his own brief comments at the bottom and posted it to his local newspaper. So each week, this MP figured in two stories in that newspaper, each of them involving a local matter, giving the impression that he was beavering away like a man possessed on behalf of his constituents. In fact, he rarely appeared at Westminster at all, occasionally turning up for a crucial vote if he was so minded.

Sometimes MPs seem to want more privileges than are accorded to those they patronisingly describe as 'ordinary people', or worse 'real people' or worse still as 'pond life'. Some MPs complain about the public school atmosphere of Parliament and its resemblance to a gentleman's club. I went to a public school and in all my 40-plus years reporting at Westminster, I have found absolutely no connection between the two. For a start, there is precious little discipline exercised in Parliament, except by the Whips, which any MP with any spirit in him will treat with disdain. If MPs feel strongly enough about an issue which is at odds with their party's official line, then they will generally tell the Whips to take a running jump – and rightly so – and vote how their conscience tells them.

* * * * *

The late Sir Ray Powell, the one-time Labour MP for Ogmore, had what was probably the most unenviable job in the House of Commons. He was the man who allotted office accommodation for his colleagues at Westminster. It was a task which had all the potential to cost you all your friends and gain you a whole host of new enemies. His internal postbag was not, therefore, necessarily a joy to read. One of the classic missives he received was from Diane Abbott, the Labour MP for Hackney North and Stoke Newington. She penned these few sad words for him: 'Dear Mr Powell: I'm chairless, deskless, roomless – and speechless.'

But Powell did have some moments to savour. Ken Livingstone was never a popular figure in the House of Commons, though he was one of the best-known. When he was leader of the Greater London Council, abolished by Margaret Thatcher, he became (behind her) the most famous politician in the land. And that was even before he arrived at Westminster. When Powell was confronted by Livingstone in search of an office, he remained deadpan. He looked up dreamily and said to the man whose photograph was splashed over the newspapers almost on a daily basis: 'Name please.' That must have stung. I understand that at first Livingstone was allocated about the worst accommodation that Powell could find.

And there was another even more striking example of the contempt in which Livingstone's colleagues regarded him at Westminster. Early in 1988, he was barred from the Commons for five days for calling the Conservative Attorney General, Sir Patrick Mayhew, an 'accomplice to murder' over the Royal Ulster Constabulary's alleged 'shoot-to-kill' policy in Northern Ireland. During the period of his exile from the precincts of the Palace of Westminster, the Labour policy review committee, of which he was a member, was due to meet in the Commons which was then, of course, out of bounds to him. So eager was he to attend the meeting, that he tried to persuade his colleagues to change the venue and hold it instead at the party's south London headquarters. But they would not budge. Livingstone then, apparently, resorted to desperate measures. He actually offered to pay the taxi fares for his nine or so committee colleagues to take them down to south London. Even then he got a dusty answer.

* * * * *

Ken Livingstone's successor as Mayor of London was Boris Johnson. Looking like a windswept haystack, Johnson bounced into politics in 2001 to embark on a short but extraordinary and explosive parliamentary career. Many of his contemporaries in the House of Commons did not know how to deal with him. So they took the easy way out and labelled him a clown and a buffoon. He certainly was not that, even though he exuded the impression of being shambolic, forgetful, chaotic and gaffe-prone.

But his so-called 'gaffes', like those of the Duke of Edinburgh, were not really gaffes at all. He merely said true things in a stark, uninhibited way which shocked the conventional elite and had the tabloid newspapers screaming at him. A dull academic called Vernon Bogdanor, Professor of Government at Oxford University, has said: 'David Cameron must hope that Boris can be muzzled and he has, apparently, appointed minders to insure against future gaffes...Conservative hopes of winning the next election depend on Boris ceasing to be Boris.'

The dry-as-dust professor doesn't get it, does he? It was because Boris was Boris and a refreshing gust of air compared with many of his workaday colleagues at Westminster that he won the mayoral election. His critics – including plenty in his own party – thought he was incapable of being serious and were horrified when David Cameron, the Tory leader, in a stroke of genius, chose him as the party candidate to fight Ken Livingstone for the mayoralty of London. Boris, to the regret of his many admirers, did, however, suddenly try to turn serious – not altogether successfully.

He had his hair cut in line with the pudding-basin style (as opposed to his former straw-coloured sheepdog look), donned suits which fitted him, polished his shoes and, worst of all, started to talk like his fellow MPs, in stilted sentences culled, no doubt, from the Westminster book of truisms and clichés and endeavoured to sound like a man with gravitas. Those who canvassed for Boris during the campaign reported that as many questions were asked on the doorstep about his hair as about his policies. That old corny issue of 'elitism' was also occasionally raised because Boris was an Old Etonian. When the former Conservative MP Harry Greenway reported to the candidate that his Eton background could become an issue, Boris replied: 'I don't give a toss.'

It all paid off. He swept Livingstone out of office – something which the Tory Party had previously thought was nigh on impossible. And so he was occupying one of the most powerful and influential posts in the country (even more so, some say, than the Prime Minister himself) with millions of pounds at his disposal. Within days of embarking on this awesome office, Boris was visited by the friendly and supportive Michael Bloomberg, the Mayor of New York. After their talks at London's City Hall, Mr Bloomberg presented Boris with an expensive crystal apple bought at Tiffany's. Boris, however, was either unaware of or had possibly forgotten about the habit of top politicians exchanging gifts after a meeting. In short, he had nothing to give the Mayor of New York in return. He rustled up a cheap T-shirt bearing on the front the map of the London underground system. It was gratefully received by Mr Bloomberg who commented later: 'It was hilariously awful, and for that reason I will always treasure it, even if I never wear it and I can assure you I won't'.

Boris Johnson, scholar that he is, has an unnerving habit, as did Enoch Powell, of occasionally answering reporters' questions in classical Latin. He sometimes inserts a Latin tag, or two, into his remarks when he is expounding on the state of the nation. All very impressive, no doubt, but not much use to your routine journalist, most of whom never advanced beyond the *amo, amas, amat* (I love, you love, he or she loves) stage, if they got even that far.

And although the improvement of public transport in the capital was one of the main planks of his election manifesto, Boris was, and remains, an ardent cyclist, able to get around London more easily and more quickly on his bike, he claimed, than he could have done in a taxi. But his mask slipped slightly over his dedicated campaign to crack down on crime when, soon after his election, he was spotted zooming across red traffic lights on his bicycle, in sympathy, no doubt, with Cameron, his leader, who a few weeks earlier had been photographed cycling the wrong way along a one-way street.

Mayor Johnson, however, could have been lost to journalism and possibly to politics as well had he demonstrated any aptitude for business. After graduating from Oxford he lasted just one week as a management consultant at LEK Consulting, explaining his rapid departure from that company with these immortal words: 'Try as I might, I could not look at an overhead projection of a growth profit matrix and stay conscious.'

I first met him when he was the Brussels correspondent of the *Daily Telegraph*. I can well remember him, in the late 1980s and early 1990s, tying both Margaret Thatcher and John Major in knots with his convoluted questions at Brussels press conferences about the incomprehensible (to me, anyway) highways and byways of the European Community. Dread spread over their prime ministerial faces whenever they saw Boris rise to question them. But in those days Boris, if not exactly meek, was far less bullish a character than he was to become. So diffident, in fact, was he that some of the hard-boiled Fleet Street reporters among the resident journalist community there felt he needed mothering against the slings and arrows of the wicked world outside! It seems laughable now.

In the House of Commons, until he retired from it as the MP for Henley-on-Thames, Johnson was one of the very few members who, when their names appeared on the TV monitors proclaiming that they were on their feet and speaking, caused other MPs to drop whatever they were doing and rush from the bars, the restaurants, and even the lavatories to hear him.

In a relatively short spell at Westminster – less than two Parliaments – Johnson rose from being a virtual nobody to become a household name and a highly recognisable figure, identified by the use of his forename only. Not many can boast that. But there is every chance that he could return to Westminster after his stint as Mayor of London is over. Until then, the Chamber of the House of Commons will be a greyer place without him, but London's City Hall will be injected with a new and sparky lease of life.

* * * * *

There are few more pathetic sights than that of a new MP standing in the members' lobby of the House of Commons, confused and alarmed, a little boy/girl lost amid the overwhelming grandeur and majesty of Parliament. A few days earlier they were bellowing through a loudspeaker at their election-saturated would-be electors, feted on all sides, the monarch of all they surveyed. Now they are cruelly brought down to size, the dazed new pupils. Lost in a myriad of corridors, not knowing which way to turn or what to do, they are pitiful figures engulfed by meaningless rules and incomprehensible procedures, and a building which makes the Hampton Court maze seem a cakewalk. Only 48 hours earlier, they were on the brink of putting the country to rights, and after that the world. Now, all these heady ambitions must take second place to finding the loo and somewhere to buy a sandwich.

All MPs complain, later on, that no one ever tells them what to do on arrival. Like first-time sex, one of them once told me, they thrash around in the dark and hope against hope that it will all come right in the end. Well, they need complain no more. Here are a few tips for the wet-behind-the-ears brigade:

The very first essential, especially if you are in the majority party, before you even unpack your bags, is to find a 'pair', an opponent to enable you to duck off votes together. An MP without a pair is unmistakable – a fretful, sleepless individual, who is compelled to live, night and day, at Westminster.

Be ingratiating, even unctuous, towards the police and uniformed doorkeepers and especially to the MP in charge of allocating office space. They have subtle powers to make your political life hell-on-earth – or the reverse.

Find out where the vote office is (for documents), the post office (for mail), and the board (for messages). Always check carefully before you respond to a call from a constituent in the central lobby. You may find yourself lumbered with a crank for hours on end.

Tear up all junk-mail, do not reply to green-ink correspondents, do not take cash for questions, and do not give your phone number to strangers; but always give it to the Press Association (I have an interest here).

Forget about your private life. You have just ended it. Whether you like it or not, your personal affairs have now become public property. So any amours on the side should be conducted with the utmost discretion, or preferably not at all. Opt for the celibate life – boring but wise.

Clement Attlee always warned newcomers to keep out of the bars. Don't forget that in Annie's Bar, a round includes everyone who is in the bar at the time. Once in this prison, you have to buy your way out. It sometimes costs hours – and a lot of money.

Should you wish to escape from the press, go to the terrace (reporters are banned). Other safe havens are the tea-room, the smoking room (it still retains its name even though no one is allowed to smoke there) and the members' dining room. But be warned: reporters tend to lurk and pounce at the most awkward moments and in the most surprising places.

If you want a reputation for being cocky, arrogant and a clever dick, make your maiden speech early. The wisest course is to wait until you know what you are talking about.

Do not try to flout and criticise rules which may seem pointless to you. If you start by antagonising the Speaker, then your life will be a misery. And recognise now that the power of the back-bencher is relatively zero. You would have more power on a parish council – and that is not a joke.

And always toe the party line. Remember, until and unless you get that great call to serve on the front bench, you are simply lobby-fodder as far as the Whips are concerned. Indeed, however grand you become, you remain the tool of the Whips, who will not care how important you think you are.

You might as well admit it now: you have surrendered your freedom and henceforth are in total thrall to the Whips.

So nice to see you!

Points of Order

The late Sir John Stradling Thomas, Conservative MP for Monmouth, was always one of the liveliest wires at Westminster and a convivial member of the pack in Annie's Bar. When he was a Minister of State at the Welsh Office, he was confronted in the Commons by a blue-in-the-face Labour MP protesting with Celtic fury that children in his constituency were having to attend schools that were more than 100 years old, with few comforts and fewer facilities.

Thomas responded: 'I have to tell the honourable gentleman that I have every sympathy with the plight of your constituents. But I have to say that it could have been far worse. After all, I attended a school that was 450 years old.' It brought the House down. The fact that he had omitted to mention that the school in question was Rugby did not go unnoticed.

Incidentally, it remains pretty obvious why John Stradling Thomas always used his middle name. His parents had presumably not noticed the potential embarrassment they were causing him by giving him the first name of 'John' when his surname was 'Thomas'. He did it for different reasons than those which caused Iain Duncan Smith, the former Tory leader, to use his middle name. That was presumably to avoid being mixed up by historical scholars of the future with the late Ian Smith the former rebel leader of Rhodesia.

* * * * *

Lieutenant Colonel Sir Walter Bromley-Davenport, a Tory (needless to say), had the loudest voice outside the drill sergeants' wing at Sandhurst – and a stately home to go with it. He barked and bellowed fit to break the rafters and, it was said, that his ancestors had been in the House for centuries on end.

Once, in the early 1950s when he was a Government Whip and the Tory majority was pretty skimpy, it was his duty to ensure that no Conservative backbenchers tried to sneak out of the premises unnoticed and thus threaten that narrow majority at subsequent divisions. Like some nightwatchman, this ferocious fellow was posted at one of the exits to ensure no one played truant. Alert as ever, he spotted a smartly dressed, well-heeled figure furtively disappearing into the night. This one, Sir Walter growled to himself, is not going to get away. So, creeping up behind the fugitive with as much silent stealth as he could command (which was not a great deal), our portly hero seized on the poor unfortunate wretch, grabbed him by the collar and booted him up the backside.

'Gotcha!' he cried with a flourish of triumph. But as he was about to embark on the mother and father of all dressings-down, he suddenly became aware of the awful truth. His glee was short-lived and turned to abject apology, an emotion which Sir Walter rarely displayed. For the man whose dignity he had outraged was not some errant Tory backbencher. It was the Belgian Ambassador to the Court of St James. Needless to say, Sir Walter and the Government, too, had to grovel supinely in order to avert an international diplomatic incident. Sir Walter returned to the backbenches, himself, metaphorically, booted up the rear.

* * * * *

Eyebrows were raised among officials at the House of Commons when they read a report by a Labour Whip concerning the conditions that his colleagues suffered while queuing up all night outside the public bill office in order to be first to submit their bills the moment the office opened in the morning. His report read: 'The snacks were poor, the ventilation worse and the smoking insufferable – but the crack was good and morale stayed high.' I bet it did. However, when officials from the Serjeant-at-Arms Department set out to investigate what appeared to be an admission of serious drug-taking by MPs within the precincts of the Palace of Westminster, he came in for a surprise. It appears that 'crack' is a north of England term for 'chatter' or 'conversation', which, until that day, had not reached the southeast of England.

* * * * *

Oliver Letwin, the Tory MP, is not the only gullible member of the House of Commons. He once let a complete stranger into his home on the pretext that he wanted to go to the lavatory. In fact, the scallywag took the opportunity to relieve Mr Letwin of some of his most precious possessions. Well, that story can probably be capped by the Old Harrovian Hugh Summerson, the former Conservative MP for Walthamstow, and once named the most romantic MP at Westminster. Summerson, whose full name is Hugo Hawksley Fitzthomas Summerson, is straight out of the Bertie Wooster or Gussie Fink-Nottle school of PG Wodehousian politics.

On one occasion he was cycling down Knightsbridge in fashionable central London when a man at a bus stop waved him down. Summerson dutifully, some might say recklessly, dismounted to listen to what this perfect stranger had to say. Needless to recount, he wanted money. He explained to Mr Summerson that he had been robbed and had no money for his fare home and so could the kind gentleman possibly oblige?

Later Mr Summerson commented on this incident: 'Being of a naturally soft-hearted disposition, and perhaps in this case rather foolish [you said it, mate], I gave him some money, whereupon honesty broke out across his face and he told me: "Actually, I am going to take it to the nearest pub and drink it."' At this point, the man disappeared into the adjacent licensed premises, leaving Mr Summerson, clutching his fevered brow, propping up his bicycle at the pavement's edge. And although Mr Summerson had possibly (although not certainly) worked out in advance that this might have been the reason for the man's approach, he was certainly startled to hear him frankly admit it. This only goes to prove what I have been saying for years: namely, that MPs should not be allowed out on their own.

* * * * *

Shortly before the 1992 general election a letter arrived at the House of Commons for Peter Mandelson MP, containing some photographs of him, no doubt for use in the campaign. The problem was that Mr Mandelson was not at that stage an MP. So the post office at the House of Commons tried to convince Peter Morrison MP that the missive was really for him – which it palpably was not. Mr Mandelson later came up with a bizarre 'explanation'. He said: 'Could the diversion of the photographs via Peter Morrison have been cleverer than at first sight, given that my name would, in fact, have been Peter Morrison if my mother had been my father and my father had been my mother.'

'The subconscious,' he added, 'works in mysterious ways.' Peter Mandelson's grandfather, of course, was Herbert Morrison, who was Foreign Secretary in Clement Attlee's postwar Labour Government.

*****

Michael Bramley, who was parliamentary editor of the Press Association towards the end of his 30-plus years in the press gallery, used to tell the story about his early days as a cub reporter on the *Worthing Herald*. One of his first jobs was to cover a concert being given in the town by an illustrious pianist. Towards the end of the concert, the pianist invited his audience to listen next to one of his own compositions which he modestly described as 'a shocking mess', according to Bramley's report in the next issue of the newspaper. The story, as written by Bramley, was picked up at the end of the week by the *Sunday Express* which, when he read it, caused the pianist some minor concern.

In fact, he wrote to the *Sunday Express* in these terms: 'I am flattered that you should have seen fit to mention me, but I have to take issue with you over a small point. It is merely that when you report me as saying "shocking mess", what I actually said was "Chopinesque". Perhaps your music critic was just a little hard of hearing...'

* * * * *

Seb Coe, the Olympic runner, who became a Tory MP and later still a life peer, arrived at Lord's Cricket Ground in the summer of 2003 and presented his ticket at one of the turnstiles, according to a story that swept Westminster. The gatekeeper took one look at the ticket, handed it back and told him: 'This is the wrong entrance for that ticket. You have to go to another entrance, halfway around the ground, I'm afraid. It will take you about 10 minutes to get there.'

Coe pulled himself up to his full (and not very impressive) height and said: 'Do you know who I am?'

At which the gatekeeper retorted po-faced: 'I beg your pardon, Mr Coe, in that case it will take you about two minutes to get there…'

Commons, a demanding but enticing paramour dealing out its own particular brand of bondage which its compliant victims find unbearably addictive.

There was one particularly poignant and telling revelation about the effect Parliament has on family life. The Conservative MP Humphrey Atkins (who died shortly after becoming Lord Colnbrook) was defending his marginal Merton and Morden seat in the 1980s. Just before the declaration of the poll, it looked as though Atkins had been beaten. He turned to his wife and two daughters to prepare themselves for defeat, and abjured them to leave the hall 'with their heads held high and proud'. But, to his amazement and joy, Atkins soon discovered that he had miscalculated. He had actually won. His glee was not shared by his daughters. They both burst into tears.

Of those who have physical dalliances in Westminster, an ex-wife of a former Labour MP described to me an amorous encounter she had with a Tory, who was a government minister. I am under a vow not to disclose their names, but I can assure you this is true. She said: 'He fell on me with the intensity of a lapsed vegetarian attacking a T-bone steak. All thoughts vanished as he caressed me expertly…A few hours later he woke me up with a cup of tea. He looked spruce and satisfied in his dark suit and silk tie. "Goodbye, my dear," he said. "I must leave you now to go to my ministry." And that was that.' It was excitement and passion followed by the ice-cold and unfriendly light of day. She occasionally saw this man again – not to speak to let alone to engage in any further dalliance. But he never, ever spoke to her, nor even acknowledged her presence.

The Press Bar has had its amorous moments, too. The next best thing (reportedly) to membership of the Mile High Club (for those who have 'made it' aloft in an aeroplane) is the Hot Bench Club, but I cannot be sure I know anybody who belongs to it. Just as well, perhaps. Rumours persist that very adventurous souls have achieved bliss on the Woolsack, where the Lord Chancellor sits in the House of Lords. I have not yet come across an authenticated instance of this having happened, although I am sure it has done. I do know, however, of a couple who did some pretty heavy petting, undiscovered, on this most holy of holies. However, I would not have thought that the prickly and lumpy nature of the horsehair with which the Woolsack ironically is filled, is not the ideal venue for amorous bliss.

There has always been what is called a subtext of sex at Westminster. One Tory MP, Ronald Bell (who once commendably said: 'The connection between humbug and politics is too long established to be challenged') actually expired, it is reported, while in congress with his secretary. But of the pretty close encounters of the amorous kind, it is also true that Westminster lips have remained uncharacteristically sealed.

So you will see – and the following pages will show it – life at Westminster is not all statutory instruments, early day motions, and debates about sewers in Budleigh Salterton. Some of what goes on at Westminster could make your hair stand on end.

Sometimes, however, and perversely, political reputations have been improved – if only temporarily – by the exposure of amorous infidelities. Paddy (later Lord) Ashdown, the one-time Liberal Democrat leader, found that his popularity ratings rose, for a short time at least, after the world learned of his illicit relations with his dull secretary. But it was a short-term gain. Astonishingly, one of his successors, Nick Clegg, actually boasted that he had slept with 'not more than 30 women', a claim that shocked some of his colleagues on the Liberal Democrat benches. They had already had one leader, Charles Kennedy, who had to quit because of his heavy drinking, and another, Sir Menzies Campbell, who resigned because he was useless at the despatch box. Now they found they were being led by a self-confessed serial stud. No wonder that Mr Clegg acquired overnight the unenviable nickname Nick Cleggover. Why can't the Liberal Democrats ever get it right?

Conversely, David Blunkett, the former Home Secretary, became regarded as a somewhat rampant billy goat and universal laughing stock over his sexual adventures and generally incongruous behaviour. It all helped to contribute to his downfall. Everybody gets into scrapes at some time or other. But it is always far more amusing when the pompous, the self-righteous and the preachers – types which abound at Westminster – are the ones who fall prey to the banana skin.

Here are a few of the incidents which enliven many a dull moment in Parliament. In the autumn of 1987, I wrote this about David Mellor, who was then a Minister of State at the Foreign Office and who was desperate to become famous: 'He will have to try much harder…' Well, he certainly took my advice. Because a few years later he was forced to resign from Margaret Thatcher's Cabinet after extramarital dalliances. But in those early days when he was obscure, he would move heaven and earth to get television cameras to point in his direction, wherever he was. 'I want to become as famous as you,' he once shamelessly said to a well-known TV reporter. Indeed, he became such a regular feature on television that his immediate boss, the Foreign Secretary, Sir Geoffrey Howe, even considered returning home from holiday early otherwise, he feared, people would forget that he ever existed. And another Foreign Office Minister at the time, Lynda (later Baroness) Chalker was telling her friends that she suffered 'severe palpitations' whenever she saw Mellor on the television or heard his voice on the radio.

But there was one incident which had about it all the features of a fast-moving Whitehall farce. It is the story of the vicar, the stripper and Labour MP Paul Boateng's ex-directory telephone number – it must rank as one of the classics of Westminster. It started at a party being attended by Julia Langdon, former political editor of the *Daily Mirror* at a house only four doors away from her own. This was a Saturday night and among the other guests was a vicar, dog collar and all, clutching his fevered brow in a state of high agitation. His problem was that he had invited

Mr Boateng, a lay preacher, to deliver the sermon at his church the following day, thus saving himself the trouble of preparing his own homily.

The deal was that one of the church worthies was to pick up Boateng from his home and chauffeur him to the church. But the problem was that the church had lost Boateng's telephone number and did not know where he lived. Miss Langdon agreed to return to her own home to start ringing round a few people who might have been able to put her on Boateng's track.

It so happened that Julia had feasted none-too-wisely at the party and that her garments felt a little tight around the midriff. And so, to ease the discomfort, she removed her skirt. There came, as there invariably does on these occasions, a knock on the door. Julia, temporarily forgetting her state of disarray, rushed to the door, opened it and found herself confronted by the agitated vicar, whose agitation became positively frenetic at the spectacle before his bulging eyes. With much ado, and trying not to look too closely, as vicars are trained to do on these occasions, he entered the premises. And at precisely that moment, there was a squawk from up aloft. It was Julia's 15-month-old son, Edward, who had chosen just this moment to launch into a minor tantrum. Julia rushed upstairs, picked the squalling lad from his cot, whereupon he promptly threw up all over her blouse. The skirtless Julia quickly became blouseless as well. She removed her top with great expedition.

Meanwhile, downstairs, where the panicking vicar was twiddling his nervous thumbs, the Langdon mobile phone suddenly shrilled out. The resourceful Man of God picked up the phone, answered it and rushed upstairs with it. Here, he was to find our heroine in a further state of disarray, like, as he put it afterwards, Fifi the Coquette. However, the shapely Julia was unabashed. She grabbed the telephone and thrust the bawling child, still throwing up with great vigour, into the reluctant arms of the vicar. But he even seemed grateful to accept this unwholesome package as a welcome means of distracting his thoughts.

But this was by no means the end of it. At that precise moment, Julia's 21-year-old live-in nanny suddenly appeared on the scene. She had heard the commotion up aloft and sportily took to the stairs three at a time to see what the trouble was. Can you imagine this innocent girl's consternation when she sees before her chaste eyes in the bedrooom – yes, the bedroom – her employer, clad only in her racy nether-garments, a vicar in a tizzy and a baby with a problem. The lengths to which some people will go to, just to get Paul Boateng to the church on time. They got the man there – but Ray Cooney, author of many West End farces, could not have devised a more devilish scenario.

And while on the subject of clothes in disarray, William Price, the late and very noisy Labour MP for Rugby, once dashed into the Commons Chamber, audibly out of breath, in the nick of time to deliver his speech for the closing 30-minute adjournment debate. But what was unusual about this was that he was clad in a voluminous and incongruous raincoat, buttoned up from neck to toe, which it very nearly reached. Needless to say, in the true British tradition, no one made any comment on his grotesque appearance, and the debate began and ended in the normal manner. Afterwards, however, a few questions were asked. It transpired that on his way to the Chamber, Mr Price had cause to visit the gents. To his horror, as he tried to do up the zip, it simply broke in his hands.

A lesser man would have panicked. How could he address the House of Commons, with the television cameras trained mercilessly on him, with his flies wide open? But Mr Price was not a lesser man. He grabbed the first raincoat he saw on a hook and wrapped it round himself. He may have looked a chump but he regarded that as the lesser of the two evils. Flashing in the House of Commons is almost certainly regarded as a very grave offence. The garment was restored to its rightful owner, who by then was looking in every nook and cranny for his property before Mr Price, bursting with apologies, suddenly rolled up.

That sort of predicament would never have happened to Enoch Powell, who always advocated delivering speeches on a full bladder, thus adding urgency and drama to the words. But not all the goings on at and around Westminster are as wholesome and innocent as that.

Nowadays, ministerial comments are made as often as not by civil servants, who literally put words in ministers' mouths, especially when some embarrassing event has to be explained away. Not least was the incident when Ron Davies, Secretary of State for Wales, was involved in some unsavoury business on Clapham Common. New Labour spin doctor Alistair Campbell told him to say to the media that this was his 'moment of madness'. It was a remark which sounded like a good idea at the time but which Davies quickly came to regret. He realised, and probably rightly, that he will always be known as Ron 'moment of madness' Davies and that inexorably the tag will figure in the first paragraph of every obituary that will be written about him.

But there is nothing new about illicit behaviour at Westminster. In Victorian times, politicians were not as prudish as you might imagine. What is now crudely called 'a bit on the side' was as rampant then as it is today. Lord Palmerston, known behind his back as Lord Cupid, was cited as co-respondent in a divorce case, having forged a relationship at the age of 79 with a Mrs O'Kane. This inevitably gave rise to the gibe 'She was Kane but was he Able?' His rival, Benjamin Disraeli, himself something of a sower of wild oats, said it was a pity that this liaison had come to public knowledge because the nation would be so impressed at his prowess that he would sweep the board at the next election. Disraeli's fears were justified. Palmerston did just that.

David Lloyd-George, too, enjoyed amours with 'streams of ladies', relationships which were not so much romantic as clinical, thus earning him the unflattering nickname of 'The Goat'. And William Ewart Gladstone, when not moralising, used to walk up to Piccadilly Circus to pick up young women of the street and take them back to Number 10, 'to save them from their sinful ways'. Disraeli is reported to have commented: 'If you are saving these girls, would you kindly save one for me?'

Even King Edward VII had his moments. He allocated a pew at his Coronation for his mistresses. It was known as 'the loose box'. One thing is certain: for hundreds of years, the House of Commons has boasted more than its fair share of womanisers and flirtatious ladies. No wonder some people have christened it the Bawdy House.

Armed Neutrality

The press gallery, I fear, has been cosying up too intimately over recent years with the politicians. The attitude of the press gallery is that we seem to want to demonstrate to the powers that be at Westminster that we are all part of what is pompously called 'the democratic process', and that we belong to a 'community' – a dread word which sticks in my very craw as I type it out.

We should be divorced, in a sense, from the politicians in a state of armed neutrality, not having a love affair with them. One of my colleagues put it to me picturesquely that the relationship between the press gallery and Parliament should be similar to that between a dog and a lamp-post. Hear! Hear!

The point was effectively made by one of my former colleagues on the Press Association, David Healy. He was asked to join some parliamentary committee. His reply: 'I am paid to report your pantomimes, not take part in them.' At the very least it should be a love–hate relationship, with the accent on 'hate'. We are – or at least I am – disinterested in the political or so-called democratic process. I am simply interested in getting stories to sell newspapers, and the Palace of Westminster happens to be the source of more stories than any other building in the UK, possibly even the world. That is why it is such a good place for a journalist to be.

It used to be just as useful to take MPs out of Parliament to get stories from them. These days, ministers have minders who only reluctantly let them out of their sight, for fear that they will commit some minor, even barely discernible indiscretion when let out on their own. Not so many years ago, it was a regular thing for political journalists to take cabinet ministers out to lunch, usually a mutually advantageous event, giving the journalist a scoop and the minister an opportunity to get something off his chest. Now, alas, it has become not unknown for ministers to have to seek permission from Downing Street before they can take lunch with a journalist. If this permission is granted then often the minister is forced to take along a civil servant as well. The presence of a civil servant obviously prevents the minister from uttering anything even vaguely interesting and the addition of another diner adds to the cost of an event which has thus become totally unproductive, so the practice of lunching ministers has become less popular.

The members' lobby of the House of Commons is one of the most fruitful places for a political reporter, although under the Tony Blair administration you got the distinct feeling that cabinet ministers had been told not to use it for fear of being browbeaten by correspondents who might trap them into saying something indiscreet or, worse, 'off-message'. It would have been unthinkable not so many years before, that a bumptious civil servant such as Alistair Campbell, who remains at heart a Labour Party apparatchik, should order cabinet ministers around in this way – and that they should, apparently, so meekly submit. Even so, it is still a useful place to haunt. Sometimes I just stand there like a whore or a length of flypaper waiting for something to stick. Usually one comes away from the lobby with a story of sorts under one's belt.

The rules there are quite strict, although they have been somewhat whittled away over the years. For instance, reporters were not allowed to bring out notebooks and take notes in the lobby, but that rule appears to have fallen somewhat into desuetude since everybody now does it. You are not allowed to run in the lobby, not that most reporters would feel inclined to. It is said that there is no need to run after an MP because another will be along in a minute, like the proverbial no. 11 bus. And here a reporter has eyes but does not see. You are forbidden, for instance, to report a punch-up in the members' lobby – and there have been brawls and scuffles from time to time. But there are simple ways round this problem. In such a case, you describe to a friendly MP what has happened (if he hasn't seen it for himself, that is) and then get him to describe it back to you in his own words.

I was once involved in a curious little lobby-related incident with an MP, Dr Alan Glyn, the Conservative MP for Windsor and Maidenhead. He told me about the case of a schoolgirl in his constituency who had been punished at school for bravely complaining publicly that children's education was being put in jeopardy by a teachers' strike. The child described the stoppage as 'irresponsible action'. Dr Glyn eagerly took up the cudgels on behalf of the girl. His intervention attracted widespread attention in the newspapers as well as on radio and television. When I next saw Dr Glyn, in the members' lobby, he pulled an envelope out of his pocket and handed it to me before he shuffled off. I opened it and found inside a £50 note, with the words 'Thank you' on a piece of paper attached to it. It was not that Dr Glyn was in the business of bribery or corruption or anything like that. He was as innocent and honourable as the day is long. He just thought, in his simplicity, that that was the way things were done, and that MPs were expected to pay for stories that appeared about them. Needless to say, I hastened after him, waving the £50 note, an article I had never seen before (or since), insisting that I could not take it. Dr Glyn appeared hurt. 'Well,' he said, 'if you don't want it, wouldn't the wife like something?'

'No, no, no!' I said, 'the wife does not want for anything,' thrusting it back in his pocket. He took it, but disappeared out of the lobby plainly thinking what an ungrateful so-and-so I was.

Dr Glyn, incidentally, was an amiable, shambling old soul, who gave the impression of having had a daily shower of dandruff. Much of the time, he seemed blissfully unaware of what was going on around him. This was exemplified by an extract from Hansard on 25 January 1989. It read: 'Dr Alan Glyn: "I support this Bill, because it enshrines in legislation some form of basis for the security services." (Hon Members: "That was last week's Bill").' And they were right. It was.

As age overtook this likeable fellow, he shuffled about the House of Commons at the speed of an elderly tortoise. I often wondered how he managed to reach the voting lobbies in time before the Speaker locked the doors on latecomers, even when he was sitting in the Chamber, but his voting record, actually, was usually quite commendable. In his last few years in the Commons, Dr Glyn became increasingly infirm. James Kilfedder, the Ulster Unionist MP, who has also sadly died, told me that when Glyn got up in the Chamber to deliver a speech or ask a question, he virtually had to haul Glyn to his feet and hold him in an armlock to keep him upright for the duration of his utterances. None of this was noticeable to other MPs or even in the press gallery. I would suggest that this heroic and Herculean performance by Mr Kilfedder was certainly worthy of a £50 note, even if my own modest exertions on Dr Glyn's behalf were not.

When I was first introduced to the mysteries of the lobby system, I was told by my mentor and predecessor, Arthur Williamson, then chief political reporter of the Press Association, that I must not talk about lobby meetings to anyone except, for some reason, my wife, who, incidentally, wasn't particularly interested. The implication was that there were meetings which did not take place in a room which did not exist and during which nothing was said – nothing, that is, for outside ears. Indeed, the lobby room might as well not have existed in the eyes of those uninitiated with the labyrinth that is the Palace of Westminster.

Various high-minded MPs have publicly expressed disgust with this 'secretive and corrupt' system. Jonathan Aitken, when he was a Conservative MP in 1986 – the year I was chairman of the lobby – buttonholed me in the members' lobby and told me in fearsome language what a disgrace the lobby system was, undemocratic and a shameful collusion between journalists and Government. He was not alone in his views on the lobby. A number of MPs have often warned that they will invade these meetings, disrupt them and then report to an astonished world all the 'corrupt practices' that go on within these four walls. But they have never done so, probably because they have been unable to find the room. It stands alone at the top of a tower, a dull, dust-laden, undistinguished room, with a fine view of the river Thames. At the back is a grotty old kitchen, filled with brooms and other lumber. To the side is another small door which leads one into a complicated structure of rafters and pipes.

This room is reached by a spiral staircase which used to be more perilous than it is now. Occasionally, parties are held in the lobby room, and on at least two occasions I witnessed reporters cascading down these stairs, having, unsurprisingly, missed their footing at the top. However, they felt no pain at the bottom.

At one such party Glenys Kinnock, wife of the Leader of the Opposition, Neil Kinnock, learned with horror that the Prime Minister, Margaret Thatcher, was soon to put in an appearance. She said she could not bear to be in the same room as Mrs Thatcher, swigged her drink down in one gulp, and beat a hasty retreat. It was a blessing that these two powerful ladies did not collide on that notorious staircase.

It always has been a widely known fact within the Westminster village and I suspect far beyond that too, that the Prime Minister's press secretary, or official spokesman as he is known today, dispensed information on an unattributable basis to lobby correspondents in the morning at 10 Downing Street and in the afternoon in that infamous lobby room. In 1986, when the *Independent* newspaper was born, its political editor Tony Bevins (son of Tory Postmaster General Reginald Bevins, who got most of the blame, unfairly, for the Great Train Robbery), decided that the paper should boycott lobby meetings on the grounds of their secrecy and because he felt that lazy reporters were being spoon-fed Government pap.

The boycott was later joined by the *Guardian* and the *Scotsman*. Their view was that they would return once these meetings were on the record (which they are now) and above board. I always thought this stand was ridiculous. Whatever Fleet Street may think, the Government rules the roost and if that is the way they want to dish out their information, then that is something the rest of us will have to live with. You get far more information from governments when they are off the record and unattributable. And what is more, what the Government tells you, or, perhaps more significantly, what it does not tell you, or indeed the way it tells you, can all be part of the story. It is not difficult to ascertain when a Government spokesman is telling you an untruth or evading an issue. But you need to be there to spot it. Lobby meetings rarely take more than half an hour, leaving plenty of time to go and check the information or get reaction to it. Those who boycotted those meetings – all have now returned to the fold – were merely making life more difficult for themselves for no good purpose. It is all very well having principles, but when they achieve nothing except to ease your conscience, then there seems to be little point in employing them. Lobby meetings can be rowdy, rumbustious occasions, with table-thumping and even insults being hurled back and forth. Sir Bernard Ingham, when he was Margaret Thatcher's press secretary, and Alastair Campbell have been the two most colourful and lively mouthpieces for their bosses in recent years. On one or two occasions, when the sun has been shining down on Westminster, lobby meetings have been held, perilously, on the roof of the Palace of Westminster, just adjacent to the lobby room. So far, fingers crossed, there have been no casualties, but as those of a nervous disposition used to say, it was only a matter of time before someone would fall off.

When I was chairman of the lobby, I was required, unsurprisingly, to chair lobby meetings. On one such occasion, when Dr David (later Lord) Owen was the guest answering questions, I fell fast asleep sitting next to him at the table. He never noticed. What he did notice and was perplexed by, was that the questions asked of him were couched in increasingly loud voices, virtually shouted at him. My colleagues were doing their best to wake me up without the great man noticing. It worked.

That chairmanship also occurred at the time when Labour were having a row with the Murdoch newspapers and childishly would not speak to reporters from *The Times*, the *Sun*, the *Sunday Times*, the *News of the World* or any other of their publications. It was a tradition, then, that on a Thursday afternoon, the Leader of the Opposition, in this case Neil Kinnock, would come to the lobby meetings to answer questions. He wrote me a letter saying that he would be willing to attend these meetings – they were always at our invitation – but that he would refuse to answer any questions from Murdoch reporters. Needless to say, this was not on. So I wrote to him saying that unless he was prepared to respond to questions from any member of the Lobby, the invitation to attend would have to be withdrawn. Mr Kinnock and I exchanged further letters, each more pompous than the last. He stood his ground and I stood mine, so the invitation was consequently withdrawn by me in my final bout of pomposity. However, Kinnock won that battle and I lost it. He held his own press meeting on a Thursday afternoon in the Leader of the Opposition's room, where he could invite whom he liked. Murdoch reporters were not on his guest list.

One of the splendid perks of being chairman of the lobby and the press gallery was that both jobs at that time qualified you for an invitation to the Buckingham Palace garden parties in July. So you put on your best bib and tucker, as did your good lady wife, and trotted along. Before I first went along I was given a very useful tip by Conservative MP Lynda Chalker. I will pass it on, because it is still as valid today as it was then. Namely, do not join the queue for food and drink. It is a strange fact of life, but at these garden parties a queue always forms at one end of the trestle table which is groaning under the weight of iced coffee, tea, sandwiches and all manner of nourishing cakes and buns. This is despite the fact that this is no ordinary trestle table: it goes on for yards, stacked for its full length with all these comestibles and with people only too happy to hand you them. Just thought I would mention it.

The terrace of the House of Commons, which runs alongside the river Thames, has been one of the great places for journalists to pick up stories. However, shortly before the end of the 20th century, the House of Commons authorities in their wisdom (such as it is) decided to ban reporters from this productive and agreeable area unless they were the guests of MPs. There had been complaints by MPs that reporters had been eavesdropping, but even more ludicrous was the suggestion that MPs were actually being bugged by political correspondents on the terrace. What was alleged – if you can believe it – was that reporters were leaving their mobile phones switched through to their head offices and then placing them in such a position that personnel on news desks could actually overhear MPs' conversations and then put them into print.

When we were permitted on to the terrace in our own right the rules were such that, as in the members' lobby of the House of Commons, we were not allowed to report what we actually saw happen there. The answer to that was to do what was done in the lobby, namely, to get a friendly MP to tell you what had happened. On one occasion, I witnessed, to my considerable surprise, a young lady rise up from the river Thames, mermaid-like, dripping and topless, and step forth on to the terrace. I gather that the security men pretty well choked on their fish fingers and dropped their dominoes when they saw this apparition appear on their monitor screens. But, mindful of the rules as ever, I metaphorically averted my gaze. What I did was to ask a friendly MP, Geoffrey Dickens (now, alas, dead) who had also witnessed this bizarre scene to describe it to me in his own extremely colourful words. Simple as that. This he obligingly did and the story went out on the Press Association wires and received prominent treatment in the newspapers the following day. The only thing that was lacking was a picture. But you can't have everything.

Equally, you needed to find a friendly and reliable MP to divulge to you the goings-on at private party meetings, transacting your business with him in dark and dusty corners. I used to pick up all the gossip from the meetings, often rowdy, of Labour's National Executive Committee (NEC). This included one gem where the then Chancellor of the Exchequer, Denis (later Lord) Healey, described a left-wing member, Judith Hart as being 'out of your tiny little Chinese mind'. Although I had complete faith in my contact, I nevertheless sweated for an hour after these splendid words were put out by the Press Association, fearing that a denial might be issued by the Treasury and I would, of course, not be able to disclose my source. Once that worrying hour was over I was happy that the story was true. However, the Chinese Government were not as overjoyed as I was and Healey was compelled to issue a grovelling apology to their embassy in London. It was all very satisfactory.

This was reminiscent of the occasion when Harold Wilson described Tory MP Peter Griffiths as 'a parliamentary leper'. Griffiths had won a seat after an allegedly racial campaign at Smethwick in 1964. Wilson was later compelled to apologise to the British Empire Leprosy Relief Association.

When Margaret Thatcher was giving a pep-talk to Tory peers in the House of Lords in a private room, I shamefully had my ear to the keyhole, trying to hear what was going on. Suddenly, to my chagrin, the door was opened from the inside, and I was knocked flying. I braced myself for a severe dressing-down or worse. But it did not happen. The uniformed official who had bowled me over, exclaimed, 'So sorry, my Lord,' and helped me to my feet. 'Please go in.' I did not argue with him. He actually ushered me into the room, where I remained as unobtrusive as I could. Heaven knows why I wasn't thrown out. Sometimes I had all the luck.

It has always astonished me why, given the number of political leaks that occur year after year, there are so few people caught at it. The cynical among us are, therefore, driven to the conclusion that some of the leaks are actually carried out by Government for its own ends. Some leaks of celebrity names from forthcoming honours' lists I am convinced are the work of the Government of the day rather than skulduggery by the few people who know the contents of these lists in advance.

Leaks, when they are not executed by the Government, usually occur for political rather than financial reasons. Usually, when such leaks are perpetrated the Government's invariable response is to claim that what has been leaked is a first draft of some project which 'is now totally out of date and meaningless'.

Sometimes civil servants with a political axe to grind have been known to leak material to selected newspapers as a way of embarrassing the Government. One of the few such cases was that of Sarah Tisdall, a Whitehall clerk, who leaked to the *Guardian* newspaper secrets about the Cruise missile programme written in memos by the then Defence Secretary, Michael Heseltine. This was plainly a political leak in which no financial reward was sought. But Miss Tisdall was quickly identified – the *Guardian* has since been accused of breaking all the codes of practice by allegedly disclosing her name – and she was tried, convicted and sentenced to six months in prison.

Leaks, some embarrassing, some not so, became a regular feature of the last years of the Conservative governments which ended with the general election of 1997. But the most significant of all was the leaking to the *Daily Mirror* of some hundred pages of Kenneth Clarke's budget. The Treasury were forced to admit that the documents leaked were genuine, and John Major, then Prime Minister, ordered a top-level inquiry. However the *Daily Mirror*, although running a huge story about the fact that they had acquired this material, decided not to publish any of the Budget secrets. The editor, Piers Morgan, said at the time that he had reached this decision 'after very careful thought', and handed the documents back to the Treasury. Some of the *Daily Mirror*'s Fleet Street contemporaries derided Mr Morgan for having acquired this massive scoop and then, astonishingly, not using it. It did seem a little odd, I must say, to boast about getting a story with which they never regaled their readers until it was public property after the Chancellor had delivered his Budget.

One of the main recipients of leaks at this time was Jack Straw, who was to become Home Secretary, Foreign Secretary and then Justice Minister when Labour were returned to power. Regularly he would call press conferences, triumphantly brandishing these prized documents in the air. No one ever discovered where or how he obtained this booty on such a regular basis.

Then there was the leak that wasn't, so to speak. The late and great Gordon Greig, who was political editor of the *Daily Mail*, possessed in greater quantities than most the essential attribute of all journalists, namely, a rat-like cunning. Once, during the days of Harold Wilson at 10 Downing Street, the Cabinet was discussing whether to reduce the age of voting from 21 to 18. And a decision had to be reached. None of us could find out after the Cabinet meeting which way ministers had decided. That is, except for Gordon Greig. In the members' lobby, he approached a couple of Wilson's cabinet ministers, and said to them blithely: 'Well, I see you have done it!'

The ministers, according to Greig, came back sharply: 'How do you know?' In fact, of course, Greig did not know – until they had unintentionally let the cat out of the bag without realising it. Greig tapped the side of his nose with his finger, as though he had secret sources, and went on his way rejoicing. The *Daily Mail* had a world scoop the next day. Needless to say, Harold Wilson was raging that the news had leaked out before he had had a chance to announce it to the House of Commons. He set up an immediate and high-powered 'leak inquiry' which, hardly surprisingly, made no progress whatsoever. The bizarre thing is, of course, that the 'leaking' ministers never realised that they were the source of the leak themselves.

Leaks, however, whether contrived or accidental, are by no means a new phenomenon in politics. I understand that the habit goes back at least to Lord Chancellor Francis Bacon, Viscount St Albans (1561-1626). At one stage, he wrote: 'As for cabinet councils it may be their motto pleus rimarum sum [I am full of leaks]. One futile person that maketh it his glory to tell, will do more hurt than many that know it is their duty to conceal.'

American presidents, as well, have been particularly affected, even afflicted, by unauthorised leaks. President Truman was driven to complain that '95 per cent of our secret information has been leaked in newspapers and slick magazines'. While President Johnson was no less perturbed. He protested once: 'This goddam town leaks like a worn-out boot.'

Even Jimmy Carter fell foul of the leak. He was once compelled to storm: 'If there is another outbreak of misinformation, distortion or self-serving leaks, I will direct the Secretary of State to discharge the officials responsible...even if some innocent people might be punished.'

Ronald Reagan, in his typical way, spoke of reading memos in the newspapers which 'I haven't even gotten yet'.

But his Secretary of State, Alexander Haig, took a pretty resigned view of leaks. He pointed out: 'In the Reagan administration, leaks were not a problem. They were a way of life. Leaks constituted policy, they were the authentic voice of Government.'

Sir Robert Armstrong, the man who was so famously economical with the truth, and who was Cabinet Secretary for much of Margaret Thatcher's premiership, took a jaundiced view of leaks, but could see the funny side of them as well. When he wrote a letter to Whitchall top brass about the importance of stemming leaks, he commented later: 'I was very sad that it took as long as six weeks for this letter to leak.'

Even in Victorian times, leaks were rampant and severely frowned upon. In 1873, a Whitehall bigwig, Sir Ralph Lingen, notified his subordinates in the sternest of terms: 'The unauthorised use of official information is the worst fault a civil servant can commit. It is on the same footing as cowardice by a soldier.' Strong stuff, that. But neither this nor any other stricture about leaking seems to have made the slightest difference to anything. Leaking, whether governments like it or not, is part of the world of politics and will never be snuffed out. In short, Westminster and Whitehall will continue for evermore to leak like an old barn roof.

Points of Order

Stephen Ross, a man with a very short fuse, used to represent the Isle of Wight for the Liberals. On one occasion I wrote a story about some late-night crisis at Westminster involving his party and said: 'The Liberal Whips have scuttled away when everybody wants them...' The excitable Mr Ross took grave exception to the use of the word 'scuttled' and protested to my superiors at the Press Association. So hot under the collar was he that a special meeting had to be called at the Commons including top brass both from the PA and from the Liberals. It struck me as being wildly over the top. But Mr Ross certainly had a reputation for blowing his top. So much so, in fact, that when he was elevated to the House of Lords, as Lord Ross of Newport, his ermined colleagues lumbered him with an appropriate nickname which has stuck ever since: Vesuvius.

* * * * *

David Hill, who was ultimately to succeed Alastair Campbell as press supremo at 10 Downing Street, was a much quieter and less bombastic operator. But he was probably just as effective, indeed probably more so than his noisy, ranting predecessor. Campbell committed the cardinal error of becoming part of the story himself, an unforgivable sin in the eyes of one of his predecessors, Sir Bernard Ingham. Indeed, Ingham was so insistent on this that if ever one of his colleagues inadvertently found themselves in a picture in a paper he or she had to pay a fine of 50p in an office charity box.

Hill had worked for Roy Hattersley, when he was deputy leader of the Labour Party, then in opposition, and subsequently for Neil Kinnock himself, the party leader. At this time, Hill lived fairly near me in Walthamstow. Occasionally, he would ring me up on a Saturday morning to tell me that he was going out for the day but that Neil Kinnock's speech could be found under the milk bottles on the doorstep of his home. Whereupon, I jumped on my wife's old boneshaker, pedalled furiously to the Hill household, picked up the speech from the doormat and filed the story from the nearby Walthamstow Central underground station.

Hill, incidentally, was an avid football aficionado and claimed to know the name of every league football ground in the country. He had probably been to most of them. He had left the service of the Labour Party after Tony Blair's massive victory in 1997 and went into private enterprise public relations work. He returned to help fight the general election campaign in 2001 and was lured back from the private sector after Campbell's decision to quit his Downing Street job in August 2003.

Despite sporting a Mexican-bandit-style moustache, Hill is by no means as ferocious as he looks. Indeed, he is a mild-mannered man who demonstrates not a jot of the deviousness and wiliness normally associated with the dubious trade of spin-doctoring.

* * * * *

Tory MP Alistair Burt was compelled to remove his trousers in front of a lady (who was not his wife) in the days when he was Parliamentary Private Secretary to Kenneth Baker, then Secretary of State for Education and Science. The diminutive Mr Burt was working away in his master's office when somehow (don't ask) his trousers split from seam to seam. Within seconds, a lady called Sandra, after receiving an urgent telephone call from the little man, hurried to the scene of humiliation. Complete with needle and thread, she invited the red-of-visage Mr Burt to remove his trousers so that she could speedily get to work on some running repairs.

* * * * *

Sometimes reporters have been known to shatter the delusions of grandeur suffered by politicians. For instance, once, when that well-known Labour trencherman Roy Hattersley was shadow Home Secretary, he was being entertained to lunch by a group of journalists. One of the reporters asked him what his two great ambitions were. Hattersley replied without hesitation: 'To become Home Secretary, which I fully intend to do once Labour is returned to power, and the other is to open the batting for Yorkshire.'

'In that case,' the reporter said. 'I should hurry up and get your pads on,' implying, correctly, that he would never in a month of Sundays make it to the Home Office. Hattersley, according to those who were present, did not see the funny side of it.

* * * * *

John Cole, the distinguished former political editor of the BBC, was once discussing a forthcoming dinner with Hattersley. It was amicably agreed that well-fed Mr Hattersley, with his reputed monumental knowledge of these matters, should name the restaurant of his choice. Then a thought clearly passed through the mind of Mr Hattersley. He asked Mr Cole: 'Why is it always assumed that I know all about restaurants and that you have a funny voice?'

'Well,' replied the self-effacing and modest Mr Cole, 'I have got a funny voice...'

* * * * *

Sir Teddy Taylor, who sat first for Glasgow Cathcart and later for Rochford and Southend East, was not only a vociferous critic of the European Union, but also a tub-thumping non-drinker. He signed the pledge on a public platform in Glasgow at the tender age of eight. 'I have never had a drop from that day onwards,' he told me, adding hastily, 'Nor before that day, of course, either.' So he was surprised to find in his Christmas stocking one year no fewer than 26 bottles of wine, seven bottles of whisky, four bottles of champagne and a single bottle of the very finest port.

'It just arrived in cascades,' he told me. 'You cannot move in my house for bottles of booze. I think that the good people of Southend assumed that just because I came from Glasgow, I was bound to be a drinker.' But, unsurprisingly, he had little difficulty in getting rid of it all, but not in the accepted manner. He actually raffled the lot to swell the coffers – of the temperance organisation the Band of Hope,

* * * * *

In the late autumn of 1987, the Tory John Watson was roused from his slumbers by his bleeper at 3am. The message from the Whips was to get to the House of Commons as quickly as possible for an urgent vote that was about to take place. He leapt from his bed, flung a tie around his neck and prepared to hotfoot it to the Commons, less than half a mile away. And, then, just before he set out, he thought to himself: 'There is something rather wrong here.' It suddenly dawned on him, as he came to his senses, that he was no longer Conservative MP for Skipton and Ripon, or indeed anywhere else, having retired from the Commons at the general election earlier that year. He returned to his bed. And in the morning he angrily telephoned the Tory Whips' office with his own urgent message to them, namely: 'Get up to date with your mailing lists…'

* * * * *

When Robert Atkins was appointed the Conservative Minister for Sport in 1990, he gave short shrift to one radio reporter who thrust a microphone in his face and inquired, 'What are you going to do to protect Britain's national sport?'

'Oh, you just keep the covers on when it rains,' the cricket-mad politician replied.

'No! No!' the impatient and frustrated reporter cried: 'I mean Britain's other national sport, not cricket.'

To which the irrepressible Mr Atkins replied: 'Oh, you mean angling…' It was one of the shortest interviews on record. Nowadays, it would seem, politicians are too nervously protecting their image to risk taking a rise out of reporters.

* * * * *

The British press gets more than its fair share of sneers for printing gossip, scandal and trivia – all of which I am totally in favour of. But in among all that, the serious news is always to be found. Not so among the reporting of important British news in many foreign papers. Some years ago the great Lord Deedes picked up a copy of the *Daily News* in Budapest expecting to see reports of Sir Geoffrey Howe's resignation from the Government and the latest intelligence on the Gulf War.

Instead, the only item relating to the UK in the entire paper was a front page photograph of a gentleman standing at Waterloo Station in his underpants. He was said to be taking advantage of a free trouser-pressing service while you wait offered to rail commuters. Lord Deedes commented: 'When abroad you will read only the silliest news about your own country.'

I remember an occasion equally as bizarre as that one. I live on the edge of Epping Forest where, until relatively recently, cattle had the right to wander up and down the roads without let or hindrance. If you drove into a cow and killed it, then you could be liable to the owner of that dead cow. On this occasion, a young motorcyclist, on a darkened, tree-shrouded road called Oak Hill, did hit a cow. He was killed, along with the cow, and the owner of the cow could have pursued the next-of-kin of the dead man for compensation.

I had an idea for a story as a result of that fatal accident. Why should not the owners of these cows be compelled to paint the horns and hindquarters of their beasts with luminous paint so that they would at least be visible in the dark to oncoming motorists. I suggested to the Labour MP Col Marcus Lipton that he should raise this matter in Parliament, which he did, even though there was not the slightest constituency interest for him in it at all. The story ran and ran, led by the London *Evening Standard* which brilliantly headlined it: 'By the light of the silvery moo…'

Some days later, a Government minister who had been visiting Kenya told me that he bought an English language newspaper in Nairobi and discovered to his disconcertion (and my subsequent glee) that this story was the only UK news item in the entire paper.

* * * * *

In 1988 two former Liberal MPs, Sir Cyril Smith (Rochdale) and David Alton (Mossley Hill), tabled a House of Commons motion lamenting the fact that some newspapers would be printing on Boxing Day thus 'burdening the British public with unnecessary boredom'. It did not seem to occur to them that it was not then, nor is it yet, compulsory to buy newspapers, whether they are boring ones or not.

Name-Calling and Narcissism

The House of Commons has been variously dubbed 'Halitosis Hall', 'A Whitehall farce' and 'the most prolific generator of hot air known to mankind'.

Aneurin Bevan said that the place provided 'hours and hours of exquisite boredom'. That was probably because he did not know where to go in the building for variety and entertainment. In fact, the House of Commons is probably the least boring edifice in London, provided you do not waste too much time in the Chamber itself, listening to second-rate backbenchers droning on, unaware, seemingly, that a five- to ten-minute speech is always more effective than a prolonged diatribe.

There is also a tendency for MPs – perish the thought – not to fulfil their pledges. For instance, the Leader of the Commons of the day may be pestered for a full-dress, two-day debate on, for instance, defence or foreign affairs. When he grudgingly surrenders to their demands, you may find that even before the first day has been completed there are no MPs left who want to speak in it, despite the clamour they had earlier made. Parliament would look stupid if such grandiose debates fizzled out early because no MP wanted to take part. So what happens is that the

Whips on both sides rampage around the Palace of Westminster, the bars, the restaurants, the terrace and even the lavatories, ordering backbenchers to get into the Chamber and deliver speeches. Things have occasionally got so desperate that men have been forced to leave the lavatory seat to keep Parliament running.

The oratory at Westminster, which is not always of the highest quality, sinks to rock bottom when this happens. It is bad enough, sometimes, having to listen to speeches which have been carefully prepared. But when an MP with no knowledge of or interest in defence, say, has to run into the Chamber, possibly still buttoning up his trousers, and address the House on a subject which has not even troubled his brain, then you are immediately reminded of your school debating society years.

However, the Chamber itself does have its moments, Prime Minister's Question Time, in particular. You emerge from the place exhilarated by the theatricality of it all, but no wiser than when you went in. Indeed, when David Cameron became opposition leader, he vowed he would put an end to Punch and Judy politics. Thankfully, he reneged on this pledge almost immediately, by launching a ferocious attack on the Government Chief Whip Hilary Armstrong, who had tried to interrupt Cameron's flow.

Even during periods when there is no election fever around, the exchanges between the Prime Minister of the day and the leader of the opposition amount to little more than political point-scoring. There is nothing wrong with that, but if you went there with the object of increasing your knowledge about, say, the economic life of Britain, you would have come to the wrong place. New facts rarely emerge. And opposition leaders very often ask the Prime Minister questions to which they already know the answer.

Before the House of Commons embarked on the daytime office hours sittings, Thursday night always used to be an event not to miss in the Chamber. Invariably there was a big debate and a raucous wind-up session between 9 and 10pm, with many MPs noisy and exuberant in a manner which suggested prolonged attendance in the Strangers' Bar during the evening. Nowadays, Thursday is a relatively dull day. As John Major once said: 'Thursday is now like a Friday, and Friday is like a Saturday.' The reason for this is that once Prime Minister's questions are over at lunchtime on Wednesday, the parliamentary week rapidly goes downhill, though Tuesdays have more recently been recaptured by the traditionalists who favour late sittings.

The style of the place has changed with the hours. The House of Commons has become drab and colourless. Time was when insults would reverberate back and forth across the Chamber like a Wild West shoot-out. Things never got so bad as they did in Taiwan at the beginning of this century when their Parliament degenerated into a brawling mass of squirming MPs, one of them clobbering his colleagues with an aluminium bar and others throwing books, shoes and finally punches at all and sundry. But occasionally there were Commons scenes which exhilarated the more bloodthirsty among us. Sometimes it was so spectacular and savage that even supporters of Millwall Football Club ('Nobody likes us and we don't care') might have learned a trick or two. But even so, one of the main attractions of Westminster remains the skilful and savage use of invective, MPs bad-mouthing one another with gusto and relish, while very rarely descending to fisticuffs.

But more recently the House of Commons is increasingly in danger of being sanitised. Sometimes an MP is rebuked and compelled to withdraw what appear to be the most harmless of remarks, which do not even really qualify as insults. For instance, the veteran Labour MP Martin O'Neill was called to order by the then Speaker, Betty Boothroyd, for describing a Conservative frontbencher, Angela Browning, as 'a second-rate Miss Marple'. As epithets go, it was on the tame side of innocent. Some might even have regarded it as a compliment. Even so, Mr O'Neill was required to withdraw the remark 'without reservation', while Mrs Browning remained remarkably unbothered by the description.

Before that, the previous Speaker, Bernard (later Lord) Weatherill, surprised the House by suddenly objecting to the use of the word 'poppycock', an innocent enough sounding term, although polyglots will be aware that it has somewhat unpleasant connotations in its original Dutch. But compare all that with the MP, the late Tony Banks, who once accused Margaret Thatcher in the Commons of 'behaving with all the sensitivity of a sex-starved boa constrictor' – and got away with it.

Nor was any action taken against the MP who described the former Conservative Home Secretary, Kenneth Baker, as 'a cruel swine'. Michael Foot, once the Labour leader, suffered no ill when he likened Norman (later Lord) Tebbit to 'a semi-house-trained polecat', an animal which Lord Tebbit, as soon as he was ennobled, promptly and proudly included in his coat-of-arms. There, indeed, seems to have been little rhyme or reason in what is acceptable and what is not. It has seemed to have depended largely on the mood of whoever was sitting in the chair at the time.

For instance, the use of the word 'twerp' has had a mixed reception. Its first recorded use was during questions to the Air Minister in 1956. It was ruled to be in order because the then Speaker assumed, inexplicably, that 'it was a sort of technical term of the aviation industry'. And when, shortly after that, the word was again used, but in the plural, it passed muster again because 'it appeared to be directed at a multiple object'. However, there was no such luck for Willie Hamilton, the anti-monarchist Labour MP, now dead, who described Prince Charles as 'that young twerp'. He was quickly ordered to withdraw the remark.

Other phrases, referring to the constituencies of various MPs, such as the 'wolf from Dagenham' (Bryan Gould of Dagenham) and the 'hamster from Bolsover' (also known as the 'beast of Bolsover', Dennis Skinner) have all passed the test. Surprisingly, too, way back in 1896, the expression 'Tory skunks' got by, but only just, the authorities observing that it was 'highly improper' but not bad enough to have to be withdrawn. However, a century later, the term 'political skunk' was ruled out of order and had to be withdrawn. But 'political weasel and guttersnipe' passed muster, and the use of the term 'rat' has sometimes been successful, sometimes not.

At the turn of the century, Paul Boateng, then a junior Health Minister, was called to order for using the term 'sweet FA'. This expression, of course, derives from the words 'sweet Fanny Adams', 19th century Royal Navy slang for packed mutton. Fanny Adams was a girl who was murdered in 1812, cut into pieces and thrown into the river at Alton, Hampshire. The expression is thus innocent enough, but those who ordain these things at Westminster plainly mistakenly thought it was just another way of using the 'F-word'.

The word 'fuck', however, has been used both in the House of Lords and the House of Commons. Possibly the most unfortunate incident was in 1988, when Mr Speaker Weatherill was having a gruelling time at the hands of some awkward MPs. He muttered, under his breath, the dread word, not intending it at all for public consumption. But there was a radio microphone nearby which, sadly for him, conveyed the expletive to the press gallery – the worst possible destination – even though MPs had not heard it.

The word was first uttered in the House of Lords on 15 November 1783 by the Earl of Sandwich who quoted the rhyme: '...life can little more supply than just a few good fucks and then we die.' This was from the *Essay on Woman*, attributed to John Wilkes but almost certainly written by his friend Thomas Potter. Some of the peers tried to egg on the Earl of Sandwich to quote it at greater length. He forbore from doing that. But he had achieved his purpose, which was that the House resolved to prosecute Wilkes 'for a most scandalous, obscene and infamous libel'. This was all part of revenge on the part of Sandwich, who had not forgiven Wilkes for an outrageous trick played on him some months earlier. Wilkes had somehow managed to smuggle a baboon dressed as the Devil into a Black Mass being celebrated by the Hell Fire Club at which the Earl attended. The beast jumped on the Earl's back, nearly causing him to suffer a massive heart attack.

It was nearly two centuries later before the first recorded use of the word in the House of Commons appeared. During a debate on the Government (Miscellaneous Provisions) Bill in 1982, not normally regarded as the liveliest measure in the world, the then hard-line left-wing Labour MP Reg Race described to his colleagues in the Chamber that there was a sex shop in his north London constituency which boasted a list of prostitutes bearing the legend: 'Phone them and fuck them!' The highly puritanical speaker George Thomas (later to become Lord Tonypandy) was outraged. He said (although not everybody believed him): 'None of us would use it in our homes' – the word, I imagine he meant, rather than the house of ill-repute.

There was also, surprisingly, a rebuke on the same occasion for the editor of Hansard, the *Official Report*, who had printed the word as 'f...' Mr Speaker Thomas called him to task for allowing even this mild hint of obscenity to appear. One wonders what the editor of Hansard was supposed to do. After all, he was only reporting what was said, and he could scarcely ignore it since the Speaker himself had made an issue of it in the Chamber.

There was more trouble and confusion and insult-hurling involving Sir Gerald Nabarro, Conservative MP for South Worcestershire and a prominent and noisy member of the standing committee on the Bill to nationalise the steel industry in the mid-1960s. It was, needless to say, a hotly contested Bill and during one angry exchange the left-wing Labour MP, Ian Mikardo accused Sir Gerald (justifiably!) of 'narcissism'.

That remark, which he actually misheard, enraged Sir Gerald, who with his fine moustache almost twitching with fury immediately and loudly appealed to the Committee chairman, Sir Harry Legge-Bourke, that he should call on Mr Mikardo to withdraw 'this offensive insult'. To Sir Gerald's chagrin, not to mention anger, Sir Harry refused. What Sir Gerald thought was that Mikardo had accused him of 'Nazi-ism'. And since the chairman's hearing was not of the highest order (nor, it appears, was Sir Gerald's), he did not spot the distinction between the two words. After considerable kerfuffle, Sir Gerald was eventually satisfied that Mikardo had not accused him of 'Nazi-ism' but 'narcissism'. He appeared to settle for that, and things quietened down. Then, Sir Gerald rose from his seat and approached me in the press box. He bent over and whispered in my ear: 'What is narcissism?' I can tell you, it is not the easiest thing in the world to have to tell one of the most narcissistic people I have ever met what the word actually means...

Then there was the case of a Labour MP who was called to order for accusing a Conservative of being a member of the SS. The MP withdrew it, but did not do his own standing any favours when he added that he thought the letters stood for 'silly sod'.

Even John Major, that most courteous of men, was forced to retract his description of the leader of the opposition, Tony Blair, as a 'dimwit'. Pretty anodyne stuff!

Compare all this with what goes on in the far more robust Australian Parliament. Paul Keating, the former Prime Minister there, the so-called Lizard of Oz, thought nothing of calling his opponents 'gutless spivs', 'sleazebags' and 'criminal garbage' – epithets which would create uproar at Westminster. But in Australia it's all part of the business. Nobody complains; the recipients of these insults just give as good as they get.

The admirable Simon Walters, later to become political editor of the *Mail on Sunday*, had a brush with Mr Keating. A few hours after this altercation, Walters stepped into a lift in which Keating was already travelling. Keating took one contemptuous look at our hero and observed coldly: 'Here comes that blowfly again...'

Walters, to his immense credit, responded quick as a flash: 'Well, Mr Keating, you know where blowflies like to hang around, don't you?' Full marks to Mr Walters...

The perception, in the country at large, of MPs is these days about as low as it could be. I think that recent surveys have shown them well below journalists (and quite right, too!) in the league tables, or rolls of dishonour as some people prefer to call them, and in some cases, I believe, even below foot-in-the-door and inertia salesmen. However, they still call each other 'honourable' or 'right honourable' in the Chamber, and long may that continue. I have always been of the view that any change in the Parliamentary procedures is a change for the worse. However, MPs, despite the veneer of extravagant courtesy, or possibly because of it, can go to enormous lengths to insult each other without actually breaking the rules.

To call a fellow MP a liar or a hypocrite would instantly bring the wrath of the Speaker on the culprit's head. He would either have to withdraw the epithet or be ordered out of the Chamber. This happened to campaigning Labour MP Tam Dalyell, who refused to withdraw his claim that Margaret Thatcher was lying over the sinking of the Argentine warship, the *General Belgrano*, during the Falklands conflict. Dalyell also described her as 'a cad and a bounder' both of them, strangely, unparliamentary words at the time.

Incidentally, being ordered from the Chamber could be seen as a good way of achieving notoriety for the backbencher. In May, 1988, just for amusement, I asked a vague acquaintance on a bus how many backbench MPs he could name who were not figures of renown. He came up with: Ron Brown (Lab Leith), Dave Nellist (Lab Coventry South-East), John Hughes (Lab Coventry North-East) and Alex Salmond (Scot Nat Banff and Buchan). And just what had all these undistinguished worthies got in common? They had all, during that period, been ejected from the House of Commons for one reason or another.

But there remain, nevertheless, many ways of calling someone a liar in Parliament without using that word and without breaking the rules. Indeed, with the rat-like cunning that most MPs possess (I know that only journalists are supposed to possess this enviable trait, but that is not true) it is so easy to circumvent these rules that one wonders why they still exist.

Churchill brilliantly got round the problem by his use of the expression 'terminological inexactitude' in the Commons in February 1906, during a discussion about slavery. And even though his unpleasant son, Randolph, later insisted that his father did not actually intend it as a euphemism for a lie, it is, nevertheless, always regarded as such, and will continue to be, by his parliamentary heirs and successors.

And again, Nye Bevan, in one of his many jousts with Churchill, avoided accusing the war leader of lying by saying that he (Bevan) was 'pricking the bladder of falsehood with the poignard of truth' during exchanges over the devaluation of the pound.

When Churchill protested that he was being accused of lying, the Speaker of the day replied: 'Oh, I thought it was a quotation.'

Churchill, too, was able to escape with impunity when on another occasion he effectively called Bevan a liar without using the word. What he said was this: 'I should think it hardly possible to state the opposite of the truth with more precision.'

MPs have also got away with using the expression 'economical with the truth', first used – amid great hilarity – by Sir Robert Armstrong, then the Cabinet Secretary, in the Supreme Court of New South Wales in November 1986. He was testifying in support of Margaret Thatcher's inexplicable resolve not to allow *Spycatcher*, Peter Wright's book on MI5, to be published in Australia. I think her obstinacy on this issue was misguided because the book, by a former MI5 officer, even though he was probably breaching the terms of his employment, was so boring and badly written as to be virtually unreadable. It had all the characteristics of a product of the infamous Circumlocution Office from Dickens's *Little Dorrit*.

Pitt the Younger once said: 'If I cannot speak standing, I will speak sitting. And if I cannot speak sitting, I will speak lying.'

To which Lord North uncharitably retorted: 'Which he will do in whatever position he speaks.'

It was Winston Churchill, again, who elegantly justified the conduct of what was called black propaganda in wartime. He said: 'In time of war, truth is so precious, it must be attended by a bodyguard of lies.' Indeed, the complete and utter adhesion to the truth seems to have been cynically disregarded over the years by a succession of eminent politicians.

Arthur Balfour once said: 'It has always been desirable to tell the truth, but seldom possible (if ever necessary) to tell the whole truth.'

Worse than that, one unnamed politician was reported to have said: 'If you ever injected truth into politics, you would have no politics.'

But cynicism did not stop there. Benjamin Disraeli once remarked that 'something unpleasant is coming when men are anxious to speak the truth' and it was Bismarck who offered this comment: 'When you want to fool the world, tell the truth.'

The one-time Labour Prime Minister, Lord Callaghan, is credited with inventing the phrase: 'A lie can be halfway round the world before the truth has got its boots on.' Sunny Jim, as he was bizarrely known, was quoting the words of a 19th century Baptist preacher, the Rev C.H. Spurgeon, even if he did not know it. And in the same year, 1976, the born-again Baptist Jimmy Carter vowed during his presidential campaign: 'I'll never tell a lie.' One commentator said rather acidly at the end of Carter's term of office: 'Though his single term was widely rated a failure at the time, that was a promise he came close to keeping.'

While Gordon Brown was never accused of lying, for different reasons his reputation crumbled with dizzying speed. Rarely can a Prime Minister have waited so long for the keys of 10 Downing Street only to see his premiership crumble into crisis within a year of securing office. That was the fate of Gordon Brown when he assumed power in June 2007, with masses of goodwill behind him. But within a matter of months, he was being labelled the worst Prime Minister within living memory and faced calls from some Labour backbenchers to quit the leadership.

The trouble with Brown is that he is a ditherer. You would have thought that after a decade as Chancellor of the Exchequer he would have grasped the importance of taking firm decisions. Soon after his 'accession', or indeed 'coronation', he let it be known that there was every likelihood of an autumn election that year, 2007. At that stage the so-called 'Brown bounce' was in effect and he could well have won that election and thus given much more authority to his leadership. But he chickened out, a move which caused his own personal popularity to plummet almost immediately. Within weeks, he had reached virtual rock-bottom and the party's prospects, once so bright, suddenly hit rock bottom too.

It was plain, especially after huge Tory successes in the local government elections, the election for mayor of London and a by-election at the so-called impregnable Labour seat of Crewe and Nantwich, that the party would by then face a drubbing at a general election. The hapless Brown was then forced on to the back foot, and it looked as though he would take that Parliament right up to the wire in May 2010 before going to the polls, precisely what Tory Prime Minister John Major had to do in 1997, when defeat stared him in the face.

Gordon Brown could not be described as a 'fun' politician. He has a dour manner, uses words and expressions most people could not comprehend, and reportedly has a ferocious temper which never exhibits itself in public. Those who have worked close to him have reported that he occasionally turns as black as thunder and bawls out those who had displeased him.

He also lost the sight of one eye in a rugby accident as a child and thus, when delivering his Budgets as Chancellor, had to place his speech on three thick volumes of bound Hansard so he could the more easily read his words. Brown would clutch these volumes with his constantly gnawed fingernails. Jokes, during his Budget speeches, were few and very far between. But it is untrue to suggest that he never smiled. He could be, and very often was, genial towards the press, even political reporters. The relationship between 10 Downing Street and the press, now that he is Prime Minister, is far less abrasive than it had been when Tony Blair was in power.

Then he had smiled ever less regularly. However, he was once 'caught' grinning in a public place immediately after what was reported to have been a ferocious stand-up row with Prime Minister Blair. It seemed an odd and inappropriate moment for a man like Gordon Brown, not noted for his cheeriness. He quickly explained himself: 'I was actually smiling, talking to my colleagues about my new baby. It was nothing to do with politics.' There were some who remained sceptical about that explanation.

Given the animosity and, indeed, the level of hatred between Brown and Blair, and the occasional snide remark about him thrown in from time to time by Cherie Blair, it was a wonder the country was governed at all, never mind efficiently. At one point in 1998 Downing Street had labelled him 'psychologically flawed'. Needless to say, the Downing Street spin machine ferociously denied that it was responsible for that insult. But it was difficult, if not impossible, to believe that it had emanated from any other source, since it had appeared in all the Sunday newspapers and was clearly the result of an unattributable briefing. Brown chose, in public at least, to ignore this jibe.

Incidentally, it says something about the inefficiency of the Tory opposition at that time, that even 24 hours after all the Sunday newspapers had splashed this remark over their front pages in June, the shadow Chancellor Peter Lilley was not even aware of it. I had encountered Mr Lilley by chance on the London underground, and when I mentioned this to him, to my amazement, he hadn't a clue what I was talking about.

Later on, Brown, in another dust-up with the Prime Minister, had apparently told him that he would never believe anything Mr Blair said ever again. This was never actually formally denied, so one assumes that it was true. Although even when something is denied, you would be very naïve to accept that denial as the truth, such a slippery bunch of people our politicians are these days.

Brown is not so much a private man as a closed-up clam of a man. It is often exceedingly difficult to have the faintest idea what he is thinking about. But he had a flair for keeping out of trouble. During all the sleazy moments which marked Tony Blair's premiership, Brown seemed never to be implicated in them. So – unusually for a 21st century politician – when he advanced towards 10 Downing Street, no amount of muck-raking (and there was plenty of it) could uncover any scandals or tittle-tattle about the man – quite an achievement. He has remained a sobersides with an untarnished pair of hands. He was the last man to engage in gimmicks or stunts designed to make him look more like 'one of the people'. He at least realised (where scores of others have not) that such activities usually end up with the subject of them looking a fool.

But he did, early in 2008, appoint a press officer specially designed to ensure that embarrassing photographs of him did not appear in the press. This person had barely got her feet under the desk when the papers – at a time when he was at a low ebb and facing demands for his resignation – all carried pictures of him standing beneath notices bearing the words 'Exit' and 'Way Out'. His image has freshened up in other ways. Brown invariably wore dowdy suits when Chancellor and refused to dress up in formal dinner attire at official banquets, deeming it 'ridiculous'. But since he became Prime Minister his suits, thanks probably to his wife Sarah, have become snappy, his teeth are suddenly far whiter, although he claims this was simply down to 'a few fillings', and he once reported, in an uncharacteristic note of levity, for all who wanted to hear, that he bought his underwear from Marks and Spencer. At last, the man is coming out of his shell! Even so, he remains a bit of an enigma. Anyone, as he did once, who talks about the 'neo-classical endogenous growth theory' is never going to be fully understood by the common herd.

Perhaps that's the way he wants it.

Some complain about the rowdiness of the House of Commons these days. Admittedly, there have been some wild scenes in living memory – notably the Northern Ireland MP Bernadette Devlin's physical and face-scratching assault on the then Home Secretary, Reginald Maudling – but none of it seems to have been on the scale and fury of events in the past. I once saw and heard the *Red Flag* being sung in the Commons Chamber as the dawn broke after a particularly vitriolic all-night sitting. But recent scenes in the Commons have really been the stuff of a tea party on the rector's lawn compared with the uproar, the fury and even the occasional blood stains on the carpets of the Chamber in years gone by. It is a place where, in its heyday, whole libraries of books, propelled by inflamed opposition MPs, have cascaded on to the heads of ministers, where punches have been thrown and where the language has sometimes been so vivid that it would have evoked gasps of admiration from the renowned fish-porters of Billingsgate.

Charles Dickens, observing the scenes of tumult from the press gallery (positively a haven of rectitude by comparison), once wrote: 'It is the great dust-heap of Westminster – laughing, coughing, oh-ing, groaning, a conglomeration of noise and confusion to be met with in no other place in existence, not excepting Smithfield on a market day or a cockpit in all its glory.' And that was on a quiet day!

However, his description might well have applied to the bizarre events in the Chamber on the night of 5 April 1949. A contemporary diarist, who plainly hugely enjoyed the rough-house brawling on that occasion (wouldn't we all?) observed with no attempt to hide his glee: 'It was quite like old times when the Irish Nationalists were still here. Altogether, a good time was had by all.' The 'good time' he described included scrummages on the floor of the House, with honourable members going at it hammer-and-tongs, simply because one MP had called another a fascist. The diarist went on, 'A socialist hit Beverley Baxter in the face. Waldron Smithers, who was well away, tried to push into the middle of the scrum, and shoved Lady Davidson out of the way. So she turned on him. He told her to shut her bloody mouth – so that was a private Conservative row.' The author leaves us to speculate whether his observation that Waldron Smithers was 'well away' was an indication of his state of sobriety or was merely a map reference. One is forced to form one's own judgement – which shouldn't take very long.

Within recent memory, Neil Kinnock, the former Leader of the Labour Party, was reportedly involved in a scuffle during a Commons division with Alfred Morris (later to become Lord Morris of Manchester), a Labour spokesman on the disabled. It was all over a disagreement on the education of handicapped children. Mr Kinnock, who once famously took on a bunch of rowdies in the calmer and more genteel surroundings of an Indian restaurant near his home in Ealing, west London, said at the time of the Commons clash: 'He started shouting very loudly in my face. Suddenly, I found his finger pointing in my eye. I responded in a mild and admonishing way.'

Which is, of course, exactly how one would expect a man of Mr Kinnock's elevated position to respond. However, those who witnessed the scene said afterwards that it was not quite how the Leader of the Opposition described it. Indeed, it took John Prescott, well-known as a thumper of voters, according to contemporary reports, to pitch in and prevent a brawl.

There was also the incident where Emanuel Shinwell, the fiery wartime minister, once contemptuously flung a penny across the Chamber at an opposing MP who, he claimed, had passed some insulting remarks about the Jews.

Writers down the years have despaired of the conduct of the House of Commons. Pepys said it contained 'the most profane swearing fellows I have ever heard in my life'. And William Hazlitt observed: 'Talk of mobs – see how few who have distinguished themselves in the Commons have ever done anything else.'

Even Robert Louis Stevenson had his reservations. 'We all know what Parliament is and we are ashamed of it,' he said.

But almost certainly the most insulting tongue for years at Westminster belonged to the late Sir Nicholas Fairbairn, who revelled in the outrageous and gloried in defying convention. He was the eccentric genius of Westminster, whose entire public life was a litany of explosive remarks, venomous invective – and yet, from time to time, courtly chivalry. Fairbairn was brazen but likeable – except to a few who found his insults too hot and too damningly true to forgive. Self-effacement was not one of his stronger qualities. Indeed, he described himself in *Who's Who*, without a scintilla of self-doubt, as 'author, farmer, forester, painter, poet, TV and radio broadcaster, journalist, dress-designer, landscape gardener, bon viveur and wit'. His invective was so sharp and so extravagant that whenever his name appeared on the television monitors, MPs streamed into the Chamber to hear what he had to say.

This was how he once described his colleagues: 'The women in the House of Commons are mostly hideous. They have no fragrance. I dislike women who deny their femininity. People like Edwina Currie. They are just cagmags [a derogatory Scottish term for women meaning a tough old goose], scrub heaps, old tattles. In the House during the salmonella debate, I reminded Edwina Currie, who set off a furore once by talking about salmonella and eggs, that she was an egg once. I said that people on both sides of the House greatly regretted its fertilisation. On another occasion, she was going on about water being poisonous if you were stuffed full of it. I replied that I did not mind being poisoned by water, but I could not bear to be stuffed by Edwina Currie.'

He had little time for the Green fraternity, whom he summed up thus: 'What's the point of saving the green-arsed dragonfly and not discussing population control?'

Sir Nicholas also had a healthy contempt for the politically correct. 'I am perfectly happy to be politically incorrect,' he observed, 'because that means not being a creep.' He particularly liked living in a castle (which he bought for £100 in 1960), he said, because you did not need to see anybody.

'The front door is still fortified by a mesh of interlocking iron bars and I am particularly proud of my oubliette, a trick staircase designed to trip up enemies and send them tumbling downstairs into the dungeon.'

He had strong, if unorthodox, views about the Olympic Games. 'I hate the Olympic Games, which is a bogus political event. I wouldn't ban the use of drugs. I would make them compulsory so that all the competitors died before they could collect their unworthy loot.'

And in yet another memorable House of Commons speech in January 1985, he spoke of Sir Iain Moncreiffe, who had tried to chat up the then Prime Minister, Margaret Thatcher, with the immortal words: 'I have always fancied you...' Mrs Thatcher, as she then was, is reported to have, in the no less immortal words of the Cockney barrow boy, 'copped a deaf 'un' to that protestation of undying love.

Sir Nicholas's political instincts surfaced at the tender age of 11. The gardener at his prep school buttonholed him in the grounds and warned him grimly: 'We are going to wipe out the likes of you.'

The youthful Nicholas immediately took his revenge. 'That resentment was unbelievable,' he said. 'I took my catapult and put out every window in the Co-op, the only symbol of socialism in range. I was thrashed within an inch of my life. Since then, I've played a large part in the destruction of socialism.'

Another political bare-knuckle fighter was the Conservative Terry Dicks, who sat for Hayes and Harlington. Dicks did not have quite the finesse – if that is the right word – of Sir Nicholas, but he was no less entertaining and just as blunt with his political enemies and his pet hates. He was lucky more than once not to find himself the subject of race relations legislation. In 1986, he denounced West Indians as 'in general bone idle...it's about time they were given a kick in the pants'. He claimed, too, that in some parts of London race relations were given priority over law and order. Dicks denounced illegal immigrants as 'liars, cheats and queue jumpers who should be sent packing'. And he demanded the birch for Scottish football hooligans, whom he labelled 'those pigs from Scotland'.

His views were no less trenchant on the arts which, he always felt, should not be subsidised at all by the taxpayer. He likened opera singers to 'overweight Italians singing in their own language' and ballet dancers as 'men prancing about in ladies' tights'. It was little wonder, therefore, that his critics denounced him, from time to time, as a hypocrite, a racist and as Stone Age man. But perhaps the most telling description of all of Terry Dicks came from the acid-tongued Tony Banks, who served as Minister for Sport during Tony Blair's first Parliament as Prime Minister.

Banks, no respecter of persons, said of Dicks: 'He is living proof that a pig's bladder on the end of a stick can be elected to Parliament.'

It has often been said how odd it is that anything to do with Europe – until very recently – could reduce the entire nation to virtual catalepsy, but could also stir and inflame passions to breaking point. On one particular occasion, Michael Foot roared across at the Geoffrey Rippon, Britain's Common Market negotiator, the awful and intimidating threat: 'You'll get a report stage, you'll see!'

Lesser men would have quailed at this sinister foreboding. But Mr Rippon stood his ground manfully, only to be shaken out of his boots by a salvo of large tomes, despatched with deadly aim from the direction of Mr Dennis Skinner, the 'Beast of Bolsover' – no stranger to boiling over, although it is more usually only verbally.

When Margaret Thatcher became a grandmother in 1989, a group of sycophantic Conservative MPs tabled a House of Commons motion congratulating her (surprise, surprise) and wishing her new grandson, Michael, a long and healthy life. Pretty routine stuff, you may think. However, Skinner was determined not to let this innocuous and happy motion go by without comment. So, as soon as he saw it on House of Commons documents, he wasted no time in tabling an amendment to it, which read: 'And this House expresses the hope that the baby will learn to crawl as quickly as the authors of this motion...' Alas and alack, the fuddy-duddies who control these things refused to allow this sentiment to appear on the Order Paper. I could not say that I was entirely surprised by this outcome. It was, nevertheless, a great pity.

Not many ministers have got the better of Skinner, let alone managed to silence him. For more than 30 years he was an obsessive taunter of the Tories and especially cabinet ministers. But as chance would have it, Prime Minister John Major was answering Commons questions on 11 February 1997, which was Skinner's 65th birthday. Years before, Skinner had indicated to his constituents in Bolsover, Derbyshire, that, unlike judges, he was not going to remain in his job as an old-age pensioner. Major, having remembered Skinner's pledge, was merciless in his taunting. You do not often see people who are both seething and sheepish at the same time, but that was Skinner's uncomfortable demeanour that afternoon. A decade later, Skinner was still there!

But possibly even more telling was the putdown inflicted on him by John Biffen when he was Leader of the Commons in Margaret Thatcher's day. He was being subjected to a salvo of insults and invective from Skinner. There came a point when Biffen felt he had had just about enough of this. And so quietly he said: 'We grammar school boys really should stick together.'

That shut him up.

TV: And Parliament Powders its Nose

The day television came to the House of Commons, 21 November 1989, was the day when the scarlet women of Westminster dominated the chamber. They had – almost to a woman and on both sides of the House – succumbed to the advice of the charm school smoothies and donned the brightest, flashiest, gaudiest reds, and dotted themselves about the Chamber like clusters of love-lies-bleeding. The 'experts' had told them that red was the colour for the cameras and they dutifully complied. Strong men, wilting under the intense heat of camera lights, applied their powder puffs (yes, powder puffs!) to their fevered brows.

The same 'experts' told the women to avoid blue at all costs. So the Prime Minister, Margaret Thatcher, turned up in the truest Tory blue on the market. It was no occasion for the coy, the humble or the modest as the TV cameras glared down on them from a great height. It was an occasion, rather, for the camera-hogs. Bob Cryer, who has since sadly died, the Labour MP for Bradford South (no shrinking violet, he), obliged the punters once again by being the first MP to speak in a televised House. It was not meant to be like that.

With the kind of agreeable but cunning ingenuity for which he was famous, he managed to extract an obscure point of order not to deny access to MPs to the Palace of Westminster. It was, in retrospect, a virtuoso performance. Cryer at once became a footnote in the history books. Incidentally, Cryer occasionally prolonged late-night debates purely so that House of Commons' staff qualified for a free cab home.

Television began with a rush of excitement from many, while greybeards who opposed its introduction feared the worst. We were told that we would get MPs playing to the gallery (they always did) and that the Chamber would quickly be transformed into some kind of TV game-show studio. There were always fears, some of which have proved justified, that it would lead to an outbreak of grandstanding, drama queens, ham-acting and general histrionics.

These fears were intensified in the months before TV arrived by the bearded, booming actor-MP Andrew Faulds, Labour member for Warley East. He suddenly started to play up in the Chamber, shouting and gesticulating at the Prime Minister, Margaret Thatcher, like some fading, declaiming tragedian. However, one of the assistant Speakers successfully brought him down to size. 'Mr Faulds,' he said, 'I do not actually detect any casting directors in the Strangers' Gallery...'

When television was first introduced, the timid, even craven, people who decided on the precise arrangements, came up with a constricting list of rules which seemed deliberately to strip the Commons of all life, all movement, all vulgarity, and all the raucousness, spite, fury, farce and fun that makes it such a splendid, savage and occasionally uncouth place: only the head and shoulders of the person speaking could be shown. Any trouble anywhere else in the Chamber was effectively a no-go area for the TV screens, even though everyone in the Strangers' Gallery, or elsewhere in the House, could clearly see what was going on.

Why, one asked, should TV viewers be denied all the fun?

Happily, rules, which have not noticeably changed over the years, seem to be treated in a far more cavalier fashion than they were at the beginning. It is now possible to watch the House of Commons, warts and all. Although, I have to confess, not quite all. For if there is a rumpus in the Strangers' Gallery, as does happen from time to time, the cameras are still banned from panning to it.

But it wasn't long before the initial excitement died down and hardly anyone watched Parliament on the box after a year or two, other than a few soundbites from the rowdiest moments of Prime Minister's Question Time. In short, Parliament is overall too tedious to interest the TV programme-makers except for specialist purposes.

Incidentally, those who opposed TV in the Commons took heart from a report from the Canadian Parliament about the televising of their chamber. The report said: 'The televising of the House rewards outrageousness and has led to orchestrated removals of MPs from the Chamber and unparliamentary language. There has been visual gimmickry – in the form of displays of national flags, singing of national anthems, and disorder by visitors in the gallery. We have experienced unparliamentary activity – for instance a display of dead salmon in the Chamber – and the abuse of privilege through slander.' But on the credit side, the report said: 'Television has helped control behaviour. We have fewer drunks in the Chamber.' Canadian television sounds a lot more interesting than parliamentary TV in the UK with all the restrictions placed on what the cameras may show.

The funniest and finest piece of parliamentary television was entirely 'illicit'. It was that splendid occasion when lesbians abseiled into the Chamber of the House of Lords. This happened when parliamentary televising was very much in its infancy and those responsible for the camerawork instinctively panned to the descending band, while their lordships and not a few ladyships registered apoplectic fury and disbelief in equal measure. Needless to say, to the glee of the viewer, this episode was shown live. And at least one television company decided to show it several times again. That is until the pompous authorities of the Palace of Westminster sternly told them it was illegal to show anything extraneous like this. They had to concentrate on their lordships' debate and ignore the interesting and exciting diversions. I suppose it is typical of Westminster that whenever – a rarity in itself – something amusing happens in the Chamber, it is immediately ruled out of order and not fit for public consumption.

* * * * *

One of the practices which televising Parliament gave rise to was doughnutting, which persists to this day. This involves half-a-dozen or so MPs crowding round a speaker, say three behind him, one on either side and a couple in front. The object of this is to suggest to the innocent viewer that a crowded House is all agog with what the speaker is saying, because that is the impression it gives on the small screen. However, a panoramic sweep by the camera would expose acres of empty green benches, with just an incongruous small huddle around the MP who is on his feet at the time.

You could call it childish and you would be right. It is also, in a very ham-fisted kind of way, an attempt to deceive. But then, as any cynic would tell you, there is nothing very surprising about that. When television came to the House of Lords, the Conservative Party 'enforcers' were worried about octogenarian Lady Elliot of Harwood. She was a regular attendee at the Lords and usually sat through debates with her eyes firmly closed. The Tories, fearful that TV viewers would see one of their most venerable members apparently in a deep slumber, suggested in the most reasonable way they could that she should move from her traditional seat to a space just five or six yards down the bench. The purpose of this, although they did not tell her, was to keep her permanently out of camera shot. However, I am glad to report that her feisty Ladyship told them to take a running jump. She was staying put, so there. And so she did.

One thing television has achieved in Parliament is the sudden popularity of the office of Speaker. For as long as people could remember, the Speakers of the House of Commons emerged, like leaders of the Conservative Party in former days, by agreement with the main parties in the House. But since television was introduced the Speaker has become the most exposed member by far of the House of Commons. That could explain why, in 2000, when Michael Martin was elected Speaker, there were some 11 other aspirants for the job. The Speaker, who was an unknown quantity outside Westminster before the broadcasters arrived, had suddenly become a telly star.

Sir Edward Heath, who was then Father of the House as its longest continuously serving Member, organised a system of voting which gave the sponsor and seconder of every candidate the opportunity to have his or her say before the victor was announced by a process of elimination. Oddly, Mr Martin was the only one of all those candidates whose sponsor and seconder were both from his own party, Labour.

All Speakers used to wear a wig until Betty Boothroyd, the first woman Speaker, announced that she would not, an example followed by her successor, Michael Martin. Now Miss Boothroyd had a fine head of hair, but Michael Martin was by no means so generously endowed. Wearing a full-bottomed wig is an arduous business, so we must have some sympathy for those who decline to don it.

Wig-wearing is not the only tradition to have faded over the years. The cry, 'I spy strangers,' given by any MP meant the immediate emptying of all the galleries, including the press gallery. The purpose used to be to enable the Commons to discuss sensitive security issues in private. Now, however, if an MP cries out 'I spy strangers' it is usually merely a delaying tactic and there has to be a vote to clear the galleries; the vote is invariably lost. Also vanished is the top hat which was worn by members raising points of order during a division. With MPs milling around the Chamber, an MP who wants to raise a point of order would be difficult to spot without a hat. But now that has gone, too.

After her retirement Betty Boothroyd broke another old custom. She moved on to the House of Lords and wrote a best-selling book about her life and experiences. That would have been impossible 20 years ago. Nobody would have bought it, because nobody would have known who she was. But whatever else television has achieved – good or bad – it certainly created a sartorial revolution in the House of Commons. Alas, it was not one which was to have any degree of permanence. Contrived scruffiness, so assiduously cultivated until that momentous first day, was suddenly no longer on the agenda.

Bruce Grocott, for instance (he later became a Lord and just before that Parliamentary Private Secretary to Tony Blair as Prime Minister), had been renowned for the casual look and the undone top shirt-button. On the day TV arrived, he was dressed with the primness of a Victorian grocer. However, dark suits – which the image-mongers say intimidate the viewer – were sparse among MPs. Instead, the accent was on light grey and medium blue, with rowdy shirts and clashing ties. The Brylcreem, the evidence of hair that had actually been combed and the forced, unnatural smile were all on parade. And Mrs Thatcher, in a speech curiously unscarred with bitterness, obligingly gave way to an unprecedented number of interveners, no doubt to enable them to tell their grandchildren that they had spoken in the House of Commons the day TV arrived there. An epidemic, dammit, even a pandemic, of bonhomie seemed to be in the utmost danger of breaking out.

But the hard-line opponents of Commons television obdurately and flamboyantly refused to step into line. Ian Gow, who made the first formal speech of the TV era, proudly proclaimed his spurning of all the advice on how to conduct himself before the cameras. Conservative MP Kenneth Hind equally made no concession to the fashion gurus. He arrived in dark suit, dark tie, and dark shoes, ostentatiously refusing to become a 'media personality'.

Labour claimed a TV victory for Neil Kinnock, and Peter Mandelson, who was Labour's director of communications, let the world know: 'He won the TV war hands down today. He was cool, measured and witty while Mrs Thatcher sounded rattled during a lot of her speech. The effect on TV was shrill and un-Prime Ministerial.' Well, he would say that, wouldn't he? as Mandy Rice-Davies once observed.

The sense of occasion on that historic day was not lost on one other regular attender of the Commons. David Blunkett's dozy guide-dog Offa, normally sloppy and somnolent during the most tumultuous debates, was on that day forever preening himself with all the dedication and vanity normally associated with cabinet ministers in the make-up rooms of television studios.

* * * * *

Just as Dolly Parton said about herself: 'It costs a lot to look this cheap,' the same applies in large measure to political image-makers. It seems that the higher the fees they charge, the more lurid are their ideas and therefore the more ridiculous they make those people whose reputations they claim to be enhancing.

William Hague probably suffered the most from over-enthusiastic backroom staff who wanted to make him appear vibrant, energetic and thrusting and succeeded merely in making him look a chump. He appeared in baseball caps – a serious error of judgement – made several high-profile visits to the Notting Hill Caribbean carnival, was seen zooming down water-chutes like a teenager and held American-style business bonding sessions in seaside hotels. These activities appalled the rank-and-file core of traditional Tories, who wanted gravitas and not childish antics. He also ill-advisedly described the old guard of the Parliamentary Conservative Party – people like Michael Heseltine, Sir Edward Heath, and Kenneth Clarke – as 'big beasts of the jungle' who no longer ran the party. He further gratuitously insulted them with the old Texan tag: 'Big hats, no cattle'.

Hague was also persuaded to give his wife Ffion a £-sign brooch to demonstrate his romantic nature. The gesture was universally mocked in the media. But it got worse when the jewellers complained publicly that it had not been paid for.

He was encouraged by well-meaning but disastrous advisers to show how macho he was – always a dangerous ploy. It was put about that as a teenager he worked as a drayman in south Yorkshire and consumed 14 pints of beer a day, and on one occasion had drunk 32 shots of rum at a single session. If this were true, he would have been a dead man. Nor did it succeed as a way of enhancing his reputation. The whole thing blew up in his face when one local publican publicly recalled that he had been nicknamed 'Fizzy Willie' because his limit appeared to have been a single half-pint of lager and lime. I cannot believe that Hague, a highly intelligent individual, thought up these ludicrous escapades himself. But I am astonished that he agreed to take them on board.

It seems, too, that the image-makers have been doing their darnedest – although not intentionally – to make David Cameron, the Tory leader at the time of writing, look stupid. Whoever thought up the idea that he should cycle to Westminster to save the planet, followed by an exhaust-belching car carrying his shoes, should have had his employment terminated forthwith. Equally his so-called 'polar-bear hugging' trip to the Arctic (with TV crews in tow) and his visit to Rwanda to help the local people there when his own Oxfordshire constituency was in parts knee-deep in flood water, were regarded as political calamities.

On another occasion, anxious (mistakenly, many thought) to distance himself from Margaret Thatcher, he bluntly refused a simple opportunity to have his photograph taken with her. Yet, a few days later he was prepared to fly all the way to South Africa, for a whistle-stop visit, to have his photograph taken with Nelson Mandela. Later he did submit (however willingly or otherwise I know not) to be snapped with Lady Thatcher at the unveiling of her statue in the members' lobby of the House of Commons.

John Major, however, kept the image men at arm's length. He said: 'I am what I am and people will have to take me for what I am. The image-makers will not find me in their tutelage.' He said that on becoming Prime Minister, he had not changed the length of his hair, the style of his suits or the colour of his shirts, adding that he was perfectly content to remain 'the same plug-ugly I always was on television.' It was not the image-makers who changed the world's perception of him, but the TV programme *Spitting Image*, which depicted him as a grey man, constantly eating processed peas on a knife.

* * * * *

Time was when politicians were highly embarrassed about having to wear make-up on television. Now, they seem to take it in their stride. I remember in the late 1980s being at the receiving end of a massive dressing-down for reporting that Neil Kinnock had borrowed the powder puff of the *Mirror*'s Julia Langdon in order to prettify himself for a television appearance.

Appearance now counts for more than the words that are uttered. A cascade of dandruff on the shoulders, a grubby cuff seen for only an instant on the television screen, can cost more votes than a dodgy defence policy ever did. Margaret Thatcher was always aware of this. She invariably wore simple clothes on television, fully aware of the dangers that if she wore anything fussy viewers would concentrate on that, rather than the message she wanted to deliver.

When, in the very early stages of his premiership, Tony Blair went on BBC television to explain the reasons for exempting tobacco sponsorship from Formula One racing and the donation of £1 million to the Labour Party by the 'king' of Formula One, Bernie Ecclestone, the Prime Minister was grossly over made-up. As he pleaded his case, he looked more like a pantomime dame than a Prime Minister. I was told by a BBC official that a member of the production team had, at the time, expressed concern that the make-up lady was slapping the greasepaint on far too liberally. She replied that the lighting was such that it had to be done in this way and they let her get on with it. But it was a grave error of judgement on her part – unless of course it was her aim to make the Prime Minister look like a painted doll.

Kenneth Baker, the former Home Secretary and later chairman of the Conservative Party, was always renowned for his sleek, some would say oily, manner. He always spoke in mellifluous tones and although he fell a little short of the abject humility associated with Uriah Heep, he was, nevertheless, a little too sugary for some tastes. However, he plainly seemed to realise this himself at one stage. He underwent a kind of self-imposed makeover in 1989, years before Botox and nips and tucks became almost a fashion imperative.

At the Tory Party conference that year in Blackpool, Baker's speech was far from his routine oiliness. He was wildly and untypically waving his arms about, in the manner of Michael Heseltine, who did it much better. His hair, normally battened down with Brylcreem, was flying all over the place. He had assumed the aura of Ken Dodd, frenzied and unkempt, shouting and declaiming. One member of the shocked audience whispered to me at the time: 'It is as though a new man has entered the Baker soul.' Just my thoughts as well.

Later on that very day, a similarly tousled Baker arrived at a television studio in Blackpool to spread the Conservative message. A make-up lady approached him and inquired sweetly: 'May I comb your hair, Mr Baker?' Baker replied: 'Yes please. BUT NOT TOO MUCH.' That said it all…

* * * *

One politician who was supremely comfortable in the television era right up until the end of his prime ministerial career was Tony Blair. He could never be accused of not milking his departure from the frontline of British politics. After announcing that he had chosen a date late in June 2007 for his last day in the Commons as Prime Minister (indeed his last day of any kind as it turned out) he embarked on a nationwide glad-handing farewell tour, reminiscent of the legendary soprano Nellie Melba. His last words in the Commons itself, after a tumultuous but basically good-natured Question Time, were appropriately, 'The end', as he left the Chamber to roars of approval from all sides of the House.

It was incongruous to see Tory leader David Cameron, who had been mauling and verbally abusing Mr Blair for months past, waving his arms about wildly, like a conductor in charge of an orchestra playing *The Flight of the Bumble-Bee* at an astonishing rate of knots, as he urged his own side to mark the Prime Minister's departure with an unprecedented standing ovation. Most of the Tories, not entirely to their credit – since they spent much of their time denigrating Mr Blair– succumbed to Mr Cameron's blandishments, but others did the honourable thing and stayed firmly in their seats, either because a standing ovation and clapping were a serious breach of convention and probably against the rules or because they felt it hypocritical to join in. The only surprise was that this great actor-manager – which is essentially what he was – did not return to acknowledge this delirious crowd with a flourishing curtain call.

In the press gallery we remained, as ever, totally neutral and disinterested, not budging an inch from our perches up above – almost all of us that is. I regret to say that Julia Hartley-Brewer of the *Sunday Express* did rise to her feet in acclamation. My view has always been that we are paid to report their pantomimes, not to take part in them.

A year on after the grand finale, Blair was busier than ever, buzzing around the Middle East in his role as a peacekeeper – not that there was, at the time, much peace to keep in the region. It was a job likely to remain unfinished right until his dying day. Blair accepted invitations to make highly lucrative speeches to audiences who, I am afraid, were sometimes far from impressed by his performances, especially after they had paid a five-figure fee to lure him to their events.

'Well,' one of his friends told me, 'you surely do not expect him to spill the beans about his premiership before his memoirs come out, do you?' Absolutely, but then you would also have expected that those organisations which shovelled so much cash into the Blair coffers would have realised, too, that he was going to deliver only run-of-the-mill material.

I do not think it can be said that, after his farewell, Blair was homesick for Westminster. He never really liked the Commons and left the impression that he went into the Chamber only when he could not avoid doing so. But one thing he did miss was a game of tennis. While abroad on his peace mission, he vouchsafed to a friend, 'God, I wish I could play some tennis. I rarely ever play.'

His great tennis opponent was Lord Levy, a highly successful Labour Party fundraiser. Levy has said that it was tennis, as much as anything else, which created a bond between them, until they appeared to fall out over the cash-for-honours affair. Another generous Labour Party donor, Sir Emmanuel Kaye, paid for a tennis court to be built at the Prime Minister's country retreat of Chequers, so important was tennis to Tony Blair.

When Blair did depart, the highly unusual element was his failure to produce a resignation honours' list, which is the prerogative of every outgoing Prime Minister. Although there was never any formal explanation for this, his close acquaintances believe that it was because Blair had faced so many accusations of 'cronyism' for placing his friends in influential positions over the years, or coating them with ermine in the House of Lords, that he thought it wise to give this one a miss.

Blair – and his wife – had a strangely ambivalent attitude towards privacy: he would 'protect' his family against so-called press intrusion, but was quite happy to go public, as it were, when it suited him. For instance, on the birth of their son Leo, in May 2000, he got photographs taken by Mary McCartney (daughter of Paul McCartney) and proceeded to sell them at £500 a time, for a cancer charity, admittedly, to newspapers. Yet when Leo was paraded in public once for his christening, there was a terrible row when press cameramen tried to photograph him, while the Blairs were happy for others, with their Box Brownies, to snap the youngster.

And while his family affairs were supposed to be strictly out-of-bounds to Fleet Street, Cherie Blair once gaily announced that he was a 'five-times-a-night' man – whether that pleased him, by implying that he was a real stud, or embarrassed him beyond measure is in doubt, although I think the latter is more likely. He was once forced to comment on it by a press photographer who asked whether he felt fit. When Blair replied: 'Very' the photographer, pursued the matter by inquiring: 'What, five times a night?'

Blair's response to this was, 'At least. I can do it more, depending on how I feel.'

One blogger at the time observed: 'He did look awfully haggard by early Friday morning.'

Meanwhile, Blair on another occasion whispered to a friend: 'Once my wife goes to sleep, it takes a minor nuclear explosion to wake her.' Perhaps, if that had not been the case, he would have been a six-times-a-night man – or even more.

Points of Order

Gerald Howarth, when he was Conservative MP for Cannock and Burntwood, was sitting in the foyer of the Central Television premises in Birmingham, waiting to take part in a TV debate on racial discrimination. He was told beforehand that also taking part in the discussion would be a black footballer with a broken arm, caused when he was attacked by a racially-motivated gang of thugs. Another character was sitting beside Mr Howarth in the foyer. After some moments' silence, Mr Howarth, anxious to strike up a conversation, inquired of his companion: 'Are you the footballer.'

'I am not,' came the huffy reply. 'I am Linda Bellos.' Linda was a left-wing political activist in London for many years before she moved to France, later to return to Britain.

* * * * *

William Waldegrave, when he was in the Cabinet, was wont to deliver gaffes, although not on the same scale as his colleague Kenneth Clarke. On being moved from the post of Health Secretary to become Chancellor of the Duchy of Lancaster, he was photographed screwing a plaque on to a wall proclaiming his new department. When the photographers, as they always do, pleaded with him to go through the motions again, and then again, he called out, with just a touch of acerbity in his voice: 'For crying out loud, I can't keep on screwing all day…' At least, to his credit, he joined in the vulgar laughter which greeted this comment.

* * * * *

I think the prize for the quickest recovery from a verbal gaffe must go to Mrs Margaret Ewing, the former Scottish Nationalist MP for Moray. She was in full flight in her constituency, proclaiming: 'My party is resolutely opposed to any attempt in Scotland to put forward any schemes for nuclear dumplings.' Then, realising her goof, she recovered with lightning rapidity. 'And when I talk about nuclear dumplings,' she said, 'I mean Tory MPs who support nuclear dumping in our land.'

* * * * *

Tony Banks had for long enjoyed a reputation of being one of the wags of the House of Commons, never wanting for a technicoloured insult or a purple passage when required. But he was, understandably, a little upset when he was approached by a Labour colleague after making a speech in the Commons. 'Tony,' he said. 'You are losing your touch. You were not as funny as usual.'

The poor man tried to explain that he was only trying to be serious for once. It's hard work being serious and portentous when you have built up an enviable reputation, as had Banks, for being one of the best music hall acts at Westminster.

* * * * *

Veteran Labour MP Sir Gerald Kaufman can always be relied on for a bon mot when required. In 1988, John Prescott, who years later was to become Deputy Prime Minister, caused untold anxiety in the Labour Party by threatening to challenge for the deputy leadership, something which would have created much political bloodshed at that point. Happily, however, he was dissuaded from doing this and pulled out with as much grace as he could muster, which was not very much.

Comment from Mr Kaufman: 'Bull withdraws from china shop...'

Prescott used to claim that there were scores of Labour supporters urging him to stand. When I asked who these might be, I was told by Prescott's wife Pauline: 'I think his mother once thought it might be a good idea for him to have a go.'

* * * * *

If you thought Parliament dealt only with great affairs of state, listen to this question tabled by Conservative MP Sir John Wheeler in February 1991: 'To ask the Attorney General whether he will make it his policy to include a comma before the year in the citation of Acts of Parliament.'

The Attorney General: 'No. The practice of including a comma in the citation of an Act serves no useful purpose, and was abandoned in 1962 on the advice of the Statute Law Committee.'

Momentous events...

* * * * *

MPs have also been known to play word games with their counterparts in the Canadian Parliament. The British MP, for instance, will pick a very esoteric word and challenge his Canadian counterpart to use it in the Chamber and thus get it into Hansard. And the challenge will be reciprocated. Money changes hands, depending whether the challenged MP succeeds or fails to get the word in Hansard within an allotted time span. When, however, the House of Commons authorities got wind of this innocent little game, they sternly rebuked the participants and put an end to it.

* * * * *

The perky lawyer Jerry Hayes was not always dressed in regulation grey at Westminster. On one occasion, he turned up in a gaudy summer suit. This, too, attracted the attention of a Government Whip, who called after him: 'When you have put the deck-chairs away, Jerry, you can go off home.' But Mr Hayes had no shame or embarrassment whatever – he once embarked on some paragliding in aid of a children's charity dressed as a chicken.

He observed obscurely to me, 'You get better headlines dressed up as a chicken than you would as a bumble-bee.' I will take his word for it.

* * * * *

Baroness Strange, who left the Conservatives to sit on the crossbenches in the House of Lords after party leader William Hague had a tussle with Lord Cranborne about Lords' reform, tended, it seems, to have witnessed Saddam Hussein through rose-tinted spectacles. During the Lords' debate on the first Gulf War, she likened the Iraqi tyrant to a character in Charles Kingsley's charming book *The Water Babies*. She said: 'When the war is successfully concluded Saddam Hussein and his supporters will like to be seen as Mrs Do-as-you-would-be-done-by. I hope someone will make that point clear.' Touching thought though it was, it never looked like a runner...

* * * * *

Dirty tricks on the playing fields of Westminster. The Parliamentary hockey team, captained by Harry Greenway, the former Conservative MP for Ealing North, was playing the Timber Trades XI and the parliamentarians were losing 1-0 at half-time. At that point the dastardly captain of the Timber Trades team, in an outburst of seeming generosity, offered the Westminster players a swig from a bottle of House of Commons whisky which Mr Greenway had given their opponents as a goodwill gesture before the game. Greenway, however, had dark thoughts that this apparently kind gesture was merely a trick to get his side to play even worse in the second half. He was almost certainly correct in holding that suspicion.

His fears intensified when during the short break his players succeeded in emptying the bottle, at a time when they should have been sucking on lemons. It was with a heavy heart that he trudged on to the field of play for the second half. However, he had not reckoned on the restorative powers of a bottle of Scotch. The Timber Traders found themselves overwhelmed by a re-invigorated side which came from behind and beat them ultimately 2-1. It was a caddish ploy which came back to boomerang painfully on its perpetrators.

And as Mr Greenway said, appropriately, afterwards: 'Bully for us...'

* * * * *

One bizarre 'achievement' of mine was to end the first Gulf War before the official closure. I had been instructed to telephone 10 Downing Street at 2.40am. I knew this meant that some big announcement was to be made. I was told that the Gulf War was officially over, but that I was not to let the story go until 3am on the dot since the announcement had to coincide precisely with an identical announcement from Washington, where it was 10pm the previous evening.

At the appointed moment, I filed the story and prepared to resume my slumbers. But to no avail. The telephone rang urgently. It was 10 Downing Street furious because I had, according to them, filed it early, thus creating a rumpus in the White House which considered it had been unfairly scooped by Britain. I swore blind that I had not put the story out early. And then, suddenly, I realised something. The clock in my bedroom in Walthamstow was five minutes fast. I had ended the Gulf War early because of my own alarm clock.

Liberal Helpings

Remember the old SDP, the movement which was going to break the mould of British politics and with its 'unstoppable momentum' was going to sweep to power? How pathetic all those brave words now sound. Within months, the SDP, with David Owen and the other Gang of Four at the helm, Bill Rogers, Shirley Williams and Roy Jenkins, had effectively disappeared from the scene.

I think the event which killed it off was the Falklands War. For a full six months, domestic politics was put away and during that period the worst of all worlds happened to that unstoppable momentum. It stopped. Otherwise, I really do think that the movement might have made some progress instead of ending up with a messy liaison with the Liberal Party and with Owen and David Steel, then the Liberal Party leader, falling out over the merger. Owen tried to keep the old SDP going. But it was an unwinnable battle. Only a handful of people stayed loyally with him and it inevitably disappeared altogether. It was this very prospect of a merger which spawned an almost identical act of stubborn bloody-mindedness to keep the old Liberal Party alive.

The leader of this campaign was Michael Meadowcroft, certainly not a man to trifle with. The Liberal Party, so far as he was concerned, had a long and illustrious history and it was not

However, she seemed far from abashed at the many uncomplimentary remarks made about her appearance. Possibly she misguidedly thought her shambolic demeanour was a lovable trait. Lady Astor once said to her: 'You will never get on in politics, my dear, with that hair.' To be absolutely fair, she did get quite a long way in politics, but she might have got even further if she had used a comb once in a while.

The Oxford University magazine, Isis, once had this to say about her: 'She is like a Shetland pony, wearing a loud yellow and blue striped dress, little tarty high-heeled shoes and the wrong sort of jewellery.'

Shirley Williams, who was to become Baroness Williams, also became known as 'The Late Member', for very obvious reasons. She had the misfortune to get on a train going the wrong way once and spent the rest of her political career, fairly or unfairly, renowned as someone who could never get anywhere on time, if she indeed got anywhere at all. I have even seen her get in a Laurel and Hardy-type muddle negotiating revolving doors at Westminster, a task which you might imagine required a bit of shove but no other skills. Only our Shirl could get it wrong.

Later on, in the early 1980s, she was doing a photo call at some event on Britain's inland waterways. She, typically, arrived late and the barge left without her, thus providing the following day's newspapers with the gift of a headline: 'Shirley Misses The Boat'.

She also missed the SDP's alcohol-riddled transport – which soon got the name the 'Train of Shame' – taking the party's mobile conference from Perth (where it had started) to Bradford (for the second session). Williams had reportedly been due to pick up the train at Edinburgh, where she had been recording a TV interview. All that was loaded on to the train at Edinburgh were two great hampers of Scotland's famously indigestible mutton pies. But no Shirley Williams. She had to be taken by road to Bradford. When we all arrived there, she gave us an almighty dressing-down for doing the story. She firmly denied missing the train, but then politicians will deny anything, even if it is staring you in the face.

going to be allowed to disappear because some Labour refuseniks (those Labour MPs who defected from the party to form the SDP) wanted to abandon the name in a merger with David Steel's party.

At that time, in 1989, the partial merger was known as Democrats (SLD), inevitably called the 'Salads' (people who give political movements new names do not think these things through properly!).

But for that oldish warhorse, Meadowcroft, who was briefly Liberal MP for Leeds West, this was not good enough. He turned up at the Salads conference in Brighton in that year, openly scoffing at the idea, widely canvassed, that he and his little band of merry men would be Banquo's ghost at the conference. He made that abundantly clear when he spoke to me, saying: 'We are no ghost. We are very much alive. And, for the record, I shall not be washing my hands in blood.' Dramatic stuff.

But that was not the end of the matter. 'It is crucial, anyway,' he said, 'to maintain the Liberal Party to prevent charlatans coming in and using the name.' It was a not very polite reference to the Labour defectors. Meadowcroft made a lot of noise, a lot of clamour but as is usual in politics the big guns won the day. The Liberal Party, the pride and joy of William Ewart Gladstone and thousands of others, had been allowed to be pulverised.

*****

Shirley Williams conducted most of her political life under the unenviable nickname of 'The Frump'. That and her ability to arrive late, sometimes at the wrong venue, to miss trains and generally be scatterbrained provided her with her own unchallenged niche in political life. She was well aware of the comments made about her own appearance but seemed to do little to put it right. Indeed, she once passed a remark about it which was as convoluted as her general activities. She said: 'I did for a long time have a reputation for looking fairly untidy and drab. I don't think it is important, but I do think it matters in public life.' But you were in public life, Shirl!

Williams, who at that time represented Cambridge in the House of Commons, lost her seat in 1979, and she quickly became disenchanted with Labour's sudden swing to the left in the years that followed. It came, therefore, as no surprise when she joined forces with those who defected from the Labour Party to form the SDP. A vacancy was created in one of the Tory-held Croydon seats in south London. It looked like a real chance for the SDP to win its first seat – those who defected from Labour had to that point merely stayed in the Commons under a different banner, without deigning to fight by-elections.

I attended a lunch at the Press Club in London where Shirley Williams was the principal speaker. Her speech was on the record and she well knew that I was there, the only reporter present. Not once, but at least twice during that speech, she said she was planning to stand as the SDP candidate in Croydon. Immediately afterwards, I telephoned this story to the Press Association. It was, although I say it myself, a good story in that a nationally-known figure was going to fight a by-election in the name of the new party which in terms of news value at the time was a hot property.

But when I returned to the House of Commons that afternoon, I found the place in uproar. When she heard about the story, Williams had immediately got on to the Press Association and vehemently denied it. Needless to say, the PA newsdesk required an explanation from me. The fact remained that she had said that, more than once in her speech and was now flatly denying it. I can only assume that she did this because she thought it would sound arrogant of her to say she would be fighting a by-election in a seat where the local constituency party choose the candidate rather than herself. For whatever reason, she denied it. I, naturally, stuck to my guns and presented my shorthand note for anyone to see.

To my glee, the *Sun* newspaper splashed the story the next day under the splendid headline: 'Shilly, Shally Shirley', a description which, I am also glad to say, stuck with her for years to come. Many other people have lambasted her with a torrent of ungallant public remarks which, to be fair to her, she has always accepted with an easy grace. No wonder the anagram of her name is: 'I whirl aimlessly.'

But in case you were beginning to doubt it, I love her dearly.

* * * * *

Parliament is not a place for shrinking violets. To make any kind of impression at all, you need an outsize ego, something which Paddy Ashdown, the one-time leader of the Liberal Democrats, possessed in good measure.

During the 1992 campaign he engaged a French television crew fluently in their own tongue. And soon after that he conducted a conversation in Malay with a couple of girls he met while campaigning in Essex. But his most memorable achievement was, I have been told, to have ordered a prawn chop suey in a Chinese takeaway in a Chinese dialect. If he was expecting everyone to greet this performance with, so to speak, a standing ovation, he was sadly mistaken. The uncomprehending Chinese staff asked him if he would kindly repeat his order in English.

Ashdown led his party as though as though it were a military platoon, as befitted a former gallant soldier. His exploits and derring-do in the Special Boat Service, as well as on the streets of Belfast and elsewhere, marked him out as a swashbuckling character straight out of the pages of *Boy's Own Paper*. The trouble was that the Westminster platoon he led with such verve and energy and military precision more resembled Dad's Army than anything else. His colleagues will tell you ruefully that he used to telephone them at all hours of the day and night with bright new ideas. That is why there was so much relief among the rank and file of the Liberal Democrats when he was replaced by the much more easygoing and laidback Charles Kennedy.

'At last we were able to get some sleep undisturbed,' one MP said.

The worst moment of Ashdown's leadership was the revelation that he had been conducting a months-long affair with his secretary, Patricia Howard. This resulted in the *Sun* newspaper emblazoning him across their front page as 'Paddy Pantsdown'.

I remember a po-faced BBC presenter, who was reviewing that day's newspapers, coyly declining to read this description of him from the newspaper for fear of causing offence. But, unfortunately for him the nickname has stuck and I am afraid it will be included in the first paragraph of his obituaries when they come to be written. That is the sad fate of all politicians who stray from the straight and narrow, however distinguished they are and however much good work they have achieved. It is always their indiscretions which follow them shouting to the grave.

Once Ashdown told the world: 'Most people think I am a rampant carnivore, but there is an oddly feminine quality of my character.' I have to say that if that was true, then he kept it well under wraps. I never detected it.

Ashdown, although like so many of his kind addicted to appearing on television and trying to look 'normal' (the technical term for this affliction is 'media tart'), was not always over-friendly with the reporters who had to slog around with him during election campaigns. Ashdown appeared to give the impression to those he hoped might vote for his party that he had to endure what some people called 'the reptiles', hot on his heels all the time, when he knew in his heart that he could not have survived without the media. At one press conference along the 1992 trail a reporter was brusquely told by Ashdown: 'I give doorstep interviews in my time, and at my place and not yours.' Humility never was his strong suit.

Ashdown was always carefully casual in his sartorial and personal approach. He never quite succeeded, it seemed to me, to be 'at ease with himself' – to borrow a John Major expression – even though, goodness knows, he tried hard enough, probably too hard. He often swaggered about with his coat trailing over his shoulder, presumably in a daily struggle to persuade the voters of his blokeishness. He did it so badly that one reporter suggested (but not to his face) that a crash course at RADA might do the trick, although I doubted it.

For pompous language, give me Paddy Ashdown any day. In one gripe about the Conservative Party's European manifesto, he denounced it as a 'visionless cul-de-sac'. In my day that would have been termed a 'blind alley'.

The Liberals and their successors, the Liberal Democrats, were also (with the obvious exception of Shirley Williams) highly fussy about how the party was presented. During the 1992 general election campaign, Liberal Party officials instructed the writing press only to report the second of two speeches which the party leader, Paddy Ashdown, was delivering in Gateshead on that day.

'And why should that be?' we inquired.

'You might confuse the television people who were geared only to attend the second event,' we were told. It hardly seemed a satisfactory explanation, and we, as you might have expected, totally ignored the instruction.

The real reason for the Liberal Democrat panic was actually cosmetic. The fuss was all over the absence of a party logo to hang on the wall behind the leader at the first meeting, but one was due to become available in time for the second meeting. You do begin to wonder, sometimes, not merely at their priorities but at their vanity as well.

Their golden-silhouetted bird logo was launched in 1991, but the party refused to say precisely what this creature with the outspread wings was. At first it was annoyingly splurged across the printed words of their press releases which looked, as a result, as though they had been doused in spilt tea. When all efforts to discover what type of bird it was had failed, we came to the unanimous conclusion in the press gallery that it was a bird of 'pray' – spelt with the letter 'a' rather than 'e'. The reasoning behind this theory was that Paddy Ashdown's whole way of political life was based on a wing and a prayer...Boom! Boom!

Dr David Owen, the one-time leader of the SDP, could also be arrogant. During one election campaign, aboard Owen's Battle Bus, a woman reporter had been kept waiting for hours for a promised interview with him. By this time, the organisation for which the reporter worked had told her not to bother with the interview. As they swept through the English countryside, a haughty lady appeared through the curtains that led to Owen's lair, sashayed down the gangway and announced to the reporter: 'Dr Owen is ready for the interview now.'

To which the said reporter was able to give this splendid reply: 'Please present the good doctor with my compliments and tell him, if you would be so kind, that I do not do interviews after lunch.' Collapse of haughty party. The reporter received a standing ovation, as the lady slunk back into the Owen cabin.

Perilous Days on the Knocker

As much as MPs moan and groan about their lot, when election time comes round, they all fight like cats to get re-elected. Campaigning is intense – ranging from humble party members licking envelopes in foetid offices via others 'on the knocker', banging on doors trying to solicit support, to would-be MPs enraging all and sundry with loudspeaker vans disturbing the peace of a spring afternoon.

The best advice, incidentally, to those who have the misfortune to find canvassers on their doorstep, is to say you will vote for them, whoever they are. That is the simplest and speediest way to get rid of them. Never start a debate with a canvasser: you will end up with your head swirling, full of statistics (almost certainly inaccurate or, even more likely, made up) and 'facts' which bear little relation to anything, least of all the truth. Sometimes it's the candidates themselves who end up in awkward situations, a cause of hilarity to all but themselves.

For instance, Peter Lloyd, the one-time Conservative MP for Fareham and a Government Whip, was preparing his general election literature for the 1987 election. He trooped along to a photographer's studio for a family picture and, against his better judgement, agreed to the photographer's suggestion that he should have a dog in the picture. Imagine his consternation, then, when he saw the family photograph in his Labour opponent's election address. It contained the same photographer's dog.

Then there was the case of Alison Jane Jack, wife of the Tory MP Michael Jack. She was banging on doors during the 1992 general election and asked one potential voter whether he would be supporting her husband on polling day. His reply: 'I have had enough of those ruddy Tories. I'm voting Conservative this time...'

The Labour candidate in Sheffield one year, Martin Flannery, confronted a woman with an excitable dog on the doorstep. 'Don't worry, Mr Flannery,' the women said. 'Tiddles won't harm you.'

'Madam,' replied Mr Flannery, 'Tiddles has his teeth embedded in my right thigh.'

You might have thought, however, that by 1992 politicians would have given up what many of them considered to be the nauseating practice of kissing babies and maintaining a fixed and unconvincing rictus smile on their faces through thick and thin. But no. This campaign demonstrated that babies, although not capable of voting, were once more a prime target of MPs. Some commentators dubbed this campaign 'The Great False Smile Spectacular', in which sincerity – which should be made one of the seven deadly sins – was all too apparent in great oily dollops.

Neil Kinnock seemed to be at the head of the baby-kissing brigade, although even he appeared to perform this unpalatable task with slightly less relish than he showed doing other things. On one occasion, he was charmed when he heard that a small boy had burst into tears because he had failed to get his autograph. The Labour leader rushed back and immediately assumed that sickly approach towards young children and babies which is the unpleasant badge of all politicians at election time. The small boy handed him a greetings card to which, with unnecessary effusiveness and cries of 'Marvellous! Marvellous! Marvellous!',

Mr Kinnock appended a flourishing signature. He patted the boy on the head and hurried away to busy himself elsewhere. I was not alone in wondering why a young schoolboy should be reduced to tears over the signature of a politician and I inquired of his mother whether her son was a politician in the making.

'Not a bit of it,' she told me. 'He wants to take it to school and sell it to the highest bidder.' One wonders if Kinnock would have returned so readily to placate this sobbing child if he had realised that he was giving a leg-up to a bit of youthful Thatcherism.

To his eternal credit, Mr Major did not join in the practice of baby-kissing. He probably was not aware of it at the time, but television shots of him during the campaign showed him actually physically recoiling, with a grimace, when presented with some grimy, glutinous cheek on which he was expected to deliver a smacker.

It was entertaining stuff, but not as good as the fun created by the lunatic fringe parties, who are best value at election time. Indeed it is a wonder that Screaming Lord Sutch, leader of the Monster Raving Loony Party, did not find himself clapped in irons. Stuffy MPs had already tried to price the growing number of lunatic fringe candidates out of the market. They passed legislation increasing the deposit from £150 to £500, in the hope and expectation that it would scare them all away. The *Observer* newspaper smugly carried this headline: 'The loony fringe dodos face poll extinction'. We were all delighted that this headline could not, as things turned out, have been more wrong. All this legislation appeared to achieve was the opposite of what was intended. To our great glee in the press gallery, the number of non-conventional candidates actually increased, including the magnificent appearance on the scene of the Monty Python-inspired Tarquin Fintimlinbinwhim Bimlim Bus Stop F'Tang Ole Biscuit Barrel who amassed 286 votes in Cambridge. This was not the ideal name for a returning officer to have to read out with the solemnity and dignity that is expected of him.

The Loonies were still around in 1992 and their manifesto for the general election included this item: 'Inserting crocodiles into the river Thames to "rescue" inebriated MPs who fall off the Terrace into the water below.' The Loonies' manifesto of 1992 also contains a number of other refreshing items which you would scarcely ever hear a mainstream politician dare to utter. For instance: 'We are serious, you know. We all perfectly well understand the big questions of the day. The trouble is, we don't know the answers.'

Although the Tories won in 1992, with the great gift of hindsight they later wished they hadn't. This hit the Conservatives very hard indeed five years later when Tony Blair cast them into oblivion and did so again in 2001, and won yet again handsomely in 2005. The thinking at Conservative Central Office was that if Neil Kinnock had won for Labour in 1992, he would have been such an unpopular Prime Minister that the nation would have reverted to the Conservatives in droves the next time round. As it happened, John Major's Government in the subsequent Parliament did not exactly cover itself with glory, but that was not entirely his fault.

Major, whose majority seemed to whittle down almost on a weekly basis (it started at 22 and had disappeared altogether by the next election) was also subject to treachery from the 'Barmy Army' of Tory backbenchers who made his life almost impossible over European issues. It was hardly surprising, therefore, that when Iain Duncan Smith, a leading light among the rebels, was battling it out for the leadership himself in 2001, Mr Major, who by then had left Parliament, asked how Mr Duncan Smith could count on loyalty from his troops when he had been disloyal to his leadership no fewer than 11 times during the 1992–1997 Parliament. But despite Mr Major's warning, Duncan Smith won the crown, only to have it snatched from him two years later, when his leadership was exposed as being feeble and, some would say, almost a gift to the Prime Minister, Tony Blair. The 'disloyalty' which Major had accused Duncan Smith of had overtaken IDS himself.

*****

I have been asked on several occasions by defeated MPs who want to return to the Commons to keep a look-out for those members who look as though they might have a heart problem or some other defect which could cause them to quit their seat early and thus create a by-election. There is no doubt that such is the eagerness of ousted members to return that they behave like vultures, circling menacingly above the heads of the ill and the infirm. And if there is a death, they will often put their application in for consideration as the next candidate while the body is still warm.

Needless to say, this does not play well with the constituency party and is, understandably, regarded as ghoulish and in the worst possible taste. Your chances are infinitely better if you wait until the deceased member is six feet under before you put in an application.

An example of this occurred in July 1988, when Graham Bright, the then Conservative MP for Luton South, was taken ill in the House of Commons and was compelled to take some time off to recuperate. While he was thus convalescing, his constituency party agent telephoned to inquire: 'Graham, just how ill are you?'

Mr Bright replied: 'I'm coming along nicely, thank you. I will be back in the House of Commons in a couple of weeks' time. Why do you ask?'

The agent told him: 'It is simply that since your illness was reported in the newspapers, I have had two or three aspiring Conservative candidates inquiring about your state of health, about the nature of the seat, the Tory majority and so on…' That caused such a shock to Graham Bright's system that he was back at Westminster within 24 hours.

The End of the Peer Show? Not for a While

It was in 1910 that Winston Churchill, then President of the Board of Trade, said the time was now right for the total abolition of the House of Lords. Some 100 years later, the Upper House found itself in the throes of a messy and mismanaged reform programme, but still in existence. To suggest, in the terminology of Wild West films, that the House of Lords is dead but it won't lie down, is a long way from the truth. Over the years, it has been a thorn in the side of governments of both Labour and Conservative persuasions even though for most of the time it has had a massive inbuilt Tory majority.

In the first eight years of Margaret Thatcher's administrations, the House of Lords inflicted more than 100 defeats on her governments, compared, astonishingly, with only five Government defeats in the Commons during that period. On some occasions, the Tory Government let these defeats stand rather than battle them out again in the Commons.

One in particular was the extension of pub hours in England and Wales from 2pm to 3pm on Sunday afternoons, which came after the Government had said it would not tamper at all with Sunday drinking hours. It was at times like this that Labour MPs, usually the bitterest enemies of the House of Lords, suddenly took a liking to the place. But those were exceptional times.

Probably the most idiotic idea to abolish the House of Lords was put forward by Tony Benn who successfully campaigned for a new law to enable hereditary peers (like himself as Lord Stansgate) to renounce their peerages. His plan, announced when he was chairman of the Labour Party at the annual conference in Blackpool, was to urge the then Labour Government to create a thousand new life peers who would then (according to his madcap idea) vote the House of Lords and themselves out of existence. The one rather serious flaw about this course of action (which never came to fruition) was that once these thousand new members of the nobility had taken their seats, they would have realised what a nice and well-rewarded life they were having, and would be hardly likely (however uncompromisingly left wing they were) to have voted themselves into the dole queue.

There are many examples of Labour MPs who vowed never to enter the House of Lords, but who ultimately succumbed to the ermine and the coronet. Clement Attlee, who was Winston Churchill's right-hand man during World War II and who became Britain's first post-war Prime Minister, was adamant he would never grace the plush red leather benches of the Upper Chamber with his posterior. He said once that if ever he became a Lord, he would call himself Lord Love-A-Duck of Limehouse (Limehouse, in east London was his first constituency). But when the call came, Attlee bottled out and became the perfectly respectable Earl Attlee of Walthamstow (his later constituency in the Commons), a hereditary title.

Attlee was not the only Labour MP who lived to regret earlier words of contempt for the House of Lords. In 1958, when the Life Peerages Bill was going through the House of Commons, Cledwyn Hughes, Labour MP for Anglesey, commented: 'This is nothing but a coat of varnish on timber which is already riddled with rot...' Years later, as the rather sheepish Baron Cledwyn of Penrhos, he at least had the good grace to say that he could hardly believe he had uttered those words in his 'callow youth': 'I think it really was what I thought at the time. Since I've been here I have come to see that the Lords can perform essential work, even though it is outdated and obsolete as it is and imperfect as is the machinery for appointing peers.'

Former Labour leader Neil Kinnock gratefully accepted a life peerage in 2004, when he had completed his stint in Europe, even though some years earlier he had described members of the House of Lords as the descendants of 'brigands, muggers, bribers and gangsters'. But everyone, I suppose, has a right to change his mind.

It was during the course of the Life Peerages Bill in 1958, incidentally, that the very Conservative peer Lord Hinchingbrooke was heard to observe: 'The great issue is not whether women should enter the House of Lords as life peeresses, but whether they should be in public life at all...' Such a comment half-a-century later would probably have put him at the mercy of the lynch mob.

Incidentally, the hereditary peers have never been the fuddy-duddies they are assumed to be by common repute. When, around the turn of the century, nearly all the hereditary peers were ousted from the Upper House, the average age of the place actually went up. It has been the life peers, many of whom have already experienced a full career in the Commons, who have for years been the biggest ageing factor in the Lords.

The House of Lords does 'enjoy' a reputation for eccentricity which to some extent is unfair. However, it has had its moments. Years ago, Lord Falkland, the 15th Viscount, alias Lucius Edward William Plantagenet Cary, used to be worried that people would consider him eccentric because he rode a motorcycle. He was at such pains, once, to impress a young woman how normal he was that he actually managed to magnify the scale of his eccentricity. 'When a young lady came as my guest to lunch some time ago, I vigorously denied her suggestion that I might, like many other hereditary peers, be a little eccentric,' he said. 'Unhappily, as I rose to my feet to pay for drinks before lunch, all my small change came down my trouser leg into my shoe through a hole which had appeared in my pocket. From that moment I was lost. I was compelled to take my shoe off in front of this young lady and turn the change out on to the table, with as straight a face as I could muster before restoring my foot in my shoe. It would have been fruitless explaining to her that a real eccentric would have put the remaining change back into his shoe.' Even so, I think, that demonstrated eccentricity of a very high order.

In June 1988, the venerable Lord Whitelaw, former Deputy Prime Minister, now, alas, no longer with us, stepped into a lift and inadvertently pressed the alarm button. The result was that bells started to ring all over the place. Some of their Lordships who had not quite grasped the situation started to totter into the division lobbies, thinking it was the sound of the electric division bell, which rings throughout the Commons whenever there is a division to summon MPs not in the Chamber to vote (it also rings in a couple of nearby pubs). Some kind soul whispered in the ears of the confused Lords that the division bell has a slightly higher pitch...

Points of Order

I have to thank the then Viscount Cranborne, now the Marquess of Salisbury, for my arrest some years ago by the police at Liverpool Street station in London on the pretext that I was, first of all, impersonating him and secondly stealing from him a dead but (as it turned out) highly nutritious pheasant.

I had been performing as Father Christmas at the Commons press gallery children's party. And since I had some Christmas fare to bring home, I 'borrowed' the GPO sack which I had been using in my Santa Claus role and filled it with bottles of wine, this single pheasant and other festive items. We, that is my wife and I, had no sooner set foot on Liverpool Street station than I sensed that my collar was literally being felt. 'Come this way, sir, would you?'

It was the voice of a large constable. It is, apparently, an offence to be in possession of a GPO sack when not an employee. So I was hustled into the police room, where, ignominiously, the contents of the sack were emptied on the table. Bottles of wine cascaded out, chocolates and this unaccompanied pheasant, to whose leg was attached a label proclaiming: 'Lord Cranborne'.

'Are you Lord Cranborne?' the constable inquired, his voice now bearing a note of deference. And then, more acidly: 'Are you pretending to be Lord Cranborne?'

I insisted that I was not Lord Cranborne, and before I could embark on my explanation, I was interrupted by the question: 'Then what, sir, are you doing with Lord Cranborne's pheasant?' I explained that Lord Cranborne's secretary, one Freda Ruthven, had given me the pheasant, but that Lord Cranborne was not to be told about it, since he had given her a brace and she did not want him to know that she was passing one of them on. The police – by now there were three of them – stared at me with disbelief written all over their faces. Meanwhile my wife was starting to panic, assuming that I would be thrown into the slammer and never see the light of day again for several years. Finally, after a number of phone calls were made, the property was grudgingly returned to me, but not the GPO sack. Instead, I had to return home, much to the relief of my wife, I might say, carting the stuff in a dilapidated bin-liner.

* * * * *

Tony Newton, the former Conservative Leader of the House of Commons and Lord President of the Council, once made a grave confession to me about his entry in *Who's Who*. He said that when he is asked to list his non-political interests at the end of the entry, he invariably writes down 'do-it-yourself' and 'gardening' – 'And then I hope that my wife never sees it…'

* * * * *

Richard Ryder, before he became Lord Ryder, was always the silent Tory Chief Whip. If a reporter made so much as an innocent inquiry of him, then there was not even the courtesy of a, 'No comment, sorry.' He simply carried on as though no question had been asked. I assume he liked to pretend that reporters did not exist. He certainly gave that impression whenever I ventured to ask him something. However, it was not always like that. Once, to his no doubt total humiliation, he virtually had to get on his knees to one Press Association parliamentary reporter.

Ryder, who at the time was undersecretary at the Ministry of Agriculture, had been engaged in a food-tasting exercise. In normal circumstances, he was a fastidious and totally correct trencher-man, but on this occasion he had managed to slop large quantities of his tucker down his expensive green tie. Shortly after this, Ryder had to appear on live television. The TV crew were not in the slightest impressed by Ryder's careless eating habits and told him so. As a result, Ryder was compelled to beg a tie-swop from one David Simpson, so that he could appear on the box without his clothing sullied by blobs of egg, gravy and cheap white wine.

* * * * *

The former Liberal Democrat MP Robert Maclennan, later to become a member of the House of Lords, gained a reputation as the most tearful MP at Westminster. He once sobbed uncontrollably when, silly ass that he was, he marched down to David Owen's home in a vain bid to get him to join the SDP-Liberal merger. Dr Owen's unsurprising and brusque refusal reduced Maclennan to unashamed and very public weeping.

Maclennan also gained notoriety for being able to make the most boring speeches in the House of Commons, quite an achievement when you consider the competition. The highlight of his career was to start a press conference in French, a bizarre thing to do in itself, and then to cover himself with glory by using that well-known everyday expression: 'The ineluctable epiphenomenon of universal wickedness'. That is one way, I suppose, to get your name in the papers.

* * * * *

I once inadvertently caused Margaret Thatcher to lose her rag, something which I had thought, in my innocence, only European bigwigs were capable of doing. I had telephoned Mr Andrew Thomson, who used to be her agent in the Finchley constituency in north London. This was just before the 1983 general election and the burden of my inquiry was about a rumour that the Prime Minister was about to 'desert' Finchley and instead to fight a Gloucestershire seat which had become vacant with a rock-solid Conservative majority built in.

Mr Thomson told me (accurately, as it turned out) that the story was rubbish but he nevertheless invited me to make an inquiry at 10 Downing Street as well, in case I didn't believe him. The remaining facts about this story came to light only after I had read a passage from the book which Mr Thomson subsequently wrote. He said: 'The inquiry was given serious attention and went all the way up the chain of command until it reached the Prime Minister. What was then transmitted back to Chris Moncrieff was a straightforward denial. But what he never knew was the effect that his inquiry had upon her. The official, whose task it was to relay the question to her, said, "She went charging about, shouting and yelling." For her, Finchley always comes first. Her loyalty to the constituency matches its loyalty to her.' I must say, I had not reckoned on being capable of rousing the lady to that pitch of excitement.

* * * * *

I remember listening to an MP describing during a House of Commons standing committee how his uncle, attending a garden party at Buckingham Palace, had discovered on the camomile lawns a type of beetle which had never been seen before and whose existence was totally unknown. The MP went on to describe how his uncle, a keen entomologist, had scooped up his find and put it in a matchbox which he deposited in his pocket. The uncle was little concerned about the pomp and pageantry of a Royal garden party and hurried off home to examine his prized specimen in more detail. I rushed out of the committee meeting to file this story, which, since it was July and the time of year when Royal garden parties were taking place, appeared in the stop-press section of the old London *Evening News*.

'Man finds "new" beetle at the Palace' screamed the headline.

I returned to the committee and at 1pm, when it finished, I approached the MP and asked him for the name of his uncle and for more details about his 'find'. To my astonishment, the MP did not know the name of his uncle, or anything at all about him except that he was an entomologist. I have to say I found this rather strange. Then he explained it all to me: 'You know this happened in 1934?' he said.

So that evening the London *Evening News* had unwittingly carried in its late news 'fudge' column the outline of an event which had happened more than 30 years earlier. Needless to say, I pursued the story no further, and quietly forgot about it. I fully expected to receive telephone calls requiring me to fill in the many missing details of this story. Mercifully, and for once, I didn't receive any.

* * * * *

Lisl Biggs-Davison told me this story about her father, the late John Biggs-Davison, a former Conservative MP. During the 1955 general election, Biggs-Davison, who was fighting Chigwell, Essex, managed to induce Winston Churchill to come and speak for him at a constituency meeting. But Churchill was suddenly overtaken by that well-known syndrome which attacks the venerable, sometimes called having a 'senior moment'. In short, the great war leader simply forgot Biggs-Davison's name. Happily (or so he thought) he spotted the name on an election poster, and in a final flourish before he sat down, he roared: 'And I am sure you will all turn out to vote for this man on polling day.' The crowd cheered, but Winston had inadvertently mentioned the name, not of Biggs-Davison, but of his Labour opponent, one Douglas Clark. Despite this embarrassing gaffe, Biggs-Davison won the seat and entered Parliament for the first time.

* * * * *

When Chris Smith was Culture Secretary in Tony Blair's Labour Government, he was once asked what he would like for Christmas. Being a modest man, he did not want to appear to be greedy, so he opted for something unpretentious. Some weeks later he was given an article to read. It said: 'The Chief Rabbi would like to see World Peace for Christmas; the Archbishop of Canterbury wants an end to World Poverty, and the Secretary of State for Culture would like a small basket of glazed fruit.'

Keeping the Show on the Road

The people who keep the show on the road in the Commons are what those normally described in the theatre as 'a strong supporting cast'. They include the police, the cleaners, the waiters, the porters and the upstairs maid. It also includes the doorkeepers – who you should not insult by describing them as 'badge messengers'. They do wear a badge, denoting parliamentary insignia, around their necks and are really Commons' attendants attending to MPs' needs, but they think the idea of being messengers is derogatory (although they do run around delivering messages to MPs). Without these different types of staff, the place would fall apart. And dealing with politicians, most of whom are considerate but many of whom have outsize egos, is not the easiest thing in the world.

The police officers and attendants at the House of Commons listen to, mark and learn the contents of each Queen's Speech with a far greater avidity than that shown by members of the press gallery. I asked one experienced officer why he was taking such careful notes of the speech as it was being delivered in the House of Lords.

He explained they were always interested in Bills likely to create long or even all-night sessions. 'I have to tell you,' he said, 'that however else Queen's Speeches are regarded by anybody else, to us they are a police overtime sheet. And this particular example looks very good indeed,' he added, shamelessly.

Incidentally, the police invariably instinctively knew when it was a teachers' lobby that was swarming around the House of Commons. They would tell you that the spelling was so bad on the green cards which visitors must fill in to see their MPs that it had to be a teachers' protest. And they were always right. However, the police also insisted that there was only one other group of people whose spelling and punctuation were even worse than that of the teachers. These were the university vice-chancellors...

I have myself, being of a timid nature, avoided run-ins with security people at Westminster, but during one alert – which, like so many of them, came to naught – a security officer went out of his way to tell me: 'I am not paid to protect the likes of you, you know.'

I was tempted to respond: 'So you are here just for the toffs are you?' But, coward that I am, I refrained, since security officers, given the high profile they now enjoy, have powers to make life exceedingly difficult for those of an awkward disposition if you rub them up the wrong way. In short, security always wins. Feeble, I know...But there's no doubt they have played a bigger role over the years.

Right up into the 1960s and a little beyond that you could get into the Palace of Westminster without showing a pass of any kind – there were, in fact, none to show. Nowadays, one's movements are constrained by all manner of electronic barriers. Many of the short cuts I used to use (illicitly) through the highways and byways of this labyrinthine palace are now no-go areas. After one security scare – they are now run-of-the-mill – security issued special passes to visitors to display on their lapel. You were supposed to surrender them on the way out.

Unfortunately, although there is only one entrance for visitors to the Palace of Westminster, there are numerous ways of getting out, so scores of these passes were not surrendered. To the fury of the security staff, these passes become 'collectibles' and even appeared on eBay. They were then replaced by bits of sticky paper which visitors are only too ready to discard once they leave the premises.

Back when one could ramble untroubled, the sheer size of the place meant that I wasn't always entirely sure where I was going. On one uncelebrated occasion, after I had been imbibing to an unwise degree in the press gallery lobby room, that mysterious sanctuary at the top of the building, I succeeded in negotiating the notorious spiral staircase that leads from it without mishap. The problem arose when I tackled the far less tricky staircase in the press gallery itself.

I descended the 15 brief flights, but instead of stopping at ground level, the common-sense thing to have done, I inexplicably carried on further and found myself wandering about the subterranean boiler-room, surrounded by a conglomeration of hissing pipes and no visible means of escape, either back the way I had come in or any other direction. I was lost. It is wondrous how speedily one can sober up when faced with such a crisis. I have no idea how long I wandered about in this alarming place. It was like a cross between Hampton Court maze and a Turkish bath. But, eureka! Just when I was being driven to the conclusion that some future generation would find my bones down there, I spotted a way out sign. For me it was the work of a moment to make my way to the open air. Well, I thought to myself, a drink would not go amiss, so I made my way over to the St Stephen's Tavern across the road to celebrate my escape. But the door was barred and bolted. Then I turned and looked up at Big Ben. It was 2.30am. I had lost all sense of time as well as direction...

* * * * *

Some of the hard-working staff in Westminster can be forgiven for misconstruing what Ministers – even Prime Ministers – say to them. Once Margaret Thatcher bounded into 10 Downing Street and casually inquired of the doorman: 'Jim, do you like to take a drink?'

Jim, assuming that the Prime Minister might be about to present him with a bottle of something from her voluminous handbag, responded with enthusiasm, 'Why, yes, Prime Minister. I do enjoy a drink from time to time, but only on social occasions, of course.'

'Well,' came the withering reply, 'so do those flowers over there...'

At round about the same time, the flirtatious Edwina Currie placed her dazzling face temptingly close to that of one of her press officers. Romance is in the air he thought. But not for long. Suddenly Edwina sniffed and inquired in haughty tones: 'Have I driven you to tobacco?'

That was the opening shot of her fearsome anti-smoking campaign.

* * * * *

Once, in the days of Margaret Thatcher, a Tory minister broke his pen in the Chamber and as a result left on the Treasury bench, in precisely the spot normally occupied by the posterior of the Prime Minster, a massive blot of black ink. After the House rose, a compendium of aerosols was brought to the scene and various liquid chemicals were sprayed on the offending smudge. But to no avail. The Department of the Environment were summoned and boffins came forth in great numbers, scratched their heads and applied yet more sophisticated medicaments. But the blot steadfastly and obstinately refused to disappear.

'Fetch in the Royal Marines! Call the Royal Navy!' the despairing cry rang out. Then in came a little old lady with a scarf on her head, a mop under her arm, a bucket in one hand and a small object in the other. And she applied that small object to the blot which, like magic, vanished on the instant. She smiled a sweet smile and said in triumph: 'That's the way to do it.' It was half-a-potato. So much for cutting-edge technology.

* * * * *

I remember going to a photo-call, limited to the Press Association, in the kitchens of the House of Commons where they were preparing a birthday cake for Margaret Thatcher. Charles Irving, the genial, if somewhat camp, chairman of the catering subcommittee, and Conservative MP for Cheltenham, had assembled an impressive array of chefs for the benefit of the cameras.

The chefs smiled and stirred vigorously over the huge bowl containing the cake-mix. Irving sashayed around the kitchen as more and more ingredients were poured into this massive confection. But, alas, at one point, one of the chefs, while stirring away, was suddenly afflicted with a bout of coughing. Those of a queasy nature might consider ceasing to read this next bit. As he coughed and spluttered, making no attempt whatsoever to remove himself from the bowl, he then proceeded, involuntarily, to spurt a phalanx of gunge from his mouth into the mix.

This, I know, is not very tasteful either to record or read, but Irving, spotting this, grabbed hold of a vast wooden spoon and stirred the whole lot into the mix, smiling and jesting the while as though nothing had happened, or at least hoping that no one had noticed this little incident. The cake baking continued apace and I recall a few days later attending the brief ceremony when the cake was presented to the Prime Minister. It was cut with great ceremony by Mrs Thatcher and Irving and she ate the first slice with much seeming relish.

I noticed that Irving managed to avoid having to eat a slice of it himself. Meanwhile, I was somewhat worried that I might get offered a slice, a pretty remote possibility. Happily, I escaped. I have always considered it, from that day to this, to be a grave mistake to go behind the scenes in a catering establishment. It is best not to know what goes on. And certainly best not to know what goes into the fodder. Restaurant kitchens, even those catering for the great and the good, are not places to be recommended for a visit by a queasy layman.

Thatcher the Fashion Icon

Cynthia Crawford, a cheerful, cricket-loving woman, was effectively Margaret Thatcher's wardrobe mistress. The clothes worn by the former Prime Minister during her last four or five years at 10 Downing Street were invariably the choice of 'Crawfie'. Mrs Thatcher listened to her and trusted her advice implicitly. Soon after Crawfie arrived at Downing Street, the Prime Minister presented to her the garments she was planning to wear for a forthcoming visit to the Soviet Union.

'You are not going to Moscow dressed like that,' she bluntly and bravely told the Prime Minister to her face. Not many would dare to do that. She then summoned the clothing firm Aquascutum to Downing Street and selected the Prime Minister's wardrobe. From then on it was Aquascutum all the way for Margaret Thatcher and it was a triumphant choice.

Crawfie ruled the roost as far as the Prime Minister's attire was concerned. In 2003, she went out and bought Baroness (as she had by then become) Thatcher a hat to wear for her husband Denis's funeral.

'I hope you didn't think it was too Ascot,' Crawfie said to me after the funeral. It was nothing of the sort. Just right for her.

Crawfie was so successful in instilling into Thatcher a dress sense that top fashion writers – including the bitchy ones – were saying (albeit reluctantly) that by 1987 Margaret Thatcher had edged ahead of Diana Princess of Wales as the person who was doing most to influence what the women of Britain should wear.

She said once: 'It's not my job to be a fashion leader, but it is my job not to be out of fashion or obviously wrongly dressed. And I must never be mutton dressed as lamb – never!' She was always deeply conscious, as Prime Minister, of the effect her clothes had when she arrived in an overseas country. 'The first impression another country has of you when you walk down the steps of an aeroplane is what you are wearing. When you arrive there may well be a guard of honour of smart, beautifully-tailored and turned-out men. You face the prospect of odious comparison if you are not very well groomed.'

But even though she loved the colour red and believed that it suited her blondeness, she rarely wore it. And there was a reason for this. She was once invited to a dinner and she borrowed what she described as a 'rather lovely evening gown. It was more lovely than anything I possessed. It belonged to a very elegant friend and was a darkish crimson red in dull-surface satin. I felt like a million dollars.' That was until the moment when the organisers presented her with a bouquet of very blue, but not true-blue carnations. They had actually been white but had been dyed blue – can you believe it? – because they were convinced that Mrs Thatcher would arrive in a blue dress.

'It was a horrible clash,' she said later. 'Ever since I have tended to wear only blue and black on official bouquet-type evenings.' No fuss, no frills and no flutter. That was always the maxim drummed home by Crawfie and followed by Mrs Thatcher. 'What you want,' the Prime Minister said, 'is a very sharp outline. You eventually come round to your own style and it has to be what suits you. I am very long-waisted and it is not always possible to find clothes to fit. I've learned never to wear anything gathered at the waist.'

In hot climates, which she did not personally favour, Mrs Thatcher used to go for bright, even frivolous colours. Invariably in these countries she would wear dresses which came to just below the knee and would usually wear long white gloves as well. This was not so much for reasons of style, but principally to preserve her skin, which often reacted badly to the sun. But her most cherished dress was a sombre, almost black creation which she wore throughout the Falklands conflict, in the Falklands Islands themselves and in New York when she addressed the United Nations.

'It brought me good luck,' she said. 'I wear it when I don't know what else to wear, and when I haven't got a thing to wear.'

Denis Thatcher, like most men, generally speaking kept his counsel on his wife's choice of clothing, but he did occasionally show a faint spark of interest. Mrs Thatcher once said of him: 'He loves the colours and he loves the pretty clothes.' But she revealed that he once did protest under his breath: 'Oh, not black again, dear...'

On one occasion when she was getting ready to speak in a local town hall, one of her staff hurried back from there to tell her that the outfit she had chosen to wear clashed horribly with the colour of the felt on the table-top. A trivial detail, you might think? Not for Mrs Thatcher, who took all these things very seriously indeed. 'I had to change out of what I had on into something else in three minutes flat,' she said.

Mrs Thatcher always insisted, wherever possible, in wearing British-made clothes. On one occasion she got into an argument with a group of journalists about clothing. She boasted that every visible item she was wearing had come from a British manufacturer. Then she went round the room asking all the male reporters where their suits had emanated from. Some of them, to their embarrassment, had to say Hungary or Romania. I sat crouched at the back of the room, hoping she would not notice me. But inevitably she did.

'And you,' she boomed at me across the room. 'Where did your suit come from?'

I stood up and nervously looked at the label on the inside breast pocket. It was with considerable relief when I was able to tell her: 'It says Marks and Spencer, Prime Minister.'

She paused and stared relentlessly for a few agonising seconds at me and at this garment. Finally she said: 'Looks more Oxfam to me...'

Handbags, of course, were her trademark, as famous as Winston Churchill's cigar or Harold Wilson's pipe. She had plenty of them, usually small but deadly. She was the person who was responsible for transforming the word 'handbag' into a verb as well as a noun. The mere spectacle of them on the table in front of her used to cause her counterparts in European Summits to quail visibly.

I was never personally handbagged by Margaret Thatcher nor, I must admit, did I meet anybody who suffered in that way either. But it was a symbol of something terrible and you always felt a trifle uneasy if you were within flailing distance of the great woman. Those who travelled with her to Brunei in 1985 will not readily forget the boat journey up a crocodile-infested river to the Sultan's palace. In between waving to the multitudes on the river bank, Mrs Thatcher was, perilously and foolishly, we thought, trailing her right hand in the water as the boat chugged along.

We were in a boat right behind her. We mused as we went along what might happen if the Prime Minister, who was leaning precariously over the edge in any event, fell in? The unanimous conclusion we came to was that Mrs Thatcher would not only win the battle with the crocodile without any difficulty but would emerge triumphantly brandishing a brand-new, brilliantly-styled handbag. Little did she know how often her name was taken in vain.

Probably the most unforgettable picture of her that I recall was when she was wearing a headscarf and an ordinary scarf billowing in the wind as she appeared out of the top of an army tank that was rumbling at full speed along Luneberg Heath in Germany. I have never in my life seen anyone look more like Snoopy, the engaging dog from the *Peanuts* strip cartoon. I remember, incidentally, being briefed about her ride in that tank shortly before she boarded it. One of my colleagues inquired innocently whether Mrs Thatcher would be in command of the tank while she was in it.

'Certainly not,' the officer replied huffily. 'The tank commander will be in command of the tank.'

'That's what you think,' the reporter rejoined. The officer, hardly surprisingly, did not see the funny side of that remark.

While Mrs Thatcher was careering up and down in her tank, they put us in a lorry behind her, bumping up and down more agonisingly than a small vessel in the Bay of Biscay. Our discomfort was added to by Bernard Ingham, the Prime Minister's press secretary, in yet another vehicle, hurling thunderflashes at us. An altogether uncomfortable outing.

Crimpers and Curling Tongs

Sidney Silverne was the House of Commons barber for many years. He would cut your hair for a mere 90p and for your money you used to get regaled by him with the poetry he used to write on his way into work on the Central Line on the underground.

Mr Silverne was meticulous in the way he addressed the great and the good. 'Would my Lord Bishop care for his parting on the right or on the left?' Or, 'Would the right honourable gentleman like me to clip his nasal hairs?' Everything was absolutely correct.

Sometimes, his starry-eyed approach to the high and mighty did leave other customers high and dry, as you might say. On one occasion Peter Willoughby, who was at the time parliamentary editor of the Press Association, was having his routine haircut when a senior peer of the realm walked in and looked about him a trifle testily. Mr Silverne, it appeared, had forgotten that this nobleman had actually booked an appointment and needed his barnet attended to there and then. The unfortunate Mr Willoughby, one side of whose head was shorn and the other side was not, was, with a few unconvincing words of apology, eased out of the chair to make way for the new incumbent. Mr Willoughby was by no means chuffed at the turn of events and stalked out of the salon, looking a bit like a highly disgruntled walking version of a 'before and after' photograph, never to return.

However, it was the women at Westminster who were Mr Silverne's real enemies. He always claimed that he was, in that well-known misnomer, a 'unisex' hairdresser and that women were welcome as clients. But very few came. It is reported that the Labour MP and subsequent cabinet minister Harriet Harman once went and was so displeased with Mr Silverne's artistry that she was forced to wear a hat, even indoors, for some weeks afterwards. That story, however, may be apocryphal and everyone that I know who patronised the place was totally satisfied with his artistry. Even so, there were those who wanted a woman's hairdresser with a more refined approach than that offered by the splendid Mr Silverne.

The fact that he had no curling tongs was apparently the clinching factor in the ultimately successful campaign by an army of women MPs to have him removed from the Palace of Westminster. That Mr Silverne went out and bought some curlers did not change anything. A petition was raised by some of his most faithful aficionados, myself included, but our efforts to save him were puny in comparison to those of our opponents. However, his departure coincided with the springing up of a number of dirt-cheap barbers, most of them having collecting boxes for the Finsbury Park Mosque near to where I live. So, for only a fraction more than Mr Silverne's tariff, I can trot along there on a Sunday morning at very little inconvenience. Mr Silverne himself went on to take up a similar post at the Army and Navy Club.

Nigel Lawson, the former Chancellor of the Exchequer, was not one of those regularly seen in Mr Silverne's emporium. In the days when he was a comfortably-rounded figure, he got the affectionate nickname 'Smuggins', which became totally unsuitable after the man submitted himself to some drastic diet and transformed into a cadaverous fraction of his former self.

On one occasion he attended a barber other than Mr Silverne

and paid the enormous sum of £15 for a haircut. For good measure he gave the barber a gratuity of 50p which fell well short of the 10 per cent usually required. The barber, until then as unctuous and subservient as hairdressers normally are, made as plain as he dare to Mr Lawson that 50p represented more of an insult than a decent tip. But Mr Lawson was unrepentant, reportedly stalking out of the shop with the words ringing in the barber's ears: 'Well, if you don't like it, stick it in a parking meter...' One presumes that this hairdresser was not a constituent of Mr Lawson's.

While on the subject of tips: MPs have a notoriously skinflint reputation in this regard – I am reminded of the late Roy Jenkins, who paid off a taxi at the House of Commons and added by way of a gratuity a threepenny piece (that is threepence of old money, worth about nothing in today's decimalised currency). The taxi driver was so incensed with this, that he hurled the coin back at Jenkins, accompanying it with the words: 'I think you need that more than I do...'

Points of Order

MPs are past masters at making themselves scarce when unwanted visitors arrive to lobby them. It is only when a general election is looming on the horizon and that their visitors are actually their constituents that many of them show much enthusiasm to respond. Under the system, visitors have to fill out green cards, stating the name of the MP they want to speak to and the nature of their business. These cards are picked up by uniformed doorkeepers who trawl the building in search of their quarry. Often enough, the MP genuinely cannot be traced, but sometimes when the MP looks at the card and does not want to bother, he will simply ask the doorkeeper to tell the visitor that he cannot be found.

Dame Elaine Kellett-Bowman, the redoubtable Tory MP for Lancaster, who had a voice like a foghorn, used not to rely on the tinkling voices of the attendants in the central lobby. Instead, she snatched the microphone herself and bellowed out the names, so there could be no mistake. After one such stentorian performance, an MP whispered to me: 'I think she once worked at Crewe station.' Dame Elaine also had a habit of sleeping athwart the doors leading into the House of Commons Chamber on the night before big parliamentary occasions. This was to enable her to be first in to 'reserve' with her prayer card the best seat in the House, when the doors opened at 8am. It was not, I assure you, a pretty sight…

* * * * *

Nick Raynsford, an expert on local authorities, housing and all things tedious, must be one of the most unspectacular MPs ever to set foot in the Palace of Westminster. He epitomises the safe pair of hands. He drones on but he never gets anything wrong, not noticeably anyway. Nobody has a clue most of the time what he is talking about, but that doesn't matter. He sounds impressive and it is a brave man who challenges him on facts. So it came as a bit of a shock to me to hear he has form – or something very close to it.

When Mr Raynsford entered the House of Commons as Labour MP for Fulham in 1986, he was greeted by PC Ken Thomas who, incidentally, was a nephew of the one-time Speaker, George Thomas, later to become Lord Tonypandy. Mr Raynsford (foolishly as it turns out) said to the officer: 'Haven't we met somewhere before?'

'Yes sir, we certainly have,' replied the officer.

'Where was that?' inquired Mr Raynsford, who by now was beginning to doubt whether it had been a good idea to embark on this line of conversation in the first place.

'I arrested you, sir. I am sure you recall,' the policeman said. 'You climbed on to the roof of the Palace of Westminster, sir, during the course of what can only be described as student high jinks.' Mr Raynsford, the officer reported back to me, shrugged his shoulders, affecting not to have the faintest idea what the PC was talking about.

* * * * *

Snappy dressing has never been a forte of MPs. And when anybody tries to keep up with fashion, he is rewarded by being mocked and pilloried in equal measure. Paul Boateng, who became the first black cabinet minister at Westminster, has always prided himself on his snazzy attire. One day, peacock-like, he was parading around the House of Commons in a wondrous designer suit, its stitching fashionably visible, when he was stopped short by the outrageous and splendid Tory, Nicholas Soames. Soames wounded him gravely by shouting after him: 'Just one more fitting at your tailor's, Paul, and that should do the trick.'

* * * * *

Labour MP Donald Anderson, who became chairman of the important Foreign Affairs Select Committee has revealed, by chance, that he possessed some of that craftiness rarely found among politicians. In May, 1990, when he was shadow Foreign Minister, I telephoned him at home to get his reaction to Prime Minister Margaret Thatcher's meeting at Chequers with President F.W. de Klerk of South Africa. I had dragged him to the telephone from the kitchen sink where he was busily engaged in washing up after the Sunday roast.

After he had given me a statement for which I was grateful and was preparing to end the conversation, Mr Anderson unexpectedly asked me whether we could carry on talking for a little longer. Well we did, chatting about this and that, and then eventually he said, 'It's all right now. We can sign off.' He explained to me later that when he came to the telephone, his wife had taken over the washing up. He realised that if he prolonged the conversation for a while, the job would be completed by the time he got off the telephone. The old rogue!

* * * * *

A House of Commons police officer, who prided himself on being able to recognise all the faces of the scores of new MPs after the 1987 general election, was embarrassed when he twice questioned the identity of Mr David Wilshire, the new Conservative member for Spelthorne.

'Don't worry, laddie,' the MP said. 'This is how you can remember who I am. Consider that in days of yore, kings used to name their bastard sons after counties, the Earl of Hereford, the Duke of Somerset, and so on. So in future when you see me coming, you can say to yourself, 'Ah here comes that bastard Wilshire', even if I do spell my name wrongly.'

* * * * *

Dr Tom Stuttaford, who used to sit as a Conservative for Norwich South in the Edward Heath era, was the only MP I came across who was an expert on the subject of flatulence. He revealed this unexpected expertise after an unedifying incident when footballer 'Gazza' Gascoigne belched shamelessly while 'performing' on live television. This inspired Dr Stuttaford to compose a powerful piece on this and related matters. He wrote: 'People, once their stomachs have been distended by wind, are much more comfortable if they belch. However, they usually need not have found themselves in this predicament, and so far as belching is concerned prevention is better than cure. People salivate when kissing, which is one of the reasons for increased borborygmus (tummy-rumbling) and there is, apparently, a desire to belch when love-making, although serious students of this subject are convinced that posture may be an important factor in the explanation of this phenomenon.'

Which all goes to show what you can achieve given a fair wind. Dr Stuttaford's departure from Westminster is mourned to this day.

* * * * *

It was Christopher (later Lord) Soames who was made Governor General of Southern Rhodesia by Margaret Thatcher in a bid to end nearly 14 years of illegality in that country. Soames did the trick. After Robert Mugabe had won the subsequent general election there, Soames returned to London for consultations. Mugabe dutifully accompanied him to the airport. And just as he was about to leave, Sir Christopher (as he then was) turned and said to the little fellow: 'Now, shorty, I hope you are not going to muck it all up while I'm away.'

* * * * *

Edinburgh Labour MP Dr Gavin Strang tabled a Commons question, way back in 1987, to Secretary of State for Scotland Malcolm Rifkind. He asked Mr Rifkind to publish a table showing the actual total populations in each of Scotland's area health boards 'broken down by age and sex'. I instantly knew precisely how they felt...

Travels of a Fitful Flea: The Hurricane in Skirts

There was never time to stand and stare at the seven wonders of the world when, sweating and panting for breath, you chased the high-speed Margaret Thatcher in relentless pursuit from one end of the earth to the other – and, it often seemed, beyond. The British taxpayer coughed up a cool £4.3 million to launch Thatcher across the seven seas during her 11 tumultous years in power. It was a bargain.

She travelled in a modest, frugal style on a Royal Air Force VC10, a venerable but trusty jet. She even insisted it flew at the most economical speed possible to save cash and fuel. By contrast, when she attended Commonwealth meetings abroad, some of the black African states sent their Armani-clad delegations in a fleet of jumbo jets – something which enraged Mrs Thatcher. Occasionally she very publicly 'handbagged' them, telling them in no uncertain terms that British aid to their countries was not supposed to be used for luxury travel by VIPs. They never explained to her the reason for this extravagance. Many African leaders – and others – were terrified that if they left their country for any length of time, a coup, bloodless or otherwise, was always a possibility, and they could find themselves returning home, no longer a VIP, simply a penniless nonentity. It did happen, to my knowledge, more than once. It was, therefore, regarded as judicious to bring along anybody and everybody who might be tempted otherwise to usurp authority in the leader's absence. This occasionally involved bringing an entire government in tow.

By contrast, Thatcher always travelled light, with the minimum of staff accompanying her. Hardly ever was there even another minister on the plane. And much of the cost of each trip was offset by the 20 or so reporters who also travelled with her on the VC10 – but paying the equivalent of the commercial fare. Once, in not the most elegant turns of phrase, the Labour leader Mr Neil Kinnock accused the Prime Minister of 'dashing around the globe like an egotistical flea in a fit'.

True or false, this fitful flea kept as tight a grip on the purse-strings as you could possibly imagine.

She careered hot-foot – like some Formula 1 supercar – across more than 50 countries during her premiership. She dodged in and out of time zones as if there was no tomorrow (or yesterday, whichever the case may be). If you blinked you missed her. That was the measure of the speed with which she flitted around foreign climes, whether in the searing heat of the tropics or the frozen, rain-lashed, hostile, treeless wastes of the Falkland Islands.

Behind her toiled a straggling, sweat-soaked, grumbling band of reporters, me among them, most of them half her age, all of them with less than half her stamina, and many in totally unsuitable clothing for the climate we were in. I encircled the globe with Mrs Thatcher several times and saw next to nothing, except hotel bedroom walls. I went to Egypt and never saw the pyramids. I went to the Falklands, and never saw a penguin. In Saudi Arabia, there was not a camel in sight. And in India, the Taj Mahal was not for me.

Life on the road with her was an endless string of inspecting sewers, touring sludge-pump factories, blasting quarries and opening (if that is what you do with them) mighty dams. Just as some people cannot walk past a pub without going in, Margaret

Thatcher had the same problem with ball-bearing factories. It was a point of honour for her not to have any fun on any of these trips. The Kenyan authorities were amazed when she refused an invitation to dally in the game reserves. She just sniffed with contempt when told that Chancellor Helmut Kohl of West Germany had spent an entire day gazing at wild animals. No sir. She had more important things to do than that. It wasn't the only occasion on which her work ethic differed from Kohl's.

Back in Europe, in a German provincial town, she was haranguing the Chancellor on some subject. Having had more than his fill of being handbagged, Chancellor Kohl suddenly informed her that he had received an urgent call to return to Bonn immediately. Off he sped in his official car. Later that day in the same town, while on a walkabout, Thatcher spotted him sitting in a café, gorging himself on ice cream and chocolate cakes. It was not his finest hour.

With Thatcher you rose with the proverbial lark and did not bed down until you were exhausted beyond belief well after the cicadas were in full throat with their frenzied nocturnal chirruping. Her day abroad started with a briefing from the local diplomatic representative, a working breakfast (those were the only breakfasts she knew), a round of talks, visits, ceremonials and inspections non-stop until a working lunch hove into view. A similar round of engagements, tumbling over each other, occurred in the afternoon, addressing the odd parliament or two, shaking a million-and-one outstretched hands, and popping into a ball-bearing factory if one was to hand, before changing (if, indeed, there was time) for dinner, a working one of course.

She did go to the Great Wall of China but only because it was impossible for even her to persuade the Chinese that she had better things to do. However, she compromised by making it look as though she was not enjoying herself. She did actually visit the Bolshoi Ballet in Moscow but only because it meant more time for talks with President Gorbachev. Indeed, their talks lasted so long during the interval of a performance of *Swan Lake* that the resumed performance was delayed a good 20 minutes, while the 'swans' positively wilted behind the curtains. That was nothing. On another occasion, to the chagrin of the delicious Raisa Gorbachev, she spent nine hours closeted in talks with her husband in the Kremlin and did not leave herself enough time even to powder her nose before swooping off to a glittering state banquet.

It fell to Denis Thatcher to provide the entertainment on the foreign trips. In Kandy, he was caught on film attempting to feed an elephant a bun through the wrong orifice. It was a moment to cherish, and one that still exists on Sri Lankan television footage.

Mrs Thatcher, meanwhile, would not even travel with a doctor – no doubt to save taxpayers' money. On the same trip as her husband's feeding misadventure, she boldly told the Singapore Prime Minister, Lee Kuan Yew, who inquired the whereabouts of her 'medical adviser': 'I would have ended up looking after the doctor.' It was a sentence she may, a couple of days later, wished she had left unsaid. For, while commissioning a dam, she was kept standing around in temperatures of around 104°F without being offered a single drink. Her attire did not help either: she was encased in a long-sleeved floral dress and sported a three-row pearl choker, not recommended wear for undertaking seemingly interminable official functions in the central highlands of Sri Lanka.

While we hacks were able to quaff gallons of 'tea' brewed in the bowels of a dilapidated, unwholesome, and highly fragrant old trash-wagon, Thatcher was afforded no such luxury. She returned to Kandy visibly wilting, pale and trembly, her voice croaking like a battalion of frogs. She blamed it on the air conditioning – a pretty feeble excuse since air conditioning was a rarity in those parts. The press, ever-mindful of our leader's health, enquired how she was standing up to the intense heat. As she snuffled and wiped her watery eyes, she croaked by way of reply: 'We are doing quite well,' spluttering into her notes on the table. Note, of course, the royal 'We'.

The following day in Colombo, she was still decidedly groggy and was assailed by a prolonged coughing fit which halted, temporarily, her best-forgotten address to the Sri Lankan Parliament. Needless to say, not a soul came to her aid. But there was nothing that large doses of hot water with lemon and honey – and perhaps just a touch of something stronger – won't cure. She was as right as the monsoon rains within 24 hours.

There was another occasion in the East when a doctor had to be provided. We were in Bombay, as it was then called, when large numbers of her entourage (although not the lady herself), mainly reporters, went sick with violent eruptions of what is generally termed 'Delhi belly'. It got so serious that the doctor in the British High Commission in Delhi was flown over to Bombay to administer to the sick. I recall John Desborough, then of the *Daily Mirror*, who was suffering badly, inquiring of me: 'Do you think it was that tuna fish salad I consumed last night?' I think most people would agree that the last place in the world to risk eating a tuna fish salad would be Bombay.

Denis Thatcher, who was not taken ill, was wise to all of this. His advice, which he gave generously to all who sought it, was never to have Scotch on the rocks in India. 'You are eating their water,' he said. 'Something to be avoided at all costs.'

I do not know what the doctor gave to those who were suffering. But whatever it was, it detonated a sort of internal bodily explosion, and after recovering from that, everybody was as right as rain again. The fallout from that bout of sickness was that there were too few fit people available to provide a respectably sized 'delegation' to attend a performance of classical Indian dancing and opera that evening. Thatcher roped in those unaffected by illness and browbeat them to attend. I was one of those. You do not say 'No' when Margaret Thatcher asks you to do something.

I think it was the longest performance of anything I have ever attended. Each exotic dance, and each excerpt from an opera, was painstakingly explained in English before it took to the

stage. I knew of people who would have given their right arm to
see this once-in-a-lifetime performance. I would not have shed
a tear to have stayed away. Nor, judging by his expression
throughout this ordeal, would Denis Thatcher – aching for a
drink and cigarette.

* * * * *

It was her late arrival at a function in Jakarta, Indonesia, which
caused the chef and his staff to break down in a corporate bout of
weeping. They had spent weeks, presumably shivering in a
massive fridge, creating an ice sculpture of the Palace of
Westminster. It was a work of art, meticulously carved and
accurate in every tiny degree. Alas, by the time the Prime
Minister arrived, this creation was little more than a puddle on
the floor. Their tantrums and tears were well justified.

   In Jakarta we attended a press conference with Indonesian
leaders which, to Bernard Ingham's considerable annoyance (and
ours), was controlled by his Indonesian counterpart. This fellow
insisted, hardly surprisingly, on calling Indonesian journalists to
ask questions and although we made a big fuss at the back of the
hall, not once did he invite any of the British travelling press to put
their questions. Ultimately, after innumerable inquiries about rice
quotas, Ingham guided the man's arm to point in our direction
and I leapt to my feet and asked Mrs Thatcher a question about
Arthur Scargill. She gave me an icy stare, and retorted: 'I didn't
come all this way to answer tomfool questions like that.' Collapse
of stoutish party.

   Later on in Bandung we witnessed the fascinating spectacle of
a British civil servant in an advanced state of hysteria. He had,
apparently, spent weeks perfecting a hotline to London for the
Prime Minister's use should the occasion arise. It had worked
perfectly in all its trials, but the moment Mrs Thatcher arrived it
went totally dead. The poor chap was in a high scream, shouting
at all around him. The locals watched this bravura performance
unimpressed and uncomprehending. Eventually someone gave

this device a sharp kick with his left boot and it sprung into action again. It was a mighty relief but, happily, there was no occasion to use it.

While in the country, the Prime Minister watched an eccentric pilot putting an ageing helicopter through a series of daring paces. We watched, too, but did our level best not to be directly under this machine. The airport manager was hugely excited by this performance. He nudged the Prime Minister and cried: 'Watch. It can do loopings.'

*****

Margaret Thatcher paid a memorable visit to Bermuda in the late 1980s, ostensibly for talks with President Reagan. The President arrived with large swathes of his cabinet complete with golf clubs. It appeared, although it was never admitted, that the President had really come along for the golf and was using Margaret Thatcher as an excuse for an agreeable weekend. Nothing very important seemed to emerge from what talks they had when Reagan could be dragged off the golf course.

Denis Thatcher, a golfing fanatic, was also looking forward to this weekend, but the style of golf favoured by the President and his men bore little relation to the traditional game which Thatcher was wont to play. The Americans would clobber the ball and then hurtle after it, hell for leather, as if engaged in some frantic race. This was called 'aerobic golf' and was not to Denis's liking at all, and he quickly withdrew from the contest.

Meanwhile, during her brief stay, Margaret Thatcher paid a visit to the British naval vessel berthed at Hamilton. We were all aboard the vessel before the Prime Minister arrived. And then suddenly, Peter Bean, one of the 10 Downing Street press officers, arrived on the scene looking harassed and worried. He sidled up to me and said: 'Calamity! I've left my red box in a cab. I can't leave the ship now. Can you try to chase it up? He can't have gone far. I've only just got out of it.' It seemed a pretty tall order, but what could I do? I hurriedly assented and disembarked. I spotted a cab receding slowly into the distance – thank goodness for the Bermuda 20 mph speed limit! I hollered after it as I ran the length of the street, to the alarm and consternation of all around me. Ultimately, panting like a grampus, I caught up with the cab and quickly saw the precious red box, full no doubt of confidential material, sitting on the back seat.

I explained to the cab driver what had happened, displayed my array of passes festooned around my neck and, to my surprise, he surrendered it to me straight away without further ado. The next problem was to return it to Peter Bean without Bernard Ingham wondering why I was in possession of an official government portfolio. Had he realised what had happened, Sir Bernard would probably have exploded there and then. I managed to keep it hidden behind my back for the next couple of hours until an opportunity arose for me to hand it back to Peter Bean surreptitiously.

That Bermuda speed limit nearly had dire consequences for Mr Bean the following day when we were departing from Bermuda. He herded us all on to the coach to take us to the airport. But the coach driver, assuming that everyone was aboard suddenly departed, leaving Peter Bean at the side of the road with no transport to get him to the airport in the short amount of time before take-off. Enterprising as ever, he flagged down a car with a woman at the wheel. He explained his plight and asked whether she would be so kind as to speed him to the airport. She assented, but speed did not really enter into it. She cruised along at a steady 18 mph while Peter Bean frantically bit his nails. 'Is it just possible,' he finally asked her, 'if you could go just a little bit faster as the aircraft takes off in 10 minutes from now?' His plea bore fruit. The driver put her foot down and now they were daringly travelling along at an illegal 21 mph.

As they 'sped' along, the driver turned to Mr Bean and said: 'My son would adore to be here with you today.'

'Why is that?' Bean inquired.

'He just loves fast cars…' she said. Happily, Bean made it to the airport – but only with seconds to spare before the hatches were closed and the chocks removed.

Sadly, some years later, after Labour's 1997 landslide victory, Bean died suddenly. He had returned to his first love, the Foreign Office, and was working for the then Foreign Secretary, Robin Cook, when he was taken into hospital with a heart complaint and unexpectedly died. He was one of the most – if not the most – honourable, straightforward and reliable Whitehall press officers it has been my fortune to work with.

Elsewhere during her visit to Bermuda, the Prime Minister had occasion to call into a group of ladies whose main purpose in life seemed to be handicrafts. I arrived early at this venue and noticed that all the women were not only sporting their best frocks, but were also wearing state-of-the-art hats, most of them highly flamboyant creations.

'Is Mrs Thatcher wearing a hat?' one of them urgently asked me as I appeared on their premises. For the life of me I could not remember, even though I had been with her earlier in the day.

However, I agreed to post myself outside so I would have a clear view of the Prime Minister when she arrived in her motorcade. As she hove into view, I yelled at the top of my voice: 'No hat!' When, a few moments later I re-entered the premises in the immediate wake of the Prime Minister, I noticed that none of the ladies were wearing their hats any more. The news, relayed by me, that the Prime Minister was hatless was enough to get them to discard their own headgear and to stuff them – and many of them had cost a fair bit of money, I would say – ruthlessly in any nook and cranny they could find to hide them away. It would certainly not have been the done thing, in their view, for the ladies of Bermuda to be parading as though they were in the Royal Enclosure at Ascot while the Prime Minister was sporting no finery at all.

On another occasion, Mrs Thatcher made the mistake of visiting a craft centre, never a wise thing to do. Inside this centre were various ladies busying themselves with needle and thread, paintbrushes and matchboxes, and seashells from the seashore. There was also one gentleman bizarrely fashioning pottery frogs.

The Prime Minister's eye lighted upon an abalone shell pendant which she rather fancied for her daughter Carol. It was to the immense credit of Mrs Thatcher that she, manfully, did not flinch on being told that this article was priced at $85, or somewhere around £60. It looked like a complete rip-off to me, an item which I would have regarded as being overpriced at 50p. However, Prime Ministers are paid to demonstrate fortitude in the face of crises like this one and Mrs Thatcher, needless to say, rose to the occasion magnificently. She instructed her hapless private secretary Charles Powell to fork out and purchase it, since such a transaction would have been altogether too sordid for the Prime Minister to have conducted herself.

Mr Powell pulled the moolah from his wallet with a very bad grace indeed, muttering under his breath as he did so: 'She still owes me for that tin of pilchards I bought for her cat in Moscow two years ago.'

Meanwhile there was yet more evidence of the acquisitiveness of the Bermudan people. One man was deputed to present to her a cedar spoon as a memento. But he refused to allow the presentation to go ahead until she had bought one of these cedar spoons herself (another $20 down the drain). Then he graciously made her a present of the second one. I should be very surprised if these two wooden spoons were among Mrs Thatcher's prized possessions.

* * * * *

One of her specialities was dynamiting dams. We were in Alor Star in the north of Malaya when she was engaged in just such a task. Everything appeared to be going smoothly as she pressed the detonating button and we all clapped our hands over our ears. But all the detonating button seemed to activate was the wail of a siren. 'It sounds as though they are all knocking off for a tea-break,' she said. We all laughed weakly except, that is, the officials who were fearful that something had gone terribly wrong.

Suddenly, there was an almighty explosion. The applause which greeted this was more out of relief, than anything else, for those whose jobs might well have been on the line if the charge had failed.

And so back to Kuala Lumpur, where we ended up on one occasion in a train driven by the Prime Minister. Can you believe it? I have to admit that I have been on other trains, before and since, where I have felt more confident than on this occasion. It was a short but faltering journey. You got the impression, with the Prime Minister at the helm, that the engine was suffering from a severe bout of hiccups. At the end of the journey, I foolishly asked the Prime Minister whether this performance on her part signalled the onset of a stop–go policy. The 'joke' was (to put it mildly) unappreciated and haughtily ignored. She then grandly dismissed her shortcomings as an engine-driver by observing: 'Someone else can reverse. I never do U-turns.'

* * * * *

My visit to the Falkland Islands with Margaret Thatcher in January 1983, just months after the end of the fighting, was a mini-drama in itself. I was drinking pints of draught Guinness in the Popinjay pub just opposite the then PA offices in Fleet Street when a call came from Downing Street.

'You have got to get to the Ministry of Defence in two hours. You are going to the Falklands. Don't worry about money. We will help you through.' Even though we were in the depths of winter in this country, I was dressed for a summer's day. John Jenkin on the PA newsdesk insisted I took his furry coat with detachable hood.

'Do not lose it,' he told me severely. 'This has been both to the North and the South Poles with eminent explorers. It is of great sentimental value.' Needless to say I did lose it, or part of it, but more of that later.

My wife Maggie came into central London with a bag containing a few shirts and things. I discovered when I got there that I had also taken to the Falklands some sun lotion (the last thing you would ever require there) and a pound of carrots which she had failed to unpack from the bag.

So, with a full and aching bladder containing large quantities of draught Guinness, I set forth in a bus to Brize Norton airbase in Oxfordshire. The others in the party were David Walter, then with ITN, and Jack Warden (*Daily Express*). Nicholas Witchell of the BBC was already in the Falklands. The driver refused to stop to allow me to spend a much-needed penny on the grass verge. I was in agony and – I am ashamed to say – had to relieve myself on the coach. When we alighted at Brize Norton, the coach was on a slight gradient, and the driver spotted this rivulet snaking its way down the aisle.

'My God,' he cried, 'What's the problem now?' He assumed that a mechanical fault had developed on his vehicle. I fled, too cowardly to tell him what it was.

We flew in a military VC10 to Ascension Island, a journey of some 10 hours. Then we transferred to a Hercules transport aircraft, a splendid crate but lacking seats, for the 16-hour journey to Port Stanley. When ultimately we arrived, I discovered to my horror that the hood of my outfit was missing. I thought briefly about John Jenkin and the fury this would cause, but I needn't have worried. On the return journey about a week later, while we were sitting in a bar on Ascension Island waiting for the VC10 to take us home on the last lap, a small brown man, bearing a silver salver, approached me and said: 'Is this yours?' And, lo and behold, on top of the salver sat the missing hood. How it had got there and how this fellow had decided it might be mine I shall never know. After all, we were several days and several thousands of miles, too, from where I thought I had lost it. But there it was. I did not let it out of my sight until I returned it to Jenkin.

Meanwhile, in the Falklands itself we followed the 'fitful flea', Margaret Thatcher, all over the place. At one remote spot she mounted a field gun, while Denis Thatcher, a former Royal Artillery man, fussed around her telling her how it all worked. She looked through the sights and called out: 'All I can see is a pair of size 12 boots.' They were her husband's. He had managed to get right into her line of fire.

A few moments later after a little more of Denis's 'tuition', she famously cried out: 'Will this thing jerk me off?' The gusty wind blew these splendid words right across to where we, a few bedraggled, shivering reporters, were witnessing this bizarre scene. Mrs Thatcher who, unlike us, had lived a cloistered life, had not the faintest idea of the import of what she had just uttered. But we had, and we've been dining out on it ever since.

The next evening, Jack Warden and I had an interview with Margaret Thatcher in the Governor's residence. As is widely known, she sets great store by buying British and has more than once given reporters a dressing-down for what she regarded as their lack of patriotism for purchasing clothes, for instance, which were not made in Britain. Well, in the Falkland Islands there are no butchers (you kill and gut your own sheep) and no hairdressers either, a matter of considerable concern to the Prime Minister. The Kelpers, as Falkland Islanders are known, apparently cut each other's hair. You are well advised to pick a close friend who has no grudges against you to do this job or this *froideur* may demonstrate itself in the haircut performed. Margaret Thatcher had arrived with an armoury of devices designed to ensure that her famous tresses were kept thoroughly disciplined despite the absence of a crimper to crimp them.

Jack and I discovered, to our considerable glee, that some of these items bore the words 'Made in Denmark'. Here was a chance to get our revenge. So, getting our priorities absolutely bang to rights, we both did garish stories. The papers, as ever, were more interested in this story than any of Margaret Thatcher's encounters with British troops in the Falklands.

When we arrived on Ascension Island for the return home, I contemplated with some despair the prospect of a booze-free

10-hour military flight in the VC10 back to Brize Norton. So I filled my pockets and my bag with as many cans of South African beer that I could safely hide away about my person. But disaster struck as I boarded the aircraft. The weight of these cans forced my trousers to descend to my heels. It was a very bad moment. My cover was blown. The illicit booty was confiscated. And you could fairly describe that leg of the journey home as a dry run.

I telephoned the newsdesk from Brize Norton. Jenkin answered the call and with that element of sarcasm prevalent among all news desks, said tartly: 'I expect you lost that hood.'

I replied, shocked to the core by such an unworthy observation: 'How on earth can you suggest such a thing?' I retorted.

* * * * *

The main problem in Malawi seemed to be the self-styled Life President, Hastings Banda. However, judging from my observations and those of others, Margaret Thatcher had on occasions to execute some nifty footwork to avoid the unwelcome physical attentions, in quite public places, of the old man. 'Groping' might be too strong a word, but he certainly seemed to get unnecessarily close to her on more than one occasion.

At a banquet in Blantyre in the Prime Minister's honour, Banda spoke interminably far into the night. The expression on the face of Denis Thatcher, absolutely desperate for a smoke and a drink as he sat through this marathon ordeal, was something I shall never forget.

On our return from Malawi I wrote a piece in a newspaper column about the trip referring, disobligingly, to Hastings Banda as 'that old buffer'. A couple of days later I received a letter from the Malawi High Commission in London rebuking me roundly for this gross discourtesy and adding that I would not be welcome if I tried to visit Malawi again. Most reporters regard it as a great feather in their caps to be banned from a country. I cannot say that I was overjoyed to be excluded.

Elsewhere in Africa, we visited a school miles from anywhere in

Kenya. Before the visit, staff at the British High Commission in Nairobi had suggested they should buy a computer which the Prime Minister could present to the school as a gift.

'Balls!' said Charles Powell, Margaret Thatcher's chief of staff.

His expletive was well and truly and happily misunderstood by the High Commission. When Thatcher arrived she was presented with a sackful of footballs to hand over to the school. You should have seen the faces of the children light up as they received this gift. Never had swearing been put to such accidental good use.

* * * * *

Few people have daunted Margaret Thatcher in her time. But one such, I believe, was Indira Gandhi. I saw them once emerging from talks in Delhi. It was as though sparks were flying from their heads. The trouble was that they both had no difficulty whatsoever in bossing men around. Indeed, they positively relished it. But give them another strong woman to deal with, then that is where the problems start.

The same happened between Margaret Thatcher and the formidable one-time Norwegian socialist Prime Minister Mrs Gro Harlem Brundtland. Some commentators have said that by comparison, Thatcher was a mere timid Barbie doll. Once, after a series of talks between the two, the encounter was officially described as 'not a meeting of sisterly minds', which suggested not just a frosty meeting but a shrieking match, which it almost certainly was. When this Nordic terror was once interviewed by a fellow countryman about Mrs Thatcher, she rolled her eyes and raised her hands in a gesture of despair.

'I do not want to answer questions about Mrs Thatcher,' she said. But then she contradicted herself, in the way that so many forceful women do. 'When you look at Margaret Thatcher you should also look at the men around her.'

Mrs Brundtland's mild-mannered, not to say docile, husband Arne Olav was a Conservative with a capital 'C' and suffered from having an exceedingly dominating wife. On one occasion she fished him out of the sea when he fell out of a boat. Some of his friends used to say that he was occasionally reduced to the status of a downtrodden housemaid. He confided to a reporter: 'I took over the home front. But only on the condition that I could do it my way. My philosophy was that the house should be clean enough to be healthy, and dirty enough to be happy. I now understand that being a housewife is a time-consuming business and it depends a lot on your tolerance. You have to say some things over and over again before you get them done.'

I think that Mr Brundtland quickly gave up the idea of standing up to his fearsome wife. It was always going to be a losing battle with a woman who routinely tamed every man she came across. Her language was that of the proverbial fishwife and just for good measure she regularly land-skied from Oslo to her home 25 miles away in the woods north of the capital.

Another difficult statesman was the Chinese leader, Mr Deng, who was certainly not the ideal guest to invite to a traditional English tea party. He indulged in long-range spitting, a habit he persisted in even when he invited Mrs Thatcher into the Great Hall of the People in Beijing for a cuppa. She was not best pleased. We, that is the press pack following Mrs Thatcher, were 'privileged' to go into the hall on this occasion to watch the pair of them taking tea. Mrs Thatcher looked distinctly uneasy as Deng several times expectorated spectacularly into the spittoon just alongside her – in fact far too near her for comfort or peace of mind as she gathered her cloak out of the line of fire.

As the reporters were ushered in, by some misunderstanding I was thought to be one of Margaret Thatcher's officials rather than a journalist, and I was led into the room in a different direction from my fellows. I soon found myself right within the Deng spitting zone, not only that but I was pushed bang into the firing line just as he was preparing to let loose another volley. It caught me square on the left cheek, like a dive-bombing mosquito. Well, there was something to tell my grandchildren: that I had been spat upon by the great leader of the Chinese People's Republic. And in fact, I did tell them. But they were not in the slightest bit impressed...

* * * * *

Sometimes, when chairman of the lobby, one has to make announcements to one's colleagues on behalf of the Government, especially when abroad. In my case, I tried to do this in as informal a way as possible.

On one occasion, we were waiting around in Moscow for Margaret Thatcher's press secretary, Sir Bernard Ingham, to brief us on her prolonged talks in the Kremlin with Mikhail Gorbachev. A telephone call came through to me from Sir Bernard saying that he would be considerably delayed because the talks showed no sign of concluding. And in addition to that, Foreign Secretary Sir Geoffrey Howe would also be unable to brief us because he had got involved with some Muscovite intellectuals and those discussions appeared to be interminable as well. We were, by then, in the briefing room, known (aptly, some people might say) as 'The Fairy Tale Room', so I mounted the rostrum to impart this information to fellow journalists, unaware there were some American reporters in the audience as well.

My language was so informal as to be disrespectful. What I said was this, after mentioning Margaret Thatcher's delay: 'Geoffrey Howe has got himself trapped with a load of Soviet eggheads and cannot escape from them, try as he might, the poor blighter...' Unfortunately, the Americans who were present assumed I was the British Government's official spokesman, something I was to discover a few days later when somebody showed me a New York newspaper.

The columnist had written: 'Never before have I seen a Government spokesman treat his ministers with such scant contempt and derision. It was a complete eye-opener to me. Quite frankly, I was shocked.'

Another strange incident involving Mrs Thatcher was in the shipyard in Gdansk, Poland, where Lech Walesa's Solidarity campaign was born. This was what eventually toppled the Polish regime at a time when communism was collapsing all over eastern Europe. Mrs Thatcher had presented Walesa with a fishing rod and other fishing tackle. Angling, in addition to destroying governments, was one of his passions.

Then we all proceeded to the shipyard where thousands of workers cheered and shouted their support, both for Mrs Thatcher and for Mr Walesa. As all this was going on, I was standing quite a way behind this pair, feverishly taking a shorthand note of the proceedings. But an Associated Press photograph of this event gave the impression that I was only inches behind them. One British regional morning newspaper ran the picture with the following caption underneath it:

'Solidarity: Lech Walesa, leader of the banned trade union, greets Mrs Thatcher in Gdansk yesterday with a dubious-looking Polish deputy premier, Mr Rakowskin, in the background.' That 'dubious-looking' figure in the background was not the Polish Deputy Prime Minister at all. It was me! All I can say is that no Deputy Polish Prime Minister would have dared to show his face in the Gdansk shipyard at that time. It would have been tantamount to risking a lynching, so hated was the Polish Government.

The Man in the Raspberry Turban

Sir Denis Thatcher, who died in 2003, was the man constantly in the shadow of his wife, always just a stride or two behind, displaying protective instincts as sharp as the most watchful professional bodyguard. In short, he was the perfect consort for the Prime Minister. He never spoke to reporters, except rarely to upbraid them or to regale them with long golfing stories and he was a constant source of support for his wife.

Once when danger loomed and the crowd became a little menacing when she was on a walkabout in Australia, he bellowed out: 'Get those bloody people out of the way, or there will be an accident!' On another occasion he bluntly told a motley band of Turkish journalists harassing his wife: 'You are an undisciplined crew – and you can quote me.'

Then, when a reporter once asked Mrs Thatcher how many people would be unemployed after a second term of Tory government, Denis – his patience stretched way beyond its normal limits – expostulated without the degree of sotto voce that he had intended: 'Bloody stupid question. The man must be thick.'

The nation at large viewed him with a kind of benevolent amusement as a harmless buffoon, partial to a 'tincture' from time to time, a man built in the Wodehousian mould of Bertie Wooster and his cronies at the Drones Club. When a snorteroo – as he used to describe a stiff drink – was not to hand, as was the case while they were yomping around the bleak and treeless Falkland Islands, he would gaze with piercing eye into the far blue yonder with that eternal and grotesque hope of all such optimists that an English country pub would suddenly spring up before him.

In fact, he was a very astute and successful businessman. *Private Eye* and others might have made fun of him, but 'buffoon' was just the wrong word to describe him. He was an industrialist of immense shrewdness, diligence and business acumen, both feared and admired by his rivals. He had uncomplicated political views which sometimes inadvertently sprang to the surface at rugby club dinners after he had partaken of a snorteroo or two. But he was unashamed of them. 'I do not pretend that I am anything but an honest-to-God right-winger,' he once observed in a rare outburst on politics. 'Those are my views and I don't care who knows them.'

He was as quietly and insistently British as his wife was defiantly so. He possessed as stiff an upper lip as ever graced the face of a true traditional English gentleman. Nor did his constant public exposure curb his tireless zest for the boardroom, the fairway and the 19th hole. He smoked shamelessly and with almost devilish contempt for those who whinge about airborne pollution and passive smoking. He once roundly ticked me off when I decided, in 1982, to stop drinking for good. I can only guess at the scale of the contempt he would have demonstrated about the decision of the press gallery in 2004 to ban smoking in pretty well every part of their quarters.

His conversation was laced with golfing jargon and his first question to new acquaintances was invariably: 'Do you play golf?' If the answer was 'No,' the conversation usually ended there and then.

At a formal dinner party in London for the Kenyans, he sat next to the Zambian High Commissioner of the day, a strikingly handsome black woman. The dessert was pineapple chunks served in a scooped-out pineapple. Sir Denis helped himself and left two chunks joined together hanging over the lip of the fruit. 'There you are,' he said cheerfully to the totally uncomprehending lady, 'all nicely teed-up for you.'

The fellow was not cut out for public life. But the mantle fell on him with remarkable ease. He readily accustomed himself to climates and great indignities with commendable calm, possibly sometimes because he was not always aware that they existed. He would walk along red carpets to the manner born, his shoulders sometimes festooned with garlands of jasmine and roses, unconcerned by what they might be thinking back home when his buddies at the 19th spotted him on television.

Near Delhi once he was obliged to pace about for some 20 minutes, a large pink maharajah-style turban wobbling perilously on top of his perspiring head like a huge raspberry jelly. 'I wish the blighters would leave me alone,' he hissed as he gingerly passed me by.

Then a cameraman asked him to pose 'with that 'at on,' to which Sir Denis replied: 'No. You are just trying to make me look a bloody fool.' The photograph was taken anyway, and was spread all over the newspapers the following day.

His genuine modesty was summed up in a classic sentence he once uttered in my hearing: 'In recent years, the name of Thatcher has attracted a modicum of fame – to which I have added precisely nothing...'

Denis Thatcher was hugely popular with the reporters who travelled around the globe with the Prime Minister and used to spend much of the time hobnobbing with us in the rear of the plane, the very bibulous end of the Royal Air Force trusty VC10 airliner in which Margaret Thatcher did most of her travelling.

Once on the plane, an intrepid reporter asked him: 'Sir, who really wears the trousers in your household?' He paused before replying: 'Young man, I wear the trousers. And I wash and iron them, too.'

And then, on another occasion as we flew over Canada, he pointed down to the earth and said: 'Do you know what they do in Canada? They do f...-all in Canada!' If that remark had got into the public domain, there would surely have been a major diplomatic incident.

The Prime Minister once spotted her husband gazing lovingly at a bottle of something or other. She sped across, presumably to stop him from making what she would have regarded as a totally unnecessary and inappropriate purchase. She assumed, understandably, that his eyes had lighted on a bottle of gin. The bottle turned out to contain barbecue sauce. He was stopped from buying it just in time.

He excelled himself in Goa where the Commonwealth Heads of Government meeting was having its 'relaxing' weekend. The principal players had been housed in a series of chalets overlooking the glistening Arabian Sea. It was idyllic. But that was not the word that Sir Denis would have used. Suddenly the tranquillity of the tropical night was shattered by a sizzle and a bang – a power cut. It happened just as Denis was trying to shave. He stormed out of his darkened chalet, razor in hand with soap and stubble still covering half his face, and roared out into the darkness like a lion: 'This place is high on the buggeration factor.' It was an observation that went down in the annals.

Contrary to common belief, Denis Thatcher possessed a quick line in repartee. More than once his nimble brainwork extricated him from a tight corner. Once at a Downing Street party he was discussing with an admiring audience an alcohol-related subject. As his audience was being enlightened, Margaret Thatcher, suddenly and silently, swooped on us. 'And what's going on here?' she inquired. 'What are we all discussing?'

We all stood there sheepishly for a second or two. But not Denis. Quick as a flash, he said: 'We are discussing the architecture of Hyderabad, my dear.' And before you could say 'Jack Robinson' we were deep into that subject with a surprisingly knowledgeable Denis Thatcher leading the way.

On another occasion, Sir Denis's 'friends' had collected him and taken him to an important rugby match. Needless to say, they had a tincture or two before, during and especially after the match. His friends ultimately delivered him home but by then he was in a fairly advanced stage of inebriation. He plumped himself down at the table and Margaret brought him a plateful of steaming soup which she had made specially. However, he was never to taste the delights of his wife's culinary handiwork. Before he had even dipped his spoon into the broth, he had tipped the lot down his trousers.

Everybody who met him loved Denis Thatcher, particularly the ladies in his wife's constituency of Finchley. They absolutely adored him and would occasionally coo at him: 'How do you keep that trim figure, Mr Thatcher?' His invariable reply to these fluttering ladies was that an occasional snort of gin, but then only in the most sparing quantities, was what kept him lithe.

Throughout his life, his love for his wife never abated. He once described her as 'beautiful, gay and very thoughtful' and could not fathom out why everyone else was not instantly bowled over by her. There was only one public note of acerbity which I can recall and even then it was an attempt by Sir Denis – not the most discreetly executed, however – to help her out of a muddle.

In Indonesia, towards the end of a seven-nation trip crammed into 11 torrid days, she was moving so fast she forgot when and where she was. After being caught in a tropical deluge, she arrived at a glitzy diplomatic reception in Jakarta, Indonesia, expressing her delight at being in Malaysia. Suddenly, but almost imperceptibly, her husband developed an extraordinary list towards his wife and hissed in her ear: 'Indonesia, dear, not Malaysia'. His style of hissing was such that not only was it picked up by the intended recipient, but was audible to all, loud and clear, within a radius of about 100 yards.

There is no doubt that Mrs Thatcher secretly admired her husband's occasionally ferocious independence of mind, so long as it did not get out of hand. 'He has got his own personality,' she once said. 'He has got his own views, and he doesn't hesitate to express them. And if, now and then, they differ from mine, so what? It all adds to the spice of life.'

However there was one of his private and outrageously and splendidly politically incorrect jokes which did embarrass her when it inadvertently slipped into the public domain. The acronym CHOGM stands for Commonwealth Heads of Government Meeting. But not to Denis Thatcher. To him the letters meant, he used to gleefully tell reporters: 'Coons' Holiday on Government Money'. Although this endeared him to his cronies, as well as to the reporters to whom he frequently regaled it, it did not entirely meet with the approval of his wife who had to deal with all shapes and sizes and colours of individuals at these gatherings. A large number of people did not find it funny at all.

On yet another occasion we found ourselves in the British Embassy in Beijing, with the Prime Minister manfully trying to trying to discuss with us the virtues of Anglo-Sino relations. However, despite her very best and stubborn efforts, the conversation veered on to a family squabble in the Thatcher household about the £1 coin which was just about due to come into circulation. A member of the public had written to Denis Thatcher grumbling about its introduction. Plenty of people used to send him their pet problems and grouses because they knew that their letters would receive a robust and personal reply from him rather than get swallowed up in the Whitehall system which would eventually, if they were lucky, issue a bland and formal reply. Denis, writing on 10 Downing Street notepaper, had replied that, despite what his wife had said, he thought the coin was a thoroughly bad idea. He described it as 'pesky' and something which would continually wear holes in the trouser pocket. It would be a trial and tribulation, he declared, adding that his wife's

Cabinet, which had approved it, would live to regret it.

The correspondent who had made the original complaint instantly made Denis's reply public. This was immediately, and probably accurately, transformed by Fleet Street into a Thatcher family rumpus over which he and she would argue over the breakfast table. So from that press conference in Beijing we learned far more that afternoon about raised voices in the Thatcher family at home than ever we did about Anglo-Sino relations.

Travelling was not always, however, to Denis Thatcher's liking. He certainly preferred to go west rather than east, and once, in an unforgettable phrase, observed: 'China is not my cup of tea.'

If anyone ever lived up to the Bard's immortal phrase 'There is nothing so becomes a man as modest stillness and humility', it was Denis Thatcher. And Margaret Thatcher herself confessed that she would have got nowhere without him. He was, she said, 'the golden thread running through my life'.

The Whispering Valet Supreme

Charles Powell served as one of Margaret Thatcher's, and later John Major's, closest advisors. It is odd that his brother, Jonathan Powell, was to occupy a similar post with the next Labour Prime Minister, Tony Blair. Charles Powell, a sort of whispering Jeeves character who shimmered in and out of situations, was invaluable both as a purveyor of commonsense advice and also as someone who could extricate his master (or mistress) from difficult situations.

At the conclusion of a choir's performance of an anthem in a Russian monastery in Zagorsk, some 40 miles from Moscow, Margaret Thatcher, horror upon horrors, started to applaud in the solemn silence of the religious gathering. But Powell, with his customary aplomb, gallantly nullified her embarrassment by clapping himself while, in the finest traditions of the valet supreme, whispered in her ears. He was always within whispering earshot of her.

On another occasion, a city mayor in Australia addressed Mrs Thatcher as 'Your Highness…' One of her staff observed behind cupped hands: 'I would have thought he would know that was wrong…'

But Charles whispered back: 'Oh, give it time, Nigel, give it time.'

His wife Carla is an extrovert, fashion-conscious Italian beauty. The story goes that he was once pacing up and down the carpet at home, waiting to use the telephone on which Carla was loudly conversing.

'Hurry up,' he tetchily told his wife. 'I want to talk to the Prime Minister.'

'Do please be quiet,' retorted the lofty Carla, 'I already am talking to the Prime Minister.'

Carla has described how she first met Charles at Oxford, when he was a clumsy, tongue-tied, awkward individual to whom social graces were unknown. 'He could speak no Italian and so we could hardly communicate,' she said. 'He did not flirt, nor make a pass at me. All he wanted to do was to take me to his room, sit me in a chair and make toast for me.'

When in 1989, the Foreign Office issued lofty advice that Mrs Thatcher should not visit the Commonwealth war graves on her trip to Japan on the grounds that it might offend the Japanese, Powell, himself a former Foreign Office man, stepped in. He immediately vetoed the advice, not only because the British people would have expected her to go but also because he knew that the Prime Minister herself would have rejected such advice with contumely. In turn, she stood by him when he got into trouble, particularly the occasion when he was discovered to be the author of a 'notorious' Chequers minute describing the Germans as aggressive, bullying and insensitive. Margaret Thatcher could not have wished for two more supportive people looking after her interests than the magnificent Denis and the shimmering Jeeves: Charles Powell.

The Lady's not for Spurning

Cherie Blair will go down in the annals of British history as the most politically active and controversial of all the prime ministerial consorts for a long time. Her predecessors, like Mary Wilson, Audrey Callaghan, Denis Thatcher and Norma Major, followed the convention of remaining strictly apolitical, barely talking to the press and sticking to the background when their spouses were in power.

That was not the life for Cherie Blair who, if anything, was more political and certainly more left wing than her husband – and no less outspoken, too, sometimes embarrassingly so. Controversy followed her around wherever she went and whatever she did. Even as Tony Blair left office, with her snide remark to journalists ('We won't miss you') as they drove out of Downing Street – she continued to attract attention and to fuel controversy.

It is now widely believed that had she found a winnable seat she would have been in Parliament with, possibly, her husband on the sidelines. And there is little doubt that, had that happened, she would have advanced a long way in the Labour Party, possibly even to Downing Street itself, so powerful is her resolve. But that is all in the realm of speculation. For years to come, political anoraks will be wondering how much sway she held over her husband while he was in office. The general feeling was always that she was a far more passionate political animal than he was.

There was one little incident, not recorded in her book, involving Nick Brown, the Labour MP who apparently voted for Margaret Beckett in the Labour leadership contest of 1994, rather than for her husband. She asked a friend: 'Nick wants to be Chief Whip doesn't he?' When she was told that he did, she replied curtly: 'Over my dead body.' Yet when Tony Blair swept to power in 1997, he immediately appointed Brown as Chief Whip, which seemed to demonstrate that Blair took absolutely no notice of his wife's opinions or that she had changed her mind in the interim.

But her tenure at 10 Downing Street was spattered with denials of things she had allegedly said or, where denials were not appropriate, apologies when things had gone amiss. For instance she fiercely denied having labelled Gordon Brown a liar over something he said during his speech to the Labour Party conference in Manchester in 2006. This was despite the fact that an American reporter asserted that she heard the word 'lie' emanate from her lips. The day after this incident, Mr Blair reduced the conference to helpless laughter when he said: 'Well, there is one thing, there is no danger of my wife running off with the bloke next door.' It was a good way of extricating her from a pretty deep hole.

And she was compelled to apologise for saying in 2002, just after a blast in Jerusalem had killed at least 19 people, 'As long as young people feel they have no hope but to blow themselves up, we're never going to make progress, are we?'

Bizarre stories about so-called new-age practices indulged in by the Blairs have always been floating around, none of which Mrs Blair has admitted as being true. Perhaps the most bizarre of all these unsubstantiated allegations was that Cherie and her husband, while on holiday in Mexico and while wearing only bathing costumes, took part in a strange rebirthing procedure which involved smearing mud and fruit over each other's bodies while sitting in a steam bath. There has also been a hardly less bizarre – and also totally unsubstantiated – claim that she took jars containing hair and nail clippings belonging to herself and her husband to a man called Jack Temple, a retired market gardener turned health guru. Apparently, Temple would 'dowse' the jars by waving a pendulum over them to detect what he called 'poisons and blockages' which could affect the couple. It was claimed by Temple, who has since died, that his pendulum could tell her when it was a good or bad time to take major decisions.

Tony Blair would no doubt have dismissed all this as 'media froth' – one of his favourite expressions – but a fair bit of press coverage which Mr Blair denounced in this way has later been proved to have some substance.

After leaving Downing Street, Cherie embarked on a speech-making circuit, coining thousands of pounds for each of her addresses. This was seen as a serious breach of convention by many, including some in her own party, who thought it wholly inappropriate for her to cash in on her years as the Prime Minister's consort, either in this way or by writing her memoirs. But she refused to bow to this or, indeed, to any other pressure to desist. She continued to insist that she was a person in her own right and not simply an appendage to the Prime Minister. However had it not been for his work, she would never have attracted any attention whatever or have been sought after at all.

Once when I was chairman of the press gallery I made an informal request to Downing Street to ask if she would be kind enough to address one of our lunches. Her spokeswoman said to me: 'You only want her, don't you, because she is the Prime Minister's wife?' I had to admit that that was true. We never heard from her again, and the invitation was simply ignored.

Mrs Blair, incidentally, is a much more attractive woman than her photographs would suggest. She simply photographs badly. She is amiable and agreeable to converse with. At one gathering, I shook hands with Mr Blair and was about to do the same with Mrs Blair. But she absolutely insisted on a kiss. I can tell you, I needed no second bidding.

Points of Order

Former Tory MP Teresa Gorman's brand of Conservatism was even more pure than that practised by Margaret Thatcher. For while the former Prime Minister would hardly have commended the profiteering ticket touts at Wimbledon, Wembley and elsewhere, Mrs Gorman's point was that people were prepared to pay the price demanded by the touts at Wimbledon. That was the market in operation and that the organisers of the event were grossly undercharging for the tickets and should not, therefore, complain if people were prepared to pay a lot more.

In fact, Mrs Gorman went so far as to write a book on the subject, tantalisingly entitled *Everybody Lives by Selling Something.* Alas, nobody would buy it. The manuscript still languishes, as far as I know, in her bottom drawer at home.

She was also an impassioned advocate for not just smaller governments but for minute government and would have been delighted to see government departments disintegrate before her very eyes. Mrs Gorman once advocated that any cabinet minister who could work his department out of business should be awarded a dukedom on the spot. She had a soft spot for the humble earthworm, a creature she saw as 'beavering about underground in a truly Thatcherite manner' holding the universe together. And, in the manner of Prince Charles and his conversations with greenery, Mrs Gorman had regular warm chats with her worms, sometimes even stroking what she assumes to be their tummies.

∗ ∗ ∗ ∗ ∗

Ann Widdecombe, the Maidstone MP, was supposed to be on holiday in Kenya, but was persuaded (I don't suppose it took much persuasion) to address local people in a far-flung village called Mivukoni. She dilated, at considerable length, on the close ties between the UK and Kenya. Those ties were about to become even closer she soon found out to her discomfiture. The village chief, proclaiming how honoured they all were by her presence, presented her with a couple of odorous goats, a billy and a nanny. At first she thought she would call them Maggie and Maidstone, but changed her mind pretty jolly quickly when she realised the adverse effect this might have on her political career. This still, of course, left her with the problem of possessing two goats in a foreign land. However, with that ingenuity for which she is justly proud, she managed to have the goats transferred 400 miles to the British High Commission in Nairobi, where they were not exactly welcomed with open arms but where they dwelt for several years before expiring.

As she observed to them at the time when she was attempting (successfully as it turned out) to sweet-talk the diplomats into providing a home for these beasts: 'They will keep you in yoghurt for years to come...'

* * * * *

When Prime Minister John Major signed the distinguished visitors' book at the British Embassy in Saudi Arabia, he bizarrely wrote, after his name, these words: '10 Downing Street, London, SW1A 2AA'. One might just have thought that the postcode, although impressive, was superfluous in this case.

* * * * *

Dr Ian Paisley once showed me a letter he had received from an aggrieved constituent who complained: 'The Government, without so much as a by-your-leave, has removed my wife's infidelity allowance...' Dr Paisley got to work and speedily arranged for the lady's invalidity allowance to be restored.

He soon got a 'thank-you' letter back from the grateful constituent, saying: 'I don't know what either she or I would have done if you had not resolved my wife's serious infidelity problem...'

* * * * *

Sir Robert Rhodes James, the late and former Conservative MP for Cambridge, was a man of immense parliamentary knowledge. But even he was shaken once when, feeling under the weather, he visited his doctor. The doctor told him after a brief examination: 'Your problem is that you are suffering from low grade flu.'

Our hero was outraged: 'Low grade flu?' he exclaimed. 'I can't have low grade flu. I'm a Tory.'

But the doctor refused to make any concessions. 'Low grade flu is what you have. It will last for about a month and there is nothing you can do about it.'

* * * * *

Sir Charles Irving, Conservative MP for Cheltenham, was on a fact-finding trip to Africa when he accidentally put his foot through the turn-ups of his trousers while studying native life in Tanzania. He asked the feisty Mrs Gwyneth Dunwoody, Labour MP for Crewe and Nantwich, whether she would do him the honour of sewing his breeks together again, but she (unsurprisingly to those who knew her as not the sort of person to carry out such a task) declined. However, she put the embarrassed Mr Irving in touch with a local African lad who did the job, although not quite in the manner of a Savile Row outfitter.

Later that day, in what he assumed was the privacy of his hotel room, Sir Charles commenced to do battle with his newly 'repaired' trousers. And what a struggle it was! The young African tailor had turned the trousers into some kind of straitjacket into which it was virtually impossible to place the legs without performing some extraordinary and painful contortions. It was while he was in this bizarre state of disarray that the door of his bedroom quietly opened and, inexplicably, a procession of Chinese tourists shuffled through and out of the other door, maintaining their inscrutable expressions and affecting not to notice the amazing posture of Sir Charles, squirming about on the floor cursing and swearing at the less than professional needlework of the apprentice tailor.

* * * * *

Tony Benn was not accustomed to being the victim of a put-down. It appears that Mr Benn, on winning the election that first took him to Westminster, publicly announced that he must lose the stigma of being an intellectual. Unfortunately for him, one of Mr Benn's former teachers overheard the remark. He bluntly told the man: 'You had better acquire the stigma before worrying about losing it.'

Willie Whitelaw also suffered from academic embarrassment. He was certainly not one of the great mathematicians of this world. Indeed, his teacher at Winchester despaired of him at the time he was taking examinations preparatory to going to Cambridge. 'The eminent mathematician who taught me adopted a realistic attitude,' said Whitelaw. '"I despair of teaching you how to solve even the simplest mathematical problem," he said.' His teacher, therefore, told him simply to learn all the formulae off by heart and apply them to all the answers.

Whitelaw, who was to become Deputy Prime Minister, explained: 'I did so and passed with the necessary credits. When the splendid teacher saw the results he was delighted. "Now," he said, "I shall never have to teach you mathematics again. You must give them up at once." He didn't and I did.'

* * * * *

Anyone who met Ruud Lubbers, the long-serving Prime Minister of Holland, would recognise him as a man of great solemnity and, it had to be said, tedium. On one occasion, I ventured from the SAS Skandinavia Hotel in Copenhagen (where a bread roll and butter cost £15 – in the 1980s) to see Lubbers being interviewed at great length by a British TV camera crew. The interview went on and on, and Mr Lubbers was his normal monotonous self. I could not understand why they were letting him ramble on. And then someone explained the camera crew were having trouble with their sound system. So when Lubbers appeared they invited him to give an interview at great length (the only kind that Lubbers gave) so they could sort out their technical problem. Lubbers, of course, like all politicians, was flattered to be picked on like this. Little did he realise that he was being exploited. But, as someone said at the time, even Dutch Prime Ministers have their uses.

Fresh Air and Fun

Party conferences, while not exactly the lifeblood of political organisations, give the rank-and-file the opportunity to make terrible speeches to a nationwide television audience. The standard of oratory is usually abysmally low and provides a good opportunity for delegates to return to the conference hall and enjoy a siesta to work off the excesses of a hearty lunch and to prepare for the evening's heavy libations. Indeed the scene in the bars of the main hotels in conference towns resembles the London underground during the rush-hour more than anything else. Sometimes physical violence is necessary to force your way to the bar. And reporters dare not retire to bed before the bar is cleared (usually about 4am) for fear of missing an 'incident' where a grandee makes a pillock of himself.

I once saw two well-refreshed Labour women fighting in the foyer of the Imperial Hotel in Blackpool, the town immortalised in the Stanley Holloway comic monologue *Albert and the Lion* as the place to go for 'fresh air and fun'. It was drinking on an epic scale. The following morning saw many delegates in a sorry state, bleary-eyed, semi-comatose, incapable of intelligent conversation and clutching cups of black coffee with trembling hands.

But things have eased up somewhat since those halcyon days. In fact, Labour's 2006 conference in Manchester was the first I had attended, in some 40 years, that did not have a bar on the premises. That would have caused rioting a few years earlier, but, amazingly, on this occasion there was not even a single complaint.

Preparing for conferences can be as tricky as running them and just as likely to lead to pratfalls. The Labour Party had a happy and generous conference policy of presenting items of jewellery to ladies who had served the party for more years than they usually cared to admit. Shortly before the 1991 conference in Brighton, a Labour Party van, complete with driver, was despatched to a famous jewellers in London's West End to pick up the items. He parked the van outside, leaving the doors unlocked and the hazard lights flashing. When, a few moments later, he had collected his precious load, he emerged in the street to find the van was no longer there.

He telephoned the police, who told him: 'Don't worry, old fellow, it won't get far embazoned as it is with the Labour red roses plastered all over it.' The van was duly placed on the stolen list. But despite the optimism of the police, the day passed into night, and the night passed into day, and there was still no sign of it. And then, some 24 hours later, a telephone call was received at the Labour Party's London headquarters in Walworth Road.

An angry voice told them: 'When on earth are you going to remove your ruddy van? It's been standing there with its doors wide open and its hazard lights flashing for the past day and night.' The caller, it is hardly necessary to say, was from the jeweller. The driver had entered the shop by one door and left it by another without realising what he had done.

* * * * *

Sometimes, and for a variety of reasons, individual reporters may be refused passes for the party political conferences. So they simply sit in their hotel rooms, watch the proceedings on television and meet their contacts – particularly the thirsty ones – in nearby public houses. Indeed, it can be beneficial to be refused admission, especially if your newspaper trumpets you as 'the man they wouldn't let in.' A scheme devised by some MPs to charge reporters a fee to attend their conferences collapsed when it became apparent that many papers would rather not attend than give money to political parties.

David Rose, lobby correspondent for the *Liverpool Daily Post,* was dumbfounded when he was told he was to be charged £10 for the package of (often impenetrable) documents required to cover the 1991 Labour Party conference.

'Ten pounds?' he gasped incredulously. 'If you are going to charge me £10 for that little lot, I am going to charge every MP that I quote in our newspaper...' A few minutes later our hero was marching off with this great bundle of documents under his arm, not a penny having changed hands. It is nice to know – but hardly surprising – that politicians so readily cave in to threats of that nature.

* * * * *

The Conservatives, for some strange reason best known to themselves, used to employ highly-paid verbatim shorthand writers to record for posterity the remorseless flow of tripe churned out at conference. In the early 1960s, one of the transcribers was having trouble with a fast-talking speaker who had an impenetrable Glaswegian accent. So at frequent intervals, the shorthand writer's colleague started to clap. And at Conservative Party conferences, clapping spreads around the hall like a particularly virulent form of measles.

Within seconds, the entire audience were applauding, even though they had not the slightest idea what or why they were applauding – the Tories are as notorious for never listening to anything anybody says on the platform as they are for cheering it anyway. The delegates return to their homes as ignorant as they were when they arrived, yet they clap everything: the more banal, the louder the applause. They even clap in their sleep. It becomes a knee-jerk mechanical response.

The trick enabled the shorthand writer to catch up with his

prey. This ingenious method was repeated about every three or four minutes until finally the speaker, flushed with success, and on a high adrenalin count, left the rostrum to a hall ringing with a standing ovation even though barely a single word he uttered had been comprehensible. That experience must have done wonders for his self-esteem.

* * * * *

I myself have twice spoken on behalf of the press at Labour conferences. It is a daunting experience because most Labour delegates are hostile towards the media and those they called 'The fat cats of Fleet Street'. Once when the admirable Trevor Kavanagh, political editor of the *Sun*, rose to speak, there were immediate protests from the floor, including one man who said, 'If you lie in the gutter with dogs, then you are bound to get fleas.' Outrageous!

In my case, I got into trouble by starting my remarks with the words 'Ladies and gentlemen', an expression not used throughout the conference. They preferred introductions like, 'Comrade chair'. The brothers booed me, so I said, 'Sorry, I'll start again,' and continued, 'My lords, ladies and gentlemen...' and got away with it. Some of them even laughed. During that speech I congratulated a senior Labour official on his return to duties after a long illness. I said he looked 'in the peak of health'. He was dead a week later.

* * * * *

Covering party conferences is not without its perils. During the Labour conference in Brighton in 1991, I was walking along the street one evening when a large man suddenly leapt out of the shadows and pounced on me, thumped me incessantly on the chest and attempted to tear the jacket from my very back. All the time he was chanting, 'F...... socialists'. Well, I thought this was a bit rich, distinctly not cricket. I extricated myself from his attentions, told him that I had nothing to do with the Labour

Party, or any other political party for that matter, and let loose a flow of Anglo-Saxon prose which, whatever it lacked in elegance, was compensated for by a directness of message which seemed to hit the target. At any rate, the chap withdrew, without so much as an apology, never mind bidding me farewell. Dammit, where are the old-world courtesies of yesteryear? I said to myself as I licked my wounds.

That disagreeable incident had echoes of something that happened years earlier at the Conservative conference in Blackpool. For some reason, the Press Association had installed the team of reporters covering the event in a hotel miles from the centre of activity, a place called the Norbreck Hydro.

We had to take a tram ride in every morning. Each day, one of the reporters paid the fares for all of us. Come the last day, the only one of us who had not paid was Leslie (Scrooge) Howcroft, now deceased, who was renowned for the shortness of his arms and the depth of his pockets. He refused to pay. And we stood firm our ground. The conductor warned us (we were fast becoming exceedingly unpopular with our fellow passengers): 'This vehicle will not move an inch farther until you pay your fares.' This, of course, would have meant immobilising virtually the entire fleet of Blackpool trams. This had absolutely no effect on Mr Howcroft or any of us. So, without further ado, the conductor slung us all off his tram with the damning words 'F...... Tories' ringing in our ears as we shambled off, cursing our colleague in language no less fruity.

It was at a subsequent party conference that I fell into the hands of the Lancashire police. Getting into party political conference halls, in these days of high security panics, is a nightmare. My problem arose when I was trying to get out of the conference hall, a day or two before the conference got underway. I was about to leave the Winter Gardens in Blackpool and found a door clearly marked 'Exit'. I made for it, pushed it open and emerged blinking into the street. I was immediately pounced on by about six burly officers and was physically detained for well over half an hour. Meanwhile, a phalanx of police cars and fire engines screamed to the scene, while ascending ranks of police officers came to stare at me.

What I had apparently done was to open a door which was alarmed, and thus sent panic messages to everyone who mattered, it seemed, in Blackpool and a wide surrounding area. The officer who was delegated to guard me acted with the diligence of a man in charge of a rabid mass murderer. But I did observe him glancing at his watch at one point and observing to himself: 'If this nonsense goes on any longer I am going to be late home for my tea.'

Then another officer, enveloped in gold braid, approached me and in severe tones enquired of me my date of birth, telephone numbers, name of employer, reason for being in the hall, why I wanted to get out and manner of entrance in the first place. Everything about me except, as I recall it, the maiden name of my great-grandmother on the maternal side. Once I had furnished these details, yet another high-ranker approached me with these tidings: 'I don't know whether they will escort you out of the premises or take you somewhere else.'

Ultimately, it dawned on them that I was far from being an interesting person, just a bumbling old fool who had blundered through the wrong door. After a huddled conference, they decided that everybody's interests would be best served by simply letting me go. But not before, of course, delivering a magisterial rebuke. I was considering gingerly telling them that it would not be a bad idea and would have saved a lot of trouble if they had put a notice on this exit saying: 'This door is alarmed' (as indeed I was). However, as I was being released from custody, I looked back briefly and saw that they had. So I came to the conclusion that meek silence was the best option at that point.

＊ ＊ ＊ ＊ ＊

Left-winger Sydney Bidwell caused a stir by inexplicably waving his arms frantically about at a Labour Party conference.

Uncharacteristically for this unassuming man, he was doing everything in his power to get himself on television. The reason for this odd behaviour was that Bidwell's six-year-old grand-daughter had lodged an official complaint with him that she had seen all his mates on television but had not yet seen her own grandfather. One of Bidwell's friends, observing these strange goings-on, went over and inquired what he was about. When Bidwell explained, the friend resolved the problem at once.

'Just sit next to that old media tart Eric Heffer, he's never off the box.' Bidwell took the hint. It worked. And his granddaughter was well-pleased.

Telephones from Hell

The problems I faced in Blackpool and Brighton, however, were as nothing compared to things which went wrong farther afield. The famous (or infamous, depending how you look at it) Euro-summit at Maastricht when the Maastricht agreement was signed certainly took its toll on me.

I managed to smash my shins to smithereens when I walked into a gargantuan flowerpot outside a hotel. After that, I scarred my thumb for life when a coffee machine emptied its contents over me. To cap all that, a butter-fingered Brussels bureaucrat dropped a pile of heavyweight European draft directives from a balcony on to my head. My credit cards were up the creek and I could find no way of paying my hotel bill. But then I had started on the wrong foot, by booking into the wrong hotel in the wrong town in the wrong country. I know that is pretty difficult to do, but I nevertheless managed it.

The biggest problem in the pre-electronic age when abroad was getting the stories back to Fleet Street. It was always hit and miss: you eventually got through, but often not before you had been reduced to a trembling wreck. Sometimes when there were long silent gaps at the stage when an operator was allegedly trying to connect you, it was advisable to sing or talk gibberish down the phone, because if, after an interminable delay, the operator 'heard' silence, she would assume you had given up and would disconnect you. Once in Armenia, I raced to the press centre and was first there to give my London number. The call never came through and I was compelled to file my story to the *Financial Times* who passed it on to the Press Association.

Filing stories from the Falklands in particular was not easy partly because, as I recall it, the local telephone exchange seemed to close down well before bedtime. However, I discovered there was a telephone on the Harwich–Hook of Holland ferry which had been requisitioned by the government for the conflict and was now moored in the bay of Port Stanley. To get there I had to sweet-talk an army sergeant to give me a lift in his small motorboat to the larger vessel. I clambered aboard this and we whizzed over to the ferry, which I also boarded quite easily. I found the captain, who showed me the phone. I dialled Fleet Street and was through in a matter of seconds. Amazing! I filed a story, spoke fairly briefly to the newsdesk and called out to the captain that I had finished my call and 'How much do I owe you?' I pulled a sodden £10 note out of my trouser pocket which was all I had. It was not only the tenner which was sodden. I was myself soaked from head to foot by this time from the trip to the vessel through these cold and turbulent waters.

The captain, a pleasant fellow, did a brief calculation and said: 'That will be £237.50p.' I blanched. My sodden tenner was not going to help much there. So I wrote out a cheque for the amount, with quivering hand, on a no less sodden cheque book. It was my first and most memorable encounter with a satellite telephone.

The next problem was to get back ashore. The little motorboat had left the spot where I could have easily stepped from one vessel into the other. By now it was alongside the ship and I was faced with the fact that I had to climb down the side on a rope ladder, still clinging to a vast assortment of papers. As I did so, I slipped from the rope and fell into the sea. By this time the mood of the sergeant in charge of the motorboat was growing less and less sunny. I had wasted an hour or so of his time and now he had to fish me out of the icy waters. The conversation on the way back to Port Stanley was, I can tell you, not particularly comradely. Fortunately, I did not have to go through this ordeal again. I discovered a telex office from which I managed to file my stories for the rest of the trip.

But the most hairy moment with 'Maggie's Flying Circus' came during an Indaba – a spectacular and raucous trade fair – in the city of Kano to the north of Nigeria. It was a splendid occasion, with riders and horses performing the most spectacular, swashbuckling deeds. Suddenly, for a reason that has so far eluded all of us, the Nigerian militia took it upon itself to attack the Downing Street staff and also the reporters who were with them. Mrs Thatcher and her close entourage were only about 10 yards away, but such was the hubbub and racket that she did not, could not, notice that anything was amiss. Bernard Ingham had a rifle barrel stuck into his stomach.

'I moved it to one side as is advisable on these occasions,' he said afterwards. The militia were waving their armoury about in a most alarming fashion. I got bashed on the top of the head and floored by the butt of a rifle. The Downing Street secretaries were in tears and most of us were starting to feel panicky. When, after some minutes, things had quietened down, Charles Reiss, of the *Evening Standard*, and I raced to where we knew there were two telephones. He took one and I took the other. By an incredible stroke of luck, I picked the 'right' phone. I actually got through to the Press Association office in Fleet Street after dialling only once. Sometimes in Africa you can dial 50 times before you get through. Needless to say, I filed my story straight away and when I had finished poor old Charles was still trying to dial through to the *Evening Standard* office. It could so easily have been the other way around.

Later in the day, BBC diplomatic correspondent Paul Reynolds gave both Charles and me a severe dressing-down for having filed this 'trivia' when there were so many more important things, like the state of its economy and balance of payments, to report about in Nigeria. We took this rebuke on the chin, but noticed later, with a certain amount of smug glee, that the BBC were using the PA copy in its entirety.

Most parts of Africa and Eastern Europe, notably Moscow, invariably presented enormous communication problems. But there was a slightly different problem in Saudi Arabia. Although the telephones worked well for international calls, the Saudis would not accept plastic or cheques for calls. They had to be paid for in Saudi currency the moment the call was finished. While you were on your call a Saudi would stand disconcertingly close to you with a stop watch in his hand, logging every second of your conversation. It was not an ideal situation.

However, we surmounted this problem in a decidedly underhand way. At sundown, the muezzin called everybody to prayer, a compulsory activity. Once they were all safely away at their devotions we would make our calls – mid-afternoon in London terms, so just the right time of day for the morning papers to receive copy. I am not proud of this.

Mrs Thatcher visited Saudi Arabia and indeed all the Gulf states in demure attire, dressed from head to foot with only her face and hands visible. When, on another occasion, she was having talks with King Fahd in the palace in Riyadh, I had a pressing need to phone the office in London. I was presented with a telephone on a silver salver and proceeded to file a story at considerable length. When I had finished I recalled, with some disquiet the Saudi system of depleting your pockets of all your cash the moment your call had finished.

My problem was that I had virtually no money on me at all and what I had was certainly not Saudi currency. However, I delved in my pocket and proffered a handful of coppers – not even the right currency – as some kind of feeble gesture of good intent. But the official to whom I made the offer (I was told later he was a form of fledgling prince) airily waved it aside and said: 'Royal Protocol will take care of that.' It was, for me, a moment of considerable relief.

But the most notorious place of all for communications with London was almost certainly Moscow. I remember on one occasion when we arrived in Moscow, we were told by press officer Peter Bean that for once the Russian authorities had set up a specially dedicated battery of English-speaking telephone operators to enable us to get through quickly to London. All we had to do was to pick up the phone in our hotel bedrooms, utter the magic word 'delegation' and we would be put through instantly to these highly-skilled operators. In fact, all our problems would be swept away. It all sounded too good to be true – as indeed it was. When we arrived at the hotel, a soulless mausoleum called the Rossiya, we picked up our phones, uttered the code word, but nothing happened. What had happened was that this battery of operators had been on duty from 9am and had sat around doing nothing all day until 8pm when they clocked off and went home.

On another celebrated occasion, I managed to get the phone to work first time in my room at that hotel. I was bellowing my story down the line, as was necessary, and suddenly I was stopped in midflow by my door opening and the arrival in my room of a ferocious-looking Russian gentleman, wearing a long nightshirt and brandishing what appeared to be a metal bar. He started belabouring me – verbally that is – in Russian. I do not speak a word of the language, but I quickly got the drift. My stentorian tones had wakened him in his room next door to mine and would I kindly shut up. It was only at that point that I realised that the time was something around 3am. We had travelled from Japan that day, stopping off somewhere in Siberia. In other words we had passed through a number of time zones before arriving in Moscow and I had lost all sense of time. The man left the room, muttering imprecations at me as he did so. My dilemma was obvious. Was I to abandon telephoning the story or carry on shouting and thus risk getting clobbered by the intruder who clearly did not relish having his sleep interrupted?

There was, of course, no alternative but to carry on, something I did without any feeling of virtue. I was, to put it mildly, scared stiff that my visitor would return and put his metal bar to painful use about my person. Unaccountably, he did not return. He probably regarded me as a dangerous lunatic and someone not to be trifled with. For that, I gave many thanks.

The lifts in Moscow seemed to be no more reliable than the telephones. I remember us once returning to base after a day out and about with Margaret Thatcher. We piled out of the coach into the Rossiya's great galumphing lift in the hope of filing our stories to London from our bedrooms. No such luck. The lift ascended about 10 feet and ground to a halt amid much alarming booming and clanging. The simple fact was that we had overloaded it – with potentially disastrous consequences. There was on the wall of the lift a Heath-Robinson-like contraption which was presumably for use in case of emergencies such as this. None of us could read, never mind speak, a word of Russian so the instructions on how to use this gadget were useless to us. However, we spotted in the lift two strangers, presumably Russian, who would no doubt help us, and themselves, out of this dilemma.

We signalled to them to get to work on the emergency telephone arrangements, but they looked at us blankly. It was our misfortune to have chosen to travel on this obdurate piece of antiquated machinery with a couple of deaf-and-dumb Muscovites. They seemed as baffled as we were by the so-called rescue mechanism and it took an hour of shouting and hollering before anyone came to our rescue. Needless to say, we all missed our first editions, which resulted in some difficult explaining to do to news editors. It also led to a resolution on my part to avoid lifts at all costs in Moscow in future.

* * * * *

I have acquired, over the years, a reputation – which I must say I have done very little to dispel – of being something of a philistine. When on one occasion we were in Madrid with Mrs Thatcher, we noticed what appeared to be an old dustbin lying on its side in the garden of one of the King of Spain's palaces.

'What on earth is that doing there?' one of our number asked.

'It will probably be a Henry Moore,' I said disparagingly by way of jest.

A Spanish press officer chipped in: 'It is a Henry Moore,' she said.

That was the first, and almost the last time I have been right about anything to do with the arts.

Soaked in Guinness as the Troubles Raged

Northern Ireland provided plenty of bizarre moments as well as hairy ones during the height of the troubles. Throughout the 1970s and early 1980s I was a regular 'commuter' there.

When Prime Minister Edward Heath appointed William Whitelaw as the first-ever Northern Ireland Secretary it was virtually impossible, on that day, to get a seat on any flight to Belfast. So, the Press Association hired a small aircraft which we boarded at Biggin Hill. Not only PA personnel were on this plane but also some journalists from other Fleet Street organisations to whom spare seats had been sold. The aircraft was jam-packed with gin when we set out. By the time we arrived it was virtually dry and its passengers in quite a turbulent mood.

The normal flying time to Belfast was round about one hour. After about two-and-a-half hours on this crate, we started to land. 'At last,' we said. 'We can now get another drink.' But it was not Belfast. It was the Isle of Man only, where we had to land to refuel. Such were the temptations of Douglas that there were moves afoot among us – not from me, I hasten to add – to 'bribe' the pilot to say he had a mechanical fault and that we could not fly on. Happily, that idea was nipped in the bud. And on we flew to

Belfast, landing there something like an hour later. Needless to say, for many of us the first port of call had to be a loo. But one of our band was so desperate that he was compelled to spend his penny on the tarmac against the tyres of the plane which had brought us. No sooner had he set about this little matter, when a small posse of security men swarmed at him from the darkness and bundled him away to a police cell. Belfast was on fire, and here was a man being locked up for relieving himself in a public place in the dark!

Another of our passengers, a few hours later, had the narrowest possible escape from death – and it was nothing to do with the terrorists. He took a lady friend up to the darkened penthouse suite of the famous Europa Hotel. He was standing as close as he could get to the lady, just by a picture window which stretched right to the floor. At one point he put out his hand and suddenly realised that there was no glass in the window. He said afterwards: 'I shiver every time I think of that...' A chilling moment.

Many of us stayed regularly in the Catholic Hamill Hotel, just opposite the Europa. It was cheap, cheerful and exceedingly rowdy. Most of the time it was relatively free from terrorist attacks. However, from time to time the Protestant thugs from nearby notorious Sandy Row used to enliven their evenings by hurling bricks through the windows of the hotel. On one such occasion I was at the bar, on the first floor, when one of these rocks hit me plumb in the chest, breaking a rib or two. That was the worst by way of physical injury that I incurred during all those years, so I was pretty lucky, I suppose. On another occasion I was at the same bar, with an untouched pint of Guinness in front of me on the counter. I was telephoning a story about a bomb which had just exploded somewhere in Belfast. A lady I knew only as Sally, from the management of the Europa Hotel opposite, was standing near me. Suddenly she shouted: 'I have heard too much about bombs and explosions. Take this!' Whereupon, she emptied the entire pint of Guinness over my head.

On another occasion I rose and went in for breakfast only to find the previous night's drinkers still at the bar. Suddenly one of them lost his balance and fell down, the rest of them following him, one by one, like human dominoes. Professional acrobats could not have been more impressive or better coordinated.

It was inevitable, I suppose, that eventually the Hamill would be blown up, and it was, on the eve of the first anniversary of Bloody Sunday. Needless to say, I was in the bar when two IRA men, waving guns at everybody, stormed into the bar, placed this lethal package on the counter and said, as was their style in those days, 'You've got 15 minutes to get out.'

I thought to myself, and said as much: 'Well, that gives us time for just one more pint.' But I quickly found I was speaking to an empty room. Everyone, staff and customers alike, had fled. I thought perhaps I should, too. So I drained my glass and high-tailed it from the premises, across the road to the Whip and Saddle bar of the Europa Hotel from where I watched the sad demise of the Hamill. The bomb did not go off for more than an hour. I had the strange experience of watching my bed half blown out of the rubble and hanging over adjacent Amelia Street, wafting in the wind.

I paid my brief obsequies, but there was work to be done. I had to get to Londonderry for the first anniversary commemoration of Bloody Sunday. Armed with a new shirt and toothbrush, I boarded a train for the city. I stayed the night, as I recall it, in a spooky private house with men running up and down the stairs all night long. You might say that I spent a fitful night there. In the morning, along with my colleagues, I joined the marchers and protesters as they proceeded through the city, including the notorious Creggan estate and into the even worse Bogside.

There were, unsurprisingly, several acts of violence on the way and missiles, some of them aflame, being hurled all over the place. It was because some buildings were burning that we decided to split up at one point – some of the others would stay in the centre of the city while I was to continue with the marchers. We were to join up and swap notes later on in the Diamond, the area in the centre of Londonderry.

The march snaked its way through the Bogside before assembling in a Gaelic football field where speaker after speaker poured calumny and abuse on the British soldiers and the British Government. I well remember a particularly virulent Republican called Maire Drum taking the stage. She was subsequently to become the fatal victim of violence herself. It was, incidentally, pointed out to us on numerous occasions that, spelt backwards her name would appear as 'murder I am', which everybody thought was highly appropriate. She ranted on endlessly about 'Brits' and 'scum' and 'sewers' and 'drains', while across the valley in the growing dark I could see parts of Londonderry ablaze. It was a fearful and wild spectacle, particularly when allied to the gruesome event, which was hatred personified, that I was attending.

It suddenly dawned on me that I was the only 'Brit' amid this exceedingly hostile and volatile crowd. I thought it advisable to keep my notebook in my pocket and my mouth firmly closed, so as not to allow my telltale Derbyshire accent expose me. Once before I had been mistaken by the IRA for an off-duty or plain-clothes British soldier, and I had no great desire to have a repeat performance.

Once the tirades had finished, everybody trooped off back to their homes, and I followed them. When we got into the Bogside proper, a rabbit warren if ever there was one, I suddenly realised that I hadn't a clue as to how I was going to find my way out of this labyrinth. So I just kept walking round in circles, up streets and down them again, with my mouth firmly closed, hoping against hope that no one would accost me as a dodgy-looking stranger. Fortunately and surprisingly, that did not happen and to my great relief after about an hour of pounding the streets, I found my way out. I have to say, that was one of those times when you feel very vulnerable indeed.

At the end of this grim day I had a telephone call from one Mavourneen McGowan, who, along with two of her sisters, had worked in the bar at the late Hamill hotel. Our conversation was hampered by the screeching of women on the line. How they managed to get on the line, I shall never know, but as soon as an English-sounding voice was heard then, as surely as night follows day, the shrieking of obscenities began. But behind all this babble, I managed to ascertain from Mavourneen that she had actually climbed through the rubble which was all that was left of the Hamill and had retrieved all my belongings from the shattered bedroom. It was not only a highly dangerous adventure on her part, but it was also astonishing that the security forces had not stopped her from doing it.

When, a few days later, I had returned to Belfast she handed me my bag, which seemed fuller and heavier than when I arrived. When I asked how this had come about, she casually said that over the years a lot of drunken reporters who had been staying there had left behind all sorts of items, including raincoats, ties and shirts. Mavourneen simply stuffed it all in my bag. So, on that occasion, even though I had irreparably lost some stuff in the explosion, I actually returned home to England with more luggage than I had arrived with. She also gave me a loaf of homemade bread, a speciality of the province. However, when my pathetic bag was on the luggage whirligig at Heathrow, the bread spilled out slice by slice, and I had to pick them up, ignominiously, as they came around.

A hotel called the City, in Londonderry, had been a regular haunt for journalists in the early days of the Troubles. Like the Hamill and so many others of that era in Northern Ireland, it did not survive. One of the most prominent figures in that hotel was a man called Lurch, simply because of the manner of his walking. Nobody ever had the faintest idea of his real name. He was, presumably, an IRA man and thus, in a sense, the hotel was safe so long as he was there. However, the management and he fell out and he was promptly sacked over some perceived triviality. It was a stupid thing to do. Two days or so later, the hotel was little more than a pile of rubble.

But when it was thriving, I recall, the papers had done stories about some shortcomings concerning the fire brigade in Londonderry. One night, rioters decided to hurl petrol bombs and gas canisters at the hotel, large parts of which were aflame. We telephoned the fire brigade but they obviously had more pressing problems to deal with – or said they had – which didn't surprise me. So we had to put the fires out ourselves with buckets of water. It taught us not to be rude about the fire brigade again.

There were other moments of grim, so-called gallows humour. At the time when the discharge of tear gas was routine, somebody said, as he stood at the entrance of the City hotel: 'I am just popping out for a breath of fresh gas...'

There were moments to relish, too, in Belfast. I remember once attending Dr Ian Paisley's famous Sunday evening services in the Ulster Hall before his own church was built. One of the rituals of these events was a silent collection in a galvanised bucket. Being a Press Association man (and thus having no views on anything at all) and also not wishing to contribute in any event, I declined with as much courtesy as I could muster when the bucket, by then half-full of banknotes, came my way. My refusal, even though nervously and obsequiously given, was regarded as a downright insult and, without further ado, I was unceremoniously frog-marched from the place by a couple of heavies.

A few days later, Dr Paisley suddenly called a press conference in the middle of the afternoon in Belfast. Most of us had been regaling ourselves in hotel bars when the summons had arrived. We all hot-footed it to the chosen venue and sat and waited for the great man. I have to say that the atmosphere in the hall, coincident with our arrival, had become deliciously foetid, a rich and pervasive mixture of tobacco smoke, whisky and the Guinness fumes which nearly everybody was exhaling. When Dr Paisley arrived, in all his majesty, he suddenly stopped in his tracks at the doorway, hit in the face, as it were, by the fragrances which confronted him.

He took a huge intake of breath and, screwing up his face into a contortion, appeared to spit it out with disgust. And then he roared: 'The breath of Satan is upon us...' It was almost impossible to take the rest of the proceedings seriously after witnessing that masterly, Shakespearean entrance.

He always had a penchant for smelling the breath of reporters whom he suspected, usually correctly, of drinking. My first encounter with him was at Stormont before he became an MP at Westminster. We had arranged to meet for an interview. As I was a trifle early, I popped, unwisely, into the bar for a snifter or two. When I returned to our rendezvous, his first request was to smell my breath. I offered him a sample and he said: 'Have you drink taken, Mr Moncrieff?' I said: 'Just two halves of draught Guinness, Dr Paisley.' 'That's two halves of draught Guinness too many for me, Mr Moncrieff,' he thundered, turned on his heels and stalked off. No interview!

Incidentally, in those days, if you telephoned Dr Paisley at his home and asked for 'Mr Paisley' you were invariably told that no such person of that name lived there. You had to say 'Dr Paisley' if you wanted an audience.

It was always better to hear him talking in Northern Ireland than at Westminster. He was, in the Billy Connolly sense 'The Big Yin' in the Stormont and successor 'parliaments' and assemblies there. But at Westminster he never achieved the political and physical dominance he enjoyed in Ulster. He once denounced a fairly prominent politician in Northern Ireland called Austin Curry, as 'chicken curry' and regularly gave the Pope and the Roman Catholic Church a hammering, flaying the 'shackles of priestcraft' and traducing 'The Scarlet Woman of Rome'. On another occasion, after a session of one of the assemblies that followed the downfall of the Stormont Parliament itself, Dr Paisley and his cronies decided to carry on a meeting of their own, illegally, as it were. They elected Mrs Paisley into the chair and carried on debating, fortissimo, among themselves.

The officials were at a loss what to do. There was no question of marching in and physically throwing them out. There had already been one punch-up in the chamber that evening and nobody (except us up aloft in the press gallery) particularly wanted another one. But the officials arrived at the perfect solution. They simply turned off all the lights at the mains and left Dr Paisley and his fellows shouting at each other in the dark. It is not often that you see (or rather hear, in this instance) Dr Paisley turning his famous 'No surrender!' war cry on its head. But this was one such occasion. Even for me, who has had great affection for this man, it was a moment to relish.

When the currencies of Northern Ireland and the Republic of Ireland were interchangeable both north and south of the border, Dr Paisley would have nothing to do – or said he would have nothing to do – with what he called 'Fenian money'. However, on one occasion when he was jingling his coinage in his hands, in the members' lobby of the House of Commons, I detected some 'southern' coinage among his change and pointed it out to him; he swiftly returned it to his pocket and sheepishly changed the subject.

Points of Order

Margaret Thatcher had a very cloistered upbringing, which was usually the reason why she sometimes made surprising remarks ('every Prime Minister needs a Willy', a reference to William Whitelaw, was a classic) and then completely failed to understand why her audience rocked with laughter.

However, to everybody's surprise she once did crack a joke which even she appeared to understand. She was talking contemptuously, during her Conservative Party conference speech in Blackpool in 1989, about the ailing centre parties of Britain. And then, recalling the heady, but short-lived glories of the one-time Liberal–SDP Alliance, she observed: 'Any woman knows, you won't get a soufflé to rise twice...' What on earth had come over her? She had delivered a joke deliberately and not by accident!

However, further research disclosed that not all was what it seemed on the surface. The joke, such as it was, had been brazenly purloined by Mrs Thatcher's speechwriters from Australia, where it had been used by Mr Paul Keating, then the Australian Treasurer (Chancellor of the Exchequer), about a Mr Andrew Peacock who was aspiring for a second time to be leader of the opposition down under. The surprising thing is that it seemed a particularly tame 'joke' for Mr Keating who became notorious for his particularly unpleasant and graphic insults, especially after he had become Australia's Prime Minister.

Incidentally, Sir Ronald Millar, who was Thatcher's principal speechwriter, admitted later that he always omitted his best lines from the first draft of a speech submitted to her. The reason, he said, was that the Prime Minister, without fail, tore up the first draft however good it was. And he did not want to see his bon mots ending up in the waste-paper basket.

*****

Sometimes, members have an unhappy (or happy, depending on which side of the fence you are) knack of making themselves look stupid. Indeed, it is a wonder, sometimes, that we do not have more MPs expiring through their own foolishness. Look at the case of Peter Temple-Morris, one-time Conservative MP for Leominster, who crossed the floor to join Labour and was subsequently made a life peer.

He explained once that when he was staying in a hotel in Quebec he was unable to sleep because of the rowdy guests celebrating in the room above his own. Let the intrepid Temple-Morris take up the story: 'I stood up on the bed and tried to thump the ceiling with a coat hanger. Alas, the bed suddenly assumed a life of its own and starting zooming about the room. Needless to say, I fell off.' The price he had to pay for that runaway bed was a painful dislocated ankle and the hire, at considerable expense, of a pair of crutches.

Another Tory MP, Jerry Hayes, known as 'The Golden Golly' because of his cherubic Shirley Temple-style locks, had an unfortunate encounter with a train. 'I had left my dictating machine on the train and rushed back to get it. As I was getting out again, the train started off and my foot went down the gap between the train and the platform and got stuck.' Fortunately, no serious injury ensued, and he later put a cheerful face on the mishap. 'My stick gave me an aura of something approaching gravitas for a while,' he boasted.

* * * * *

The city of Derby, my birthplace, must have some embarrassing memories for certain prominent politicians. On one occasion, Sir Geoffrey Howe, then Foreign Secretary, visited the city and parked himself in a chair, which promptly collapsed. The portly fellow landed on the floor with his limbs and his dignity splayed all over the place and could not fail to hear the suppressed mirth of those he was about to address. But it didn't end there. For some unaccountable reason, after Sir Geoffrey had managed, with difficulty, to raise himself from the floor and to restore some at least of his dignity, for some unaccountable reason the owners of the chair invited him to sign the wreck of it. What they had hoped to gain from that I cannot possibly imagine.

But there was an even more humiliating incident than this in Derby. The short-lived SDP was in the middle of one of its mobile conferences, which started in Cardiff, moved on to Derby and after that finished in Great Yarmouth. Dr David Owen, who was the effective leader of this party, wandered into the press room where he was immediately seized on by a reporter from the *Derby Evening Telegraph*.

The reporter started the interview by being violently sick all over Owen's tailored and no doubt hugely-expensive suit. The reporter, demonstrating an unnatural burst of speed, disappeared from the scene like a flash of lightning never to be seen by Dr Owen again. Meanwhile, Dr Owen (unusually for him) was left totally speechless and hastily disappeared himself.

*****

Early in 1989, the British ambassador in Romania, a Mr Hugh Arbuthnott, was reportedly 'manhandled' by the militia in a provincial town called Cluj. As a result of this, their ambassador in London, Mr Stan Soare, was summoned to the Foreign Office for a ticking off and to apologise on behalf of his Government. He refused. Instead he discounted the story as told by the British ambassador, saying that Mr Arbuthnott had himself 'mistreated and insulted' the militia after he had been rebuked by them for driving the wrong way down a one-way street, all of which Mr Arbuthnott fiercely denied. It transpired that the road was actually a two-way street. After the incident and in a bid to fabricate the evidence, the Romanians at dead of night craftily erected a 'No entry' sign at one end of the street. However, no doubt because it was dark, the chap who put up that sign was unaware that another man was blissfully putting up a similar sign at the other end of the street. All of which made it a no-way street. Thanks to the incompetent zeal of the Cluj Highways Department, Mr Soare was compelled to grovel.

* * * * *

When Tory MP Robert Boscawen was Comptroller of the Royal Household, part of his duties were to write out a report of the day's proceedings in the House of Commons and present them to the Queen. After he had been doing this for some months, the Queen casually mentioned to someone that Boscawen's handwriting was so bad that she could never read a word of his reports and, indeed, had ceased trying.

* * * * *

As we have seen, sometimes even Margaret Thatcher did not know where she was. The most celebrated and embarrassing occasion was when she thought she was in Kuala Lumpur when, in fact, she was in Jakarta, Indonesia. However, there was never any danger of Sir Alec Douglas Home falling into that trap, either when he was Prime Minister or Foreign Secretary. Whenever he alighted from an aircraft, wherever he was in the world, his wife, Elizabeth, used to follow him just a pace or two behind on the tarmac, chanting the name of the place at which he had just arrived.

For instance, I once heard her saying on arrival in China: 'Peking, Alec, Peking, Peking, Peking,' thus ensuring that he would avoid wounding his hosts by beginning his remarks with the words: 'It is nice to be back in Moscow again...'

* * * * *

Some years ago, as I was walking along the colonnade into the Palace of Westminster, I noticed a tall, gangling figure approaching me. It was, or so I thought, Sir Eldon Griffiths, Conservative MP for Bury St Edmunds, a man rarely seen in the House, who became known as the MP for California because of his frequent trips to America. However, seeing him approach I greeted him with a chirpy, 'Wotcher, cock!' as our paths crossed. Griffiths, if a little intense at times, is normally, however, a genial sort of character.

But on this occasion, he gave me the hard stare. Bonhomie, usually one of his endearing traits, was noticeably absent. Frigidity was the order of the day. And then I realised my mistake. It was not the amiable Griffiths I had greeted so impudently, but his doppelganger, Ian Smith, the one-time leader of the Rhodesian rebellion and a man I had never met. No wonder I got the icy-cold treatment. He was not a man given to frivolity, especially from some strange upstart.

∗ ∗ ∗ ∗ ∗

The future baroness Ewart-Biggs could not understand what all the fuss was about when – as plain Mrs Biggs – she visited Algeria in 1963. She was feted wherever she went and was the focus of curiosity, attention and admiration. Suddenly all this ended and she became just another nonentity again. What had happened was that the local population assumed that she was the wife of the Great Train Robber, Ronald Biggs, who had just been arrested for his part in the crime. When the Algerians discovered she was nothing of the kind and merely the wife of British diplomat Christopher Ewart-Biggs, they totally lost interest in her.

∗ ∗ ∗ ∗ ∗

Lord Young, the former Trade and Industry Secretary, learned the hard way that you do not trifle with Margaret Thatcher. Some time after the salmonella in eggs scare provoked by Edwina Currie, he warned the then Prime Minister at the dinner table that she should not take a portion of unpasteurised camembert. Mrs Thatcher's hackles flared. She tapped the table with the handle of her knife and bluntly told the quivering peer: 'I am neither old nor pregnant.' A few months later, Lord Young was shunted unceremoniously into an obscure job at Conservative Central Office.

Enoch the Unflinching

Enoch Powell was, in my book, the most straightforward and honourable politician I dealt with during nearly half a century at Westminster. He was a man who stuck rigidly to protocol and had an almost religious attachment to tradition. He dressed in a sombre manner: dark suits and a homburg hat, whatever the weather. And he would never allow the 'modernisers' to get within shouting distance of him.

For Enoch Powell, there was no such thing as image. He was always simply John Enoch Powell, straight as a die, unflinching in the face of threats resulting from those of his policies – particularly on immigration – which were seen by his enemies as inflammatory.

It was the so-called 1968 'Rivers of Blood' speech (a description which he utterly detested and denounced as totally inaccurate) which ended for ever his political career on the front bench. Tory leader Edward Heath sacked him from the shadow cabinet on the telephone after that speech and from that moment onwards, Powell remained a backbencher. The two men never spoke together again. Indeed, Heath's detestation for Powell was if anything more venomous than his well-known dislike of Margaret Thatcher. I once saw Heath fly into a rage when, at his Salisbury home, one intrepid reporter ask whether he kept in touch with Powell. Often, political opponents become quite friendly in retirement. Not these two.

Unlike most politicians of his stature, Powell would travel on the London underground and often engage in conversation with people who could barely believe he was there. He once told me that people had sometimes gone past their stop on the underground, so fascinated were they at seeing him. He was, in his heyday, both the most popular and the most hated politician in the land.

The highest political office he held was Minister of Health. Yet, in the late 1960s and the 1970s he was easily the most famous, controversial and (his enemies would say) notorious politician in Britain. But although he invariably looked, and sounded, stern, he possessed some rather incongruous but appealing habits. He would, in private conversations, use words like 'spiffing', expressions straight out of early 20th century schoolboy novels. He also had a passion for family picnics and hated having his hair washed, a chore which his wife used to carry out from time to time. He did not exactly struggle like a small, whimpering child, but it was nevertheless a very difficult operation to perform.

He would never indulge in political activity on a Sunday and was even wont – if you can picture it – to dance a jig when something happened of which he approved. During the 1970 general election campaign, when he was successfully defending his seat at Wolverhampton South West, Powell was speaking at Tamworth about the decision announced by the Canadians to float their dollar, an event which, he said, caused him to dance a jig. I assumed, when I did a report on that meeting, that Powell was merely using a figure of speech. So, imagine my surprise when some days later, towards the end of the campaign, I did an interview with Pamela Powell, his wife, she mentioned this fact, saying: 'When he heard the news about the Canadian dollar on the wireless, he jumped up from the breakfast table, where he had been digging into a boiled egg, and danced a jig around the room.' He had really done it! So the moral there, was that if Enoch Powell described his personal reaction to a political event, you believed what he said, because he did not deal in metaphors or fantasies.

Incidentally, before that interview with his wife began, in their then Wolverhampton home, Powell said he would allow me half an hour, and not a minute more. He then disappeared into another room. Precisely 30 minutes later, he returned, as promised, saying, somewhat to my disconcertment: 'I heard every one of your ham questions.'

He confined almost the entirety of that campaign to his constituency and the West Midlands. The only visit he made farther afield was to Eltham, in southeast London, where he went to support an old acquaintance, a right-wing Conservative, a product of what was disdainfully known as the 'Hackney School of Toryism'. John ('Jack Boots') Jackson, a journalist, was the candidate – an unsuccessful one as it turned out – and the meeting which Powell attended proved to be one of the most unruly of his entire campaign. Eggs and other missiles were hurled at him, while Powell sat steadfastly on the platform, flinching neither to right nor left. Then, suddenly, a big, burly man, with huge commotion, charged up to the front from the back of the hall, bellowing abuse as he did so and hurling chairs aside en route to the platform. There, he thrust his face into Powell's face and unleashed a stream of abuse, but once again the politician remained totally unmoved until his would-be assailant was dragged away.

Reporters stayed in Wolverhampton's Connaught hotel, owned by the late Tory MP Sir (later Lord) Harmar Nicholls, father of Sue Nicholls, the actress who played Audrey Roberts in *Coronation Street*. This convivial hotel was very close to the local Conservative constituency party headquarters. Each morning, I would parade early outside these offices, in the hope of catching Powell as he went in for a comment on whatever issue, to do with the election or not, which was current that day. He invariably obliged, thus giving me an early morning story, which pleased my newsdesk no end. On those occasions, as I pottered up and down the street, waiting for my quarry to arrive, he would describe me as being 'like an Edwardian dandy parading along the esplanade before breakfast in the morning, seaside air...'

One sunny afternoon, during that campaign, when we had no meetings to cover, I repaired to the launderette, which was only a few doors down from his home. I chucked all my stuff in the machine and took my shoes and socks off and threw the latter in the machine as well. As I sat there sockless and reading a newspaper, I was suddenly tapped on the shoulder. It was Mrs Powell, inviting me round to their house while my washing whizzed round.

So in I went, shoes on but no socks, while Powell showed me round his very fine walled garden. If he noticed my odd attire, which I am sure he did, he had the courtesy not to mention it. Powell had always refused to give out to reporters his Wolverhampton telephone number, even though his London number was in the telephone book. On this visit to his Wolverhampton home I sneakily 'clocked' that telephone number and wrote it down on a piece of paper when he wasn't looking. But, although it was a prized possession, I was always too nervous to use it afterwards. I never once rang him at his Wolverhampton home even though I was the only reporter, so far as I was aware, to have that number.

Needless to say despite, or possibly because of, all the contumely he attracted, he was re-elected with ease. But it was the last time he was to fight Wolverhampton South West. By the time the February 1974 general election was looming, Powell had totally lost faith with Edward Heath. He accused the Prime Minister of having betrayed the nation and of going beyond his 1970 undertakings by leading Britain into Europe – a policy which Enoch Powell opposed to his dying day. And he spoke contemptuously in one speech of choosing between 'the man with the boat [Edward Heath] and the man with the pipe [Harold Wilson].' But he went much further, doing what very few politicians would do today: he resigned from the Conservative

Party and, at the last minute, said he would not, therefore, be fighting in Wolverhampton South West, and in fact went on to support the Labour candidate in that constituency.

He was good enough to give me this totally sensational story first. To my delight, but not surprise, it was splashed all over every paper and news bulletin in the land, and beyond. That evening, the Press Association picture desk wanted a 'today' photograph of him and he agreed to this over the telephone. When I asked if I could go along with the photographer, he said, 'No, you've got all you needed...'

Well, I went, nevertheless, and when after we had knocked at his door (you had to do it in a coded way, because he was subject to so many threats from his political enemies), he saw me with the photographer, he said: 'You can come in, but if you so much as utter a word, I will throw you and the photographer out...' Some moments later, upstairs, while the photographer was sorting out his equipment, Powell, bizarrely, asked me about my father, who had sent a letter to Powell, prompting the politician to begin a correspondence which lasted some time.

That presented me with a problem. Mindful of his earlier injunction, I wondered whether by opening my mouth in reply he would instantly dismiss us both from his presence. He seemed to get a little irritated as I stood there mute, so I, with great trepidation, replied. Happily, for the first time in his life, no doubt, and probably the last time, he did not fulfil his pledge or threat, call it what you will.

It was at this time that the real hatred between Heath and Powell began to flourish. There is no doubt that Powell's influence and popularity with the electorate had played a large part in Heath's victory in 1970. And Powell's decision to refuse to support him in February 1974 had an equally big effect, in my view, on Heath's downfall in that election. I remember sitting in Powell's office, alongside him at his London home, while he 'honed' a sentence to express his sheer contempt for Heath. After toying with the words for some moments, he finally lit upon: 'I took him in, and I put him out.' As he did so, he jumped in the air, with a cry of triumph.

Astonishingly, nearly a quarter-of-a-century later and only months before he died, Powell repeated that sentence, word for word, in his by then quavery voice, during a radio interview. Later still, he was to tell me over the telephone that he was 'all washed up', an incongruous term to emanate from such a great man. He died a few weeks later.

But to return to 1974. By the time the October general election campaign was underway, Powell had joined the Ulster Unionist Party, although he continued to say that he would live and die a Tory. And he was also fortunate in finding a seat to fight, South Down. On one occasion he discovered, to his shock, that he was speaking at a meeting just across the constituency boundary, in North Down, a mistake which, typically, he blamed on himself but which, of course, was the fault of his constituency election helpers.

It was during this campaign that I, and a few of my journalistic colleagues, actually caused Powell to stop in his tracks while in full oratorical flight. He was speaking in the Orange Hall of the small township of Rathfriland in his constituency. Several of us had piled into a car to be driven there from the town of Gilford, which was effectively his constituency headquarters. It was getting dusk, and our driver misjudged a sweeping bend in the road. We found ourselves on the wrong side of the road, with another car careering towards us. It looked as though a horrendous head-on collision was about to happen. But our driver swerved suddenly, missed the other car by inches (the thoughts of the occupants of that car must have been the same as ours) and we ended up on the grass verge, crashing into a tree. There was an appalling silence for a few seconds, then we eased ourselves up and discovered that although we were all shaken up somewhat, we were otherwise all right.

We pushed the car away from the tree and, to our utter amazement, it still worked. So on we drove to Rathfriland. By now it was dark, but we easily found the Orange Hall, piled out of the car and ran into the brightly-lit room. We were late because of our mishap and Powell was in full flight on the platform. We had made a bit of a commotion as we entered and Powell looked sharply in our direction. And, to our amazement, he stopped dead in his tracks and his wife came rushing off the stage towards us. And then we realised why. We looked at each other and saw that we were all covered in blood, from head to foot, like some bedraggled and beaten army, something we had not been able to see in the dusk and the dark outside. It was all superficial. None of us was seriously hurt at all. But we certainly did not present a pretty spectacle at that meeting. Never before or since had I seen Powell so discomfited during a speech.

When Enoch Powell was a candidate for the Conservative leadership in the 1960s, he secured only 15 votes, something which made him deeply downcast. At the time, I remember, Jasper More, Conservative MP for Ludlow, told me that he had voted for Enoch on that occasion 'merely to stop the man being humiliated...' That must have made it even worse for Mr Powell... He maintained to his dying day the 'not ignoble' ambition of one day leading the Conservatives, an ambition never to be fulfilled.

He died on 8 February 1998 at the age of 85, after a long period when his physique deteriorated but his mind remained as alert and clear as ever. A few hours before he died Mrs Powell told him in his hospital bed that she was just popping out for a bite of lunch. Powell inquired: 'What about my lunch?' She told him he was on a drip.

'That's not much of a lunch,' he replied. Those were among the last words he ever uttered.

The Slow-Motion Downfall of the Iron Lady

Margaret Thatcher's downfall was a long, drawn-out affair. It really began some years before that historic day when those she subsequently described as 'treacherous' brutally dispatched her, out of power and out of office.

It was in mid-December 1985, when I was acting as Father Christmas at the Parliamentary press gallery children's party, that I received a call from the Press Association office about a burgeoning crisis concerning a relatively small company in the west of England called Westland Helicopters. They had been in serious financial difficulties. Yet what should have been no more than a routine problem in the life of the Government grew into a massive and virtually uncontrollable crisis which caused the resignation of two cabinet ministers and at one point looked as though it might even bring Margaret Thatcher down as well.

All of the Cabinet – with one important exception – were seeking an American package to save this ailing company. The odd one out was Defence Secretary Michael Heseltine, who wanted a European solution. And he was determined he would not be overruled. Despite all the rules about Cabinet solidarity and unity, Heseltine campaigned openly against his colleagues. It ended with his dramatic walkout from the Cabinet, both he and Margaret Thatcher incandescent with rage. The formal exchange of letters between Prime Minister and departing cabinet minister didn't take place, which is probably unique. Thatcher had never liked Heseltine and later was to do everything in her power to stop him becoming her successor as leader. But Heseltine had a lot of friends in the Parliamentary Conservative Party and, at that time, to oust him from the Government might (or so she thought) have had dire consequences for her later on.

The story was bubbling along nicely and indeed was threatening to boil over. But before it did, there was a strange incident in which I was involved. On Boxing Day, I was telephoned at home by Heseltine. He asked me whether I had heard about his family holiday due to take place in Nepal over the New Year. I said I had not. Then he said: 'Well, I'm not going on it after all.' The reason was not difficult to ascertain. He plainly did not want to be out of the country and to allow Mrs Thatcher to throw out his European proposal in his absence, which she surely would have done. The fact that he was proposing to cancel this holiday for this reason was certainly worth a story, so I asked Mr Heseltine if he would provide me with the details. He said, to my surprise, since he had started this conversation, that he could not.

'I can't tell you,' he said. 'You'll have to get it from the Ministry of Defence duty press officer.' The conversation then took an Alice-in-Wonderland turn. 'He doesn't know about it either,' continued Heseltine, 'but if you ask him, he will ring me, I will give him the facts, and then he will tell you.' It was one of those bizarre episodes which demonstrated the occasional strange, not to say frustrating, nature of reporting political affairs.

Since I had no option to do otherwise, I fell in with what was beginning to look like a bureaucratic nightmare. The press officer's response was far from encouraging. 'Do you know what day it is?' he inquired sternly. And answering his own question, he said: 'It is Boxing Day. And if you think I am going to bother a cabinet minister with this sort of trivia and drivel, you have another think coming. Ring back on Monday.' I pondered this for a minute or two and telephoned Heseltine at his home, reporting failure and the stubbornness of the press officer in refusing to play ball.

'Bloody hell!' said Heseltine. And then, after a pause, he said: 'Leave it to me. I will ring the press officer, give him the information and if you telephone him in 10 minutes or so, he will have all you need for your story.' Fair enough, I thought. But it did just cross my mind that life would have been a lot simpler if Heseltine had himself given me the facts in the first place. However, politicians do not usually like to take the short cut if there is a long way round available. And so I bided my time for 10 minutes and telephoned the press officer back. What I got was something I had not in the least expected. The press officer gave me what can only be described as the mother and father of all dressings-down.

'I thought I had made quite clear,' he said, 'that the Secretary of State was not to be troubled on Boxing Day about a matter of so little importance and here you are, ringing him up. I despair sometimes.'

My apologies were grovelling. He grudgingly accepted them, but with a very bad grace and with an even worse grace he gave me the details which I, of course, already knew. Never has so much hot air been generated in pursuit of a handful of paragraphs in the following day's newspapers. But that was not the end of it.

Two years later I was sent to Portsmouth to address a bevy of Government press officers. I started to recount the Heseltine episode and noticed a man in the front row turning an interesting shade of puce. It dawned on me that this was the press officer on that fateful Boxing Day morning. And it was the first time he had realised that his own Secretary of State was actually stitching him up. But I was too far into the story to abort it, so I had to go on to the bitter end. When I had finished, and to avoid a confrontation with this outraged party, I affected to look at my nonexistent watch and announced to the assembled company that I had no more than 10 minutes to spare to catch my train. And with that, I vanished unscathed into the Portsmouth night.

To return to the fray. Early in January 1986, the storm was raging, some thought out of control. One afternoon, I was telephoned by Colette Bowe, chief information officer of the Department of Trade and Industry, the Secretary of State of which was Leon Brittan, Heseltine's sworn enemy. She leaked to me a letter which Solicitor General Sir Patrick Mayhew had written to Heseltine pointing out the advantages and disadvantages of the proposal for a European solution to the problem. This was a lawyer's letter and had no political content. However, what was leaked to me – and I was unaware of this – were the minuses of Heseltine's plan and not the pluses. In short, it was a totally one-sided leak.

I put the story out, and telephoned Heseltine at his desk in the Ministry of Defence to tell him what had happened. He went spare with outrage. He hit the roof and sounded homicidal. When it became clear that not only had a leak from a law officer taken place, but it had been so biased, MPs were further enraged. Attorney General Sir Michael Havers threatened to resign. And even Margaret Thatcher wondered whether it might bring about her downfall, too, coming in the wake of all the other ramifications of the Westland affair.

Some people believe that it might well have done, had Neil Kinnock, the Labour leader, performed better in the subsequent debate in the Commons. Kinnock had never had such an opportunity to damage and possibly destroy Thatcher, but even his friends said he was far from at his best. Margaret Thatcher, who herself had confided to friends that she feared she might no longer be Prime Minister by 6pm that night, had been saved by Kinnock's failure to capitalise on the story. But it has never become public knowledge whether or not Thatcher herself was aware of, or authorised, the leak which was to have such massive consequences. Heseltine was to march out of the Cabinet in a rage on 9 January – partly because of the leak, but also because his relationship with Thatcher was so poor and he disagreed with her plans to save Westland – and some days later, Mr Brittan fell on his sword. He went on to become a European commissioner, a post which, bizarrely, has become a safe haven for several British MPs who have left their posts under a cloud. Thatcher had been damaged, but not irreparably.

Three years later came the Nigel Lawson affair, which weakened her further. At 5.50pm on 26 October 1989, the telephone rang for me in the Press Association office in the House of Commons. It turned out to be a call which was to enrage the Prime Minister beyond measure. Lawson, the Chancellor of the Exchequer, had been growing increasingly irritated and then furious by continual sniping from Sir Alan Walters, the right-wing monetarist economic guru. Sir Alan, whom Margaret Thatcher claimed to be a family friend, went so far at one stage as to describe, in public, Lawson's policies as 'half-baked'. It was more than the man could stand. There had been much talk at Westminster about Lawson's anger at the conduct of Sir Alan, but Thatcher, who regularly consulted the guru on economic issues, did or said nothing to stop it, while still indicating her total faith in Lawson as Chancellor. Indeed, she went so far once in the Commons as to describe to unbelieving MPs that Lawson's position was 'unassailable'. It was just the sort of hyperbolic word which politicians regularly use when trouble is brewing. And sure enough, trouble did brew.

Hours before his call to me, Lawson marched into the Prime Minister's office and told her he had had enough and was quitting. The resignation of a Chancellor of the Exchequer is a massive blow to any Prime Minister, but Mrs Thatcher sailed through the subsequent Question Time in the Commons without giving the slightest impression that anything was amiss. We in the press gallery had no inkling about what had happened. It was that phone call – one of the smartest things Lawson ever did – which brought it all out into the open. When I picked up the telephone an unknown but authoritative voice checked my identity and then proceeded to deliver a statement down the line, to the effect that Lawson was resigning – a huge story!

When he completed the statement, my first reaction (which he was prepared for) was to check its bona fides. He told me that if I rang a certain number and gave a code name, I would be put through to someone in the Treasury whose voice I recognised, and who would confirm it. This I did. And at precisely five minutes to six, a PA flash 'Lawson resigns' was running on the wires. As soon as that flash landed on news desks, phones rang everywhere and everyone in the press gallery started to run around in circles, thundering about like demented elephants. I imagine that was happening at 10 Downing Street as well.

We discovered later that Downing Street was planning to call lobby journalists to a meeting in the Commons at 7.30 pm that evening to announce Lawson's resignation and to name John Major as his successor as Chancellor of the Exchequer. Lawson was aware of this, but cleverly pre-empted Downing Street, by coming on early to me and thus ensuring that his spin rather than Downing Street's was on the story. Downing Street brought forward its meeting of lobby reporters, but it was by then too late. The story was already running and the Downing Street version of events was merely tagged on at the end. Nigel Lawson had scooped the Prime Minister. Not many people could claim to have done that.

Thatcher had already been severely shaken that year by a little-known Tory backbencher, Sir Anthony Meyer, who mounted a 'stalking horse' challenge to Thatcher. I can claim, or confess to playing some part in altering history, in that it was an interview I did with him which caused him to mount this challenge. He implied that he would challenge her and when that interview appeared in the papers and on TV, he had no option but to do so. Meyer was furious with me, feeling I had misrepresented him. After the battle, he came up to me again and apologised for losing his temper a few weeks earlier. He said that, after all, he did think I had been accurate and if I had not done the interview, he would never have stood against her.

A total of 314 Tory MPs voted for her and 33 against. But when the spoilt papers and abstentions were calculated, they showed that no fewer than 60 Tories had not supported her – one-sixth of the parliamentary party. This was for her a grave humiliation. Meyer said at the time: 'People started to think the unthinkable.' And things went from bad to worse.

The gruff voice over the telephone was that of Bernard Ingham, Margaret Thatcher's press secretary. He said to me: 'Will you be there in 10 minutes' time because I may have something to tell you?' 'Of course,' I said, already feeling the adrenalin running for what had all the prospects of being something big. So I set up a 'PA news flash' header on the computer screen and waited... and waited and waited.

It was early in 1991 when Margaret Thatcher's future was starting to look bleak. Many people in the Conservative Party, both inside and outside Westminster, were beginning to think that it was time she stepped aside. She considered herself indestructible – how vain that was to prove to be – and either she was not aware, or pretended not to be aware, that her popularity was waning.

Well, a week may be a long time in politics, but 10 minutes is an eternity – ask any reporter. Eventually, the call came. It was the resignation of Sir Geoffrey Howe, who had been demoted from Foreign Secretary to the empty title of Deputy Prime Minister. His decision to quit was as much a shock to Mrs Thatcher as it was to the press gallery, even though we had known that he was bitterly disappointed at having been removed from the Foreign Office.

Only a few hours before I received this call from Bernard Ingham, Howe had simply asked to see the Prime Minister for what appeared to be no more than a routine call. The bombshell exploded and the PA news flash set the House of Commons afire with activity, even though Parliament had prorogued that very day. Ingham, who throughout the turmoil and anguish of Mrs Thatcher's dying weeks in 10 Downing Street, remained a sterling friend of the Press Association, filled me in with the details, including the Prime Minster's reaction (shock), and the tone of the meeting (grim). Even so, Mrs Thatcher said that she accepted Howe's resignation 'more in sorrow than in anger' and claimed that the differences between the two over Europe were not so great as the departing minister had claimed in his letter of resignation.

Labour leader Neil Kinnock reacted to the news with scarcely concealed glee. He said that Thatcher had got what she deserved, having treated Howe like a 'doormat'. The resignation created an almost tangible premonition that this could be the beginning of the end of Thatcher's reign. Then Ingham telephoned again. 'If you were to slip quietly round to No. 10,' he said, 'you might just hear something to your advantage.' Needless to say, I hot-footed it round there from the House of Commons to be handed the exchange of letters between Sir Geoffrey and the Prime Minister – with a little more 'colour' and guidance from the master thrown in for good measure.

'I shall not object if you dictate a few PA "rushes" from my telephone, if you are so minded,' he said, thus adding to my bliss at being the only reporter with the story – and more important, the means to get it across without delay. Within seconds, the words were singing through the ether on the PA wire and with Sir Geoffrey mute (through laryngitis) and my colleague on the PA lobby team, Paul Bromley, filling in the background from the PA's Fleet Street headquarters, the story was done and dusted with great expedition. You could say that this was really the point at which the bell started to toll for Margaret Thatcher. Indeed, events began to move with scaring rapidity.

A few days later, Ingham telephoned me at my home one Saturday morning. 'Have you heard about a letter Michael Heseltine has written?' he inquired. I had to admit that I was unaware of it. Downing Street had obviously got wind of it and since Heseltine was regarded as 'Public Enemy Number One' they were desperate to get their hands on to it. I made a few enquiries and discovered, among other things, that Heseltine had conveniently departed for the Middle East after having sent the letter to just a handful of Sunday newspapers, not including the Press Association. The letter had, unusually, been given direct to newspaper editors rather than the political correspondents themselves, which would have been the normal procedure. So at that stage some of the reporters on papers to whom the letter had been sent were themselves not even aware of it. I eventually managed to get hold of a copy of the letter which Heseltine had addressed to his Henley Constituency Conservative Association. It complained about Thatcher's 'strident' attitude towards Europe.

The relationship between Thatcher and Heseltine had never recovered from Westland, and Downing Street never lost an opportunity to slag him off whenever the occasion arose. And here was such an occasion. Ingham duly delivered to me some trenchant words about Heseltine, underlining the fact that the one-time Defence Secretary had 'scuttled off' to the Middle East and out of reach when he knew that the flak would soon be starting to fly. The story was therefore running on the PA on the Saturday morning, complete with the Thatcher 'salvoes' against him, hours before Heseltine wanted it to appear first – in a selected few Sunday newspapers of his choosing.

Although, on the face of it, it may seem to be of little importance to anybody that the story appeared in the way it did and not how Heseltine had wanted it to appear, this was, in fact, a considerable blow to him. It meant that the story was angled on Thatcher's fury rather than giving Heseltine an unchallenged run in a few newspapers before reaction started to come in. And this was followed by a series of telephone conversations with loyal cabinet ministers who had been orchestrated to say to me, in effect, what a splendid person the Prime Minister was and what a bounder was Mr Heseltine to commit this foul deed. Downing Street was robust and sparky in its onslaught. But Thatcher should have been aware by now that this was not just an isolated gripe on the part of Heseltine. It was an initial and sinister shot across the bows of her leadership. The uproar showed no signs of abating, although there was, unsurprisingly, no word from the instigator of all this, Heseltine himself. Not yet, anyway.

And then, out of the blue a few days later, I received a call from the Henley Conservative Assocation during which I was given the text of their reply to Heseltine's letter. It was couched in diplomatic Whitehall-ese and seemed, at first blush, innocuous enough. But I suspected that in its deliberately stilted way it probably represented a king-size rebuke to their MP. Rather than rush to that judgement myself, I telephoned the constituency party office.

I said: 'Is this a rebuke?' The party official at the other end replied: 'I think you will have to draw your own conclusions.' Then I heard (I swear it) him wink over the telephone. I needed no more confirmation. I quickly did draw my own conclusions hot and strong, writing a story which began with the words: 'Michael Heseltine was at the receiving end of a massive dressing-down from his own constituency party for his "arrogant" criticism of the Prime Minister.' The story was snapped up by the evening papers and the morning papers took the same line once they had read the PA version.

A few hours elapsed and, hardly surprisingly, Heseltine was on the telephone from Tel Aviv, furious at the way the story had been handled. You could have argued that he might have been able to handle it better himself, from his own point of view that is, if he had stayed in the country. But he shouted at me down the line: 'You said it was a rebuke. Now, because the PA said it was a rebuke, everybody else will say it was a rebuke. Well, it was not a rebuke. It was the reverse of a rebuke.' He was certainly right about one thing: that the papers and the television news bulletins would follow the lead initially taken by the PA.

I thanked him for his call, but there was certainly not a case for my having to apologise or retract anything that had appeared on the PA tape. In fact, his call had come at precisely the right time. I was by then racking my brains to find a new angle for the night lead story for morning newspapers. The call was an answer to a desperate reporter's prayer. The story opened with: 'A furious Michael Heseltine tonight angrily rejected accusations that his own constituency bosses had denounced his attack on the Prime Minister...' I suppose you would call it a score draw.

Meanwhile, the recently-resigned Geoffrey Howe had by no means finished with his one-time boss. On 13 November, just a fortnight after his departure from the Cabinet, he delivered the devastating resignation speech which visibly bleached the colour from Mrs Thatcher's face as she sat there listening to her former Foreign Secretary calmly tearing her apart, limb from limb. Neither she nor anyone else had any conception that such a mild-mannered man could harbour such venom. Had she known, I have no doubt she would have left the Chamber before Howe rose to his feet. You could hear gasps from MPs all over the House as Howe, in his low, monotonous voice, vented his spleen on the leader, her knuckles by now as white as her face.

The most damaging remark was his vivid cricket metaphor relating to British negotiations on European Monetary Union in Europe: 'It is rather like sending your opening batsmen to the crease, only for them to find, as the first balls are being bowled, that their bats have been broken before the game by the team captain.' Nobody had heard anything like it before. Everybody knew, the moment Howe sat down, that Thatcher was now, politically speaking, on Death Row.

From that moment the drama moved swiftly forward. Heseltine certainly wasted no time. He invited me and a couple of TV camera crews to his London home near Victoria station and made the historic announcement that he was about to challenge Mrs Thatcher for the leadership, basing his campaign on a review of the hated poll tax.

He said: 'I am persuaded now that I have a better prospect than Mrs Thatcher of leading the Conservatives to a fourth election victory and preventing the ultimate calamity of a Labour Government.'

My immediate reaction was to ask his wife Ann: 'Please may I use your phone?' Within seconds, almost, the story was flashing around the world.

Downing Street was probably not surprised by this dramatic turn of events, but it was certainly extremely apprehensive, and had good reason to be. Thatcher's popularity within the Parliamentary Conservative Party was waning and an outright win on the first ballot was by no means assured. The rest is history. Thatcher won the first round, but was four votes short of the outright win which would have avoided a second ballot. The PA scooped that result too. I had induced a friendly Labour MP, Nigel Griffiths, to hold a telephone open for the PA in the committee corridor of the House of Commons just outside the room where the counting was taken place. The reason for this was that these are phones which only MPs are allowed to use. So when the result came out, I sneaked into the phone booth, snatched the receiver from Nigel Griffiths's obliging hand, and spat out the result to PA copy-takers at the other end before officialdom had time to pounce on me and eject me from the box.

Mrs Thatcher had, arrogantly some say, gone to Paris on voting day. Had she stayed in London, she might well have picked up that vital handful of votes. Yet even if she had, her authority would still have taken a damaging, possibly irrevocable, body blow. Her fellow ministers and some trusted backbenchers, as we now know, persuaded her that if she continued the fight against Heseltine (as she had vowed in Paris that she would) Heseltine would certainly have beaten her and become Prime Minister. To be beaten by anyone was bad enough, but by Heseltine in particular, was more than she could stomach. So the next morning, after a tearful night, she withdrew, after being told the grim news that many MPs had decided to switch their vote to Heseltine in the second ballot.

The day after those anguished meetings, the phone rang in the PA office in the House of Commons. It was answered by our secretary Mary Dunphy-Howe. When I heard it was Bernard Ingham again I ran across the room, dropping my notebook en route. I snatched the phone from Mary and grabbed from her hands a piece of notepaper, which she tried to cling on to. It was a letter she had just impeccably typed out. In our tug-of-war, the letter tore in two. So I had a drama at each end of the telephone.

'You might wish to do a flash,' said Bernard. I was braced for what was coming: 'Thatcher resigns' – the flash was zooming round the globe within seconds. Not far behind it, I blush to say, came that fine old cliché: 'An era has ended...'

When later, more candidates, including John Major and Douglas Hurd, threw their hats into the ring, Mrs Thatcher, although with no great enthusiasm, announced that she was backing Major. She felt that he was the only one who could stop Heseltine from moving into 10 Downing Street, something she would have found impossible to live with. She was, as usual, right. Later, Mrs Thatcher made known how lukewarm she was about supporting Major. When a reporter asked her why she had done this, she replied simply: 'He was the best of a poor bunch.'

Ultimately she had to go. And when she left Downing Street for the last time as Prime Minister, alongside her husband Denis, tears welled in her eyes. The Iron Lady had cracked.

Galloping Major to the Rescue

John Major, although he continued to be derided and even reviled by right-wing members of the Conservative Party for years after he left office in 1997, was the most likeable, friendly and kindly of the Prime Ministers with whom I have had to deal. I have, indeed, to thank him for saving my life on the Great Wall of China.

Unlike Margaret Thatcher, he was not averse to accepting invitations from the host country when abroad to visit their tourist sights and he had done so in China. On this occasion, I found myself straggling behind the party, so I broke into a trot to catch up with them. Unfortunately for me, the trot developed into an uncontrollable sprint downhill and I was hurtling towards the edge of the Wall above somebody's collective farm and, very probably, to an early death, when I was grabbed by Mr Major, who galloped smartly to his right and mercifully halted me in my tracks. It was an exceptional piece of fielding which would have been a credit to any test cricketer. In short, he didn't drop me.

After that incident, I was immediately given my own personal Chinese Special Branch minder, dressed as all of them were in the manner of the bowler-hatted Homepride flour men. Whether I was granted this privilege because they assumed I had become a threat to the Prime Minister – it could have looked from some angles, I suppose, as though I was lunging at him – or that they thought I was off my rocker, I still don't know. Almost certainly the latter.

By that evening we had left China and were back in Hong Kong. I telephoned the newsdesk in London, as one routinely does, to enquire what they wanted from me, and the duty news editor, John Jenkin, immediately said: 'What's all this about you and John Major in fond embrace?' I was perplexed for the moment, and then I realised that he was talking about the incident on the Wall. But how did he know? That question was quickly answered.

'Associated Press have filed a picture of you and John Major clutching one another fervently, like young lovers,' he said. I hastily explained that although it might have looked like that, that was not the case at all. Needless to say, I was required to write a caption for the picture, now framed and hanging in pride of place in our front room.

I have many examples of Mr Major's kindnesses of which, of course, the life-saving incident was the principal one. One example was at the Victoria Falls in Zimbabwe. After he and his wife Norma had gazed upon this spectacular sight, the couple were taken into a cool, roped-off tent to refresh themselves with cold drinks. I was standing outside, bedraggled, sweating in the intense heat. Mr Major emerged from the tent with an iced drink in hand and gave it to me. Not many Prime Ministers would have bothered to do that. And when his son James married the actress Emma Noble in the crypt chapel of the Palace of Westminster, the press were kept at bay because the wedding had been 'bought up' by a glossy celebrity magazine – something which, I gather, Mr Major Snr did not wholly approve of. We were not even able to get a copy of the order of service, and stringent efforts were made by the magazine's heavies to shield the bride from our prying gaze, although their machinations were not a hundred per cent successful.

John Major, when he emerged from the chapel, quickly appreciated our problem. He gave me a copy of the order of service, a prized possession at the time, I can tell you, and some good quotes. And when I called across from behind the barrier: 'Miss Noble!' she retorted, 'Mrs Major if you please...' I do not know what the magazine paid out for the exclusive rights of the wedding, but if the coverage in the newspapers the following day was anything to go by, the minders had made something of a shambles of their job.

John Major is a cricket fanatic. At school, aged 10, he was given out lbw for a duck after what he described as 'a perfectly straightforward defensive stroke in which the ball had hit the middle of the bat. I looked at the umpire in dumbfounded dismay and discovered later in physics lessons that he really was as blind as a bat.'

When he was working for the Standard Chartered Bank in Nigeria, he made his highest ever score of 77 not out while playing for Northern Nigeria at Jos in the mid-1960s. He looked to be en route for a century.

'Alas,' he said later, 'the possible 100 was wiped out by the mail plane arriving a day early and landing at square leg.' The players had to scuttle hurriedly from the pitch as the aircraft zoomed in.

The scorebook recorded: 'Major J. 77 not out. Plane stopped play' – probably a unique scorebook entry in the annals of cricket. That was the nearest he ever got to a ton.

John Major once said to me in the garden of his Huntingdon home during his period as Prime Minister: 'You may or may not know this, but I am vice-president of Surrey County Cricket Club: by far the most important post I hold.' He subsequently became its president.

On one occasion, Major and his entourage, plus scores of soldiers, were having dinner in a barracks in Sarajevo. Suddenly there was an alarming rapping on the door. 'Were the Serbs at the city gates?' We asked ourselves tremulously. The door was opened gingerly by an orderly, who was given a piece of paper by the messenger outside. This was handed to Major, who unfolded it and perused it with a face that became graver and more ashen every second. He stood up, piece of paper in hand, and a hush fell around the room.

'Bad news,' he said. We braced ourselves for what was to come. 'I am devastated to have to announce that – we have been beaten by the West Indies.'

His passion meant that one of the advantages of travelling round with John Major was that, in whatever far-flung part of the world you happened to be, 38,000 feet in the air, or in the Malayan jungle, you could always guarantee being abreast with the latest cricket scores. And in the football season, he always made sure that the Chelsea result came through.

John Major was also persuaded to play in a cricket match in front of Fleet Street's finest (always a risky thing to do) in Harare, during the Commonwealth Heads of Government meeting in Zimbabwe in 1991. At first, understandably, he was unwilling to play for fear of making a fool of himself. However, Gus O'Donnell, his bright young press secretary (later to become Cabinet Secretary) persuaded him, against his better judgement as he said at the time, to pad up and take part. It proved to be the right decision. Major batted impressively in a match in which the batsmen were expected to retire after a certain number of overs at the crease, if they had not already been dismissed. Major successfully held his ground for the allotted time. I have to say, without much pride, that I bowled to Major in the nets on that day. My pride and joy was an unplayable 'killer' leg-break, which I had been perfecting. He hit it out of the ground.

Such was his knowledge of the sport that Major claimed that he was able to distinguish between the Surrey Bedser twins, Alec and Eric. If that was the case – and I had no reason to doubt him – he must have been one of the very few people, even among their close associates, who could. They invariably wore identical clothes. One would start a sentence and the other would finish it. I interviewed them once at the Oval cricket ground. When I first met them Alec was carrying a plastic bag. That was how I was going to know which was which when they answered the questions.

But apparently while we were walking back into the pavilion, and unnoticed by me, Alec had handed the bag to his brother Eric. So I conducted the entire interview under the misapprehension that Alec was Eric and vice versa. However, when it came to writing the story, that did not seem to matter since their views, like their appearance, were indistinguishable from one another.

Throughout their lives, the Bedser twins were virtually inseparable and spent only a handful of days apart from each other. On once such occasion, John Major told me, when Alec was touring Australia with the MCC, he went to the airport at Melbourne to meet Eric, who was to join him on the tour. To everybody else's astonishment, but not to theirs, it transpired that Eric emerged from the aircraft wearing identical clothes to those his brother was wearing that day. Uncanny, or what?

In May 1997, immediately after he had relinquished the Prime Ministership following Tony Blair's landslide victory, John Major went straight to the Oval to watch his beloved Surrey play the British Universities in a Benson and Hedges one-day match. And when he appeared on the BBC Radio 4's *Desert Island Discs* in January 1992, he said that the luxury item he would take to his hypothetical exile was a full-size replica of the Oval cricket ground.

He told the presenter Sue Lawley: 'It would be lovely. The sun will shine, the grass will grow and the pitch will be beautiful. I will be able to bowl on it and bat on it, with a bowling machine, to my heart's content.' It was one of the more unwieldy luxury items on the programme.

One of the mysteries – now cleared up – about John Major was that although he speaks with a very clear diction and does not appear to speak at any great speed, shorthand writers, including the experts who provide the virtually verbatim Hansard official report, have always found perplexing difficulties in keeping up with his delivery. Then it dawned on them. If you listen carefully to Major delivering a speech you will notice that, unlike any other speechmaker I have ever come across, there are absolutely no 'ers' or 'ums' in his delivery.

The other great mystery was for many the story of his affair. Everyone asks journalists, 'But you must have known about Major's dalliance with Edwina Currie?' But, no. It was the best-kept political secret I can remember. And anyway, if we had known, we would have written it up.

But John Major was essentially a gentleman. When he left Downing Street in 1997, he left a bottle of champagne and a note of good wishes for his successor Tony Blair. His wife Norma was similarly impeccable in her approach. Just as Denis Thatcher had been before her, she was the ideal consort for a Prime Minister. She subsequently, and deservedly so, became a Dame, largely because of her charitable work. She was also hugely knowledgeable about opera.

But whatever her many qualities were – and they were manifold – she never considered herself a political animal. That was why both she and John Major would get justifiably angry when, as occasionally happened, some sections of Fleet Street cruelly teased her about her alleged shortcomings in this area. She had much to deal with in his rise to the top.

She said at the time: 'I do not regard it as a particularly joyous occasion. I took several months really to sort it out. Things were happening to me that I was not prepared for.' It certainly was not something she had expected to happen and it was a considerable shock to her to find herself bathed in the spotlight of Fleet Street attention. She was derided, totally unjustifiably, by those who made uncalled-for criticisms of her dress sense. She was genuinely upset by the comparisons some people made between her and Hillary Clinton. But she was certainly not the cowering mouse that many people assumed her to be.

Once, at the Commonwealth Heads of Government meeting

in Harare in 1991, the formidable Hella Pick, the not-to-be-trifled-with diplomatic editor of the *Guardian*, approached Mrs Major and said with as much warmth as she could muster – which was not a lot: 'It is high time that you and I ceased to be strangers.'

Mrs Major looked her in the eye a trifle scornfully and replied without hesitation: 'Don't worry. I am quite happy with things the way they are.' A feisty woman...

Points of Order

I telephoned Labour MP Michael Meacher in January 1992, when he was shadow Social Security Secretary, inviting him to comment on Prime Minister John Major's New Year message. Mr Meacher began like this: 'The Government's welfare and social security safety net is full of holes...' What did he expect it to be full of?

* * * * *

Bernard, or more familiarly Jack, Weatherill (later Lord Weatherill), who was Speaker of the House of Commons during much of Margaret Thatcher's 'reign', always carried a thimble around with him to remind himself of his humble origins as a tailor. In fact he was not so humble as all that. He once had to run up an emergency pair of breeches for King George VI, no less. His life's motto was taken from the Sioux prayer: 'Great spirit, teach me not to judge another until I have walked two weeks in his moccasins.'

* * * * *

One of my favourite MPs was Sir John Gorst, a Tory who had a fair percentage of Russian blood coursing through his veins. Sometimes he was quiet and brooding and on others explosive. He once described himself as a pessimist and subject to black moods. But his dark side, which his friends sometimes attributed to the Russian in him, rarely showed itself at Westminster.

'I don't like the House of Commons,' he admitted once, 'because essentially political life is cooperative life and I am not a very good member of a team. I am not particularly clubbable. I am rebellious and that does not get you very far in politics. I don't feel very English.' In fact, his maternal grandfather was a colonel in the Czar's Imperial Guard and Sir John was probably the only Conservative who showed sympathy for the striking miners. His support (although not necessarily one hundred per cent) made him for a time a highly unpopular figure in the Conservative Party.

Sir John also once confessed: 'I had a very unhappy childhood, largely because my mother was miserable and she communicated that to me.' Even so, he was on the right wing of the Conservative Party on many issues and supported the rights of sportsmen to tour South Africa during the apartheid years. And in the 1970s, he fought a long and often lone battle on behalf of the management of a small north London firm, Grunwicks, whose entire staff were on strike – with the indefensible and sometimes physical support of members of the Labour cabinet: Shirley Williams, who subsequently defected to the SDP, actually appeared on the picket line when she was a member of the cabinet.

Sir John's background, in political terms, was enigmatic. He was educated at Ardingly College, where he was reportedly socialist-inclined, and at Cambridge he was regarded as being pro-Liberal. And he was originally turned down as a candidate by Conservative Central Office 'on the grounds that I had never done anything to prove that I was a Conservative'. However, he unsuccessfully fought Chester-le-Street in 1964 and Bodmin in 1966 before winning Hendon North in 1970. He was to lose the seat in the Labour landslide victory of 1997.

Sir John was also a founder-member of the Middle Class Association, whose objectives, he said, were to protect a 'persecuted, vilified and sneered-at minority' of managers and the self-employed. But, typically for him, this was, to use his own words, 'a political disaster' for him. He admitted: 'It caused considerable irritation to the people I had wanted to influence.' He was the sort of man who, by his own admission, never seemed to be able to win.

* * * * *

It is the booming voice of Spencer le Marchant, a huge and bluff Tory opposition Whip at the time, which you can hear if you play a recording of the vote of confidence which James Callaghan lost by a single vote in 1979. Spencer was one of the tellers and this moment of glory for him – the vote which destroyed the Callaghan Government and paved the way for Margaret Thatcher – was something he talked about constantly in the few years he had to live.

I remember round about the same time visiting his constituency in Buxton where the magnificent Opera House, which had lain dormant for many years, was being reopened with a right regal flourish. I stayed at Spencer's home that night and, since I had to be away early, he woke me before dawn with, not a warming brew of Earl Grey, but a large tumbler of Glenfiddich. Not a man to do things by halves. Then he drove me, hell for leather, over the Derbyshire moors to reach Macclesfield in time for the first train. Suddenly, he jumped on the brakes, even though the road was apparently clear ahead. I was all but hurled through the windscreen. When I recovered my composure, I enquired what the problem was.

He said: 'Look down there.' I complied. And there was a grouse sedately walking across the road in front of us. 'Remember, remember,' he said to me. 'It is only 11 August today.' A glorious stickler for the rules…

* * * * *

The question was often raised: how did Mikhail Gorbachev rise to the top of the Soviet system when he appeared to be so amiable and lacking in the kind of ruthlessness generally associated with previous Soviet leaders? That old, unsmiling and dour Soviet warhorse, Gromyko, came up with the answer in a conversation with Denis Healey, the former Labour Chancellor of the Exchequer.

Gromyko told him: 'Gorbachev has a nice smile, but he also has teeth of steel…'

* * * * *

One thing about members of the European Parliament is that they keep themselves to themselves and scarcely bother anybody. That is why, although a substantial minority of people might just be able to name their Westminster MP, hardly anybody knows the name of their MEP. In 1989, Sir Cyril Smith, the portly Liberal MP for Rochdale, decided to make his contribution to his party's Euro-campaign in Lancashire East by purchasing space in a local newspaper and inviting the electorate there to vote for the candidate representing his party. When Sir Cyril was halfway through dictating the words for the advertisement, he suddenly realised that he had not the faintest idea of the name of his own local candidate! A few discreet phone calls gave him the answer he required. The name was Mike Hambley. I fully believe that he remains as obscure today as he was then.

* * * * *

Sir Nicholas Lyell, the former Conservative Solicitor General, was telling me about an antenatal clinic he visited in his former mid-Bedfordshire constituency. On the wall was a notice to young mothers about the benefits of vaccinations and other postnatal care. Above it was the caption: 'Remember, the first year of your life is the most dangerous.'

Beneath it, someone had scrawled: 'The last is not without its hazards, either.'

* * * * *

Ron Brown, the former Labour MP for Edinburgh Leith, whose antics in the Commons included breaking (accidentally) the Mace and (allegedly) sharing a shower with a lady in the Palace of Westminster, had a spot of bother once with the constabulary in Glasgow. He was marched into a police cell after brandishing a fist at the Prime Minister, Margaret Thatcher, who was on a visit to Glasgow. On being challenged by the police, Brown refused to promise not to do it again.

But when, as a result of this aggressive attitude, the Glasgow police took him in charge, they did not believe him when he said he was a Member of Parliament.

'Never heard of you,' they scoffed after he had given them his name. Then he disclosed that he was an Edinburgh MP and not a Glasgow one. 'That explains it,' the officer said. And marched him off to jail. Incidentally, Mr Brown once told me that he was convinced that the routine advice given by every news editor to his reporters was this: 'Make it short. Make it juicy. Make it up.' Bless the man.

The Raging Bull

If ever there was a banana-skin politician, his name was John Prescott. Yet although he slithered and slid all over the place, he emerged unbruised and unscathed by all his many misfortunes. It is a source of amazement to many people that a man who had no public speaking abilities whatsoever, whose command of English was virtually nonexistent and who had a temper like a raging bull should not only have been appointed Deputy Prime Minister, but should have survived in the job for more than a decade.

His sexual appetite appeared to be as enormous as his addiction to food – his memoirs published in 2008 revealed that he had been stuffing his face for years, particularly with the kind of 'trash' food which dieticians are constantly warning us of. Once a week on television, during Prime Minister's Question Time, he could be seen slumped inelegantly on the front bench, his eyes half- or sometimes even fully-closed, his mouth downturned, his paunch sticking out, looking for all the world like a lump of indigestible stodgy pudding. Not a pretty sight.

Tony Blair had scores of excuses, had he wanted, to sack Prescott: his sexual cavorting with his secretary, Tracey Temple, his brawl with a farmer who threw an egg at him, his failure until reminded to pay council tax, for which he was ministerially responsible, to name but a few. So why did Blair tolerate him? I think it was because Prescott was among the very few Labour frontbenchers who had actually had a 'real' job before he entered Parliament – he was a steward on the liners – whereas nearly all his ministerial colleagues had merely been political researchers or advisers, or union officials, from the day they left school. Dumping John Prescott would have enraged the not-inconsiderable number of Labour backbenchers who viewed the New Labour concept with horror. Whenever there was a problem about Prescott, Tony Blair simply laughed it off: 'It's just John being John,' he would say.

Prescott hated the press, denouncing them contemptuously as 'penny scribblers', although I have to admit that he more than once gave me a lift in one of his famous two Jags.

His mangling of the English language was often so ludicrous that sometimes one was compelled (wrongly I believe) to think that he did it deliberately as part his 'persona'. Once he had to make a sombre, late-night statement in the Commons about some atrocity during the Bosnia conflict. The name 'Milosevic' occurred frequently during the statement and the subsequent exchanges. But Prescott's inability to get his tongue round the name, from start to finish, caused embarrassing strangulated guffaws to echo through the Chamber during what was supposed to be a grave event. Once he recalled sitting next to the lively columnist Petronella Wyatt at a lunch, describing her later as 'Petrofino or Peregrino, or something like that.' He always, either through ignorance or devilment, wrongly pronounced the name of his great enemy Peter Mandelson, whom he once likened to a crab fished out of the River Thames. Prescott always referred to him, usually with a snort of contempt, as Mr Mendelssohn, like the composer famed for his *Wedding March*.

But his masterstroke was his speech at the Labour Party conference in 1993 in support of the then leader, John Smith, on the issue of 'one member one vote' – so that the leader would be voted for by individuals rather than through the block votes up to then wielded by unions. His harangue was incomprehensible from start to finish. I was sharply reminded of the gibbon enclosure at London Zoo. However, it was the only speech I ever heard which made no kind of sense, a garbled hotchpotch of gobbledegook, yet which served its purpose. He was rewarded with a standing ovation (a rare event at the usually sullen Labour conferences) for a speech in which barely a single word was understandable yet which had the delegates trooping off to vote for Mr Smith. It was a pea-souper of a speech, a triumph of obscurity of which even Gordon Brown might have been proud.

But his hot temper was not confined to stroppy voters throwing missiles at him. Once he emerged from the House of Commons tea room, puce of visage, looking for a fight with me – although I didn't have at the time a clue what he was shrieking about. Well, what ensued wasn't strictly a fight: it was a wild swinging of arms, his grizzled face close to my own and an impressive repertory of expletives, delivered with all the decibels he could muster and which caused the ladies within earshot to blush profusely.

'Bloody fearless you call yourself do you?' he bellowed at me. 'Bloody fearless? You won't get away with this.' His agitated, rotating clunking fists were nearly shaving my chin. I was lucky to escape without a black eye or a thick ear. I worked out the problem later. I had written a column for the Press Association saying something rude about him. It had appeared in his local newspaper, the *Hull Daily Mail*, which, unknown to me, trumpeted the piece with the words across the top of the page: 'Chris Moncrieff: Fearless Westminster Correspondent'. 'Fearful' might have been a more appropriate adjective.

Incidentally, I do wonder about that tea room. MPs who enter its portals in a calm frame of mind often emerge from it distraught and angry. It is probably something they put in the tea.

On another occasion, Prescott was making a speech at a 10 Downing Street reception. He was ridiculing something I had written in the Parliamentary *House Magazine* to the effect that some politicians were clever, or devious, enough to tell the truth and tell a lie in the same sentence. I was in the audience, trying to hide away, but he spotted me. 'There's the bugger there,' he said. And then he summoned me on to the platform to explain myself. Not my favourite moment.

Prescott was always ambitious. More than once he sought election to high office in the Labour Party, notably the deputy leadership when Neil Kinnock was leader. I remember Kinnock raging at him for having the temerity to offer himself for election. I can well understand why: a Kinnock/Prescott leadership duo would not exactly have been a dream ticket. They would have put Morecambe and Wise in the shade and Kinnock's deputy was the more acceptable Roy Hattersley.

I recall once, when Prescott was seeking support to stand, he told his audience at a Labour Party conference fringe meeting that scores of people were urging him to put himself forward. I was standing at the back of the hall, next to his lovely wife Pauline. I asked her who all these 'scores of people' were. She replied: 'I don't know. I think it's his mother…'

Like most other Labour MPs, Prescott always boasted about his working-class roots, although I have often wondered why they boast about something which they can't help and into which they are born willy-nilly. One day, he told people that he had decided to become middle class. The poor blinkered soul could not take on board the truth that a son of toil remains a son of toil whether he wears an Armani suit or overalls. John Prescott, whether grouchy or smiley, certainly added to the gaiety of the nation. Even so, I would advise people to keep a discreet distance from him when he has been drinking tea in the Commons tea room.

Who Goes Home?

The expression 'Who Goes Home?' is the cry that reverberates and echoes around the House of Commons at the end of each day, and when the debates have stilled. The stentorian-voiced policemen and doorkeepers have been doing this for centuries. The custom dates from the time when it was necessary for members to go home in parties, accompanied by linksmen for common protection against footpads and cutpurses who infested the streets of London. The cry has carried through until the present day. One hopes the modernisers, hell-bent as they are on removing all tradition from Westminster, will keep their meddling hands off this ancient custom. But I wouldn't count on it.

At least the House of Commons still has and always will have, an abundance of eccentrics, people with swollen egos, the odd clown and a few bad apples, too. But we must not forget that it is the vast majority who do not seek the limelight, who do not rack their brains for sound-bites and who avoid reporters like the plague, who are the backbone of the place and almost certainly the most effective MPs. Tedious, maybe, but very worthy. But there are more than enough odd-balls there to keep even Fleet Street happy.

Gordon Brown, who became Prime Minister in June 2007, is a

typical son of the manse and certainly does not fall into that category. He is often depicted as gruff and dour, whereas in reality he is an amiable and genial chap. But he is the last person to find himself on the front page of the *News of the World*. He keeps out of trouble and thus out of the diary columns. In his bachelor days, when he went on holiday he filled his bag not with Mills and Boon, but with a library of tomes on economic theory and the like. His commitment to – even obsession with – politics seriously affected his romantic life. One of his former girlfriends, Princess Margarita of Romania, summed up the situation when that relationship ended: 'I never stopped loving him, but one day it didn't seem right any more. It was politics, politics, politics, and I needed nurturing.'

However, David Cameron, the Tory leader at the time of writing, is much more promising material. He has a marvellous knack of making a complete pillock of himself. You get the impression that if a banana skin is waiting for him on the pavement, he will unerringly and automatically step on it and send himself flying. A man who can cycle to work, with the objective of saving the planet, and is followed by a gas-guzzling chauffeur-driven car carrying his shoes has all the hallmarks of Mr Bean about him. Since then, he has ridden his bicycle the wrong way up a one-way street, and cycled the wrong way round a traffic island. This is a good start, and we look forward to many more such pratfalls in the future.

But you do wonder, sometimes, about the mindset of some MPs. I used to do a lot of business, many years ago, with Sir Brian (later Lord) Mawhinney, a former Northern Ireland Secretary and Conservative Party chairman. Later, a mutual friend was to tell me that Mawhinney had deliberately had nothing to do with me for 20 years because I had, apparently, let him down over something all those years ago. I was totally unaware of his boycott on me and every time our paths crossed I greeted him cheerfully. But since I heard that news, I started to greet him even more effusively and fulsomely than before. I haven't a clue what it was that upset him, but no doubt, one day, it will all come clear.

One of the finest MPs who graced Westminster since World War II was the late Tory Geoffrey Dickens. He was a fine man, popular on all sides of the House, a past-master at quick-witted comedy, but, as he would be the first to admit, he was no leader of men. Once a magazine ran a poll, asking Conservative MPs who they would like as their new leader. The MPs entered into a conspiracy and overwhelmingly voted for Dickens, a plainly ludicrous idea. The magazine quietly dropped the poll.

He telephoned me at home one day, and could hear the tinkling of the ivories in the background.

He inquired: 'Is that the wife on the piano?'

I said, 'No, it's the cat stalking up and down the keyboard.'

'Oh,' he said, 'she's got a very nice touch...'

That says it all.